I0187668

Only Connect

UTE INDIANS
ELKHEAD HOMESTEADERS

ONLY CONNECT

CREATING AND SUSTAINING COMMUNITY

BELLE ZARS

Only Connect: Creating and Sustaining Community

For information about this title or to order other books and/or electronic media, contact the publisher:

Nauwa Press
www.nauwapress.com
nauwapress@gmail.com

ISBNs:
978-1-7351225-0-2 (hardcover)
978-1-7351225-1-9 (softcover)

Printed in the United States of America

Cover photo credits:
Young Ute woman and baby on horseback, circa 1911-1915. Stephen Olop photographer. Denver Museum of Nature and Science.
Ute children posed for studio portrait by William Henry Jackson, circa 1890. National Museum of the American Indian, Byron Harvey, III Collection of Exposition and Portrait photographs.

The book title, Only Connect, is from Howards End by E.M. Forster. The longer quote reads, "Only connect! That was the whole of her sermon. Only connect the prose and the passion, and both will be exalted, and human love will be seen at its height. Live in fragments no longer."

for Carmen

Contents

Introduction

Sit still in the grass on a hillside in a clearing in the sagebrush. Look up at the sky, that vast blue bowl, bottomless and weightless. Watch the towers of cumulus clouds drag shadows across the land, the little fleecy bits speeding toward the horizon. The weather can come quickly and with dramatic force. There is nothing to soften the changes in temperature, the hard winds, the bright sunshine. Clouds race in, the sky grows dark, rain splatters down, the dust jumps in little saucers, the clouds move on, the sun beats down. Very little monotony here—few gradual soakings, subtle shades or gentle breezes.

Far down the hill there is a line of trees along the creek; otherwise, the land is covered in sage and oak brush, blue stem, and mule's ear. There is no human sound, and yet a presence is felt nearby. A rutted road, a pile of logs, a rusted metal washtub, a bar of concrete, a dried leather shoe, a piece of glass, a metate, an arrowhead, a shard of pottery. People used to be here. They picked chokecherries, hunted deer and elk, worked in fields, tended livestock, danced in the schoolhouse, and walked over the crusted snow to visit neighbors. The land stretches away, rolling, tucking and folding, heaving up a pile of rocks, falling steeply into a narrow creek bed that twists and swerves in a giant S toward the big river to the south and west.

Bears Ears country, later known as Elkhead, Colorado, located in the northwestern corner of the state, is an immensely beautiful place. It was part of the last open land held by Native American Indians, and also one of the last places opened for homesteading. The Ute came here every summer, thriving on the abundant game, wild berries, and Yampa roots. When the U.S. government removed these Indians to a reservation in 1880, settlers from around the United States and the world moved in to claim what they called "free" land, eventually forming a community. The Ute had lived communally for perhaps as long as 10,000 years; the homesteaders, by contrast, left behind a life somewhere else and in the parlance of the day, "struck out on their own." In a very short time, however, they became a group with their own identity: Elkheaders. As they pulled together in a harsh climate on geographically isolated land, they also developed their own local culture, traditions, and values. They searched for land and water and managed the conflicts inherent in a land rush. They built homes, barns, fences; they planted gardens and crops and survived the long hard winters. They constructed their own roads and telephone lines. They played music and danced together; they shared work, knowledge, and materials. They formed a school district and a few years later, in 1915, built a fine rock schoolhouse that doubled as a community center. For the first-through-twelfth-grade school they scoured the country for the best educated and most enthusiastic teachers they could find.

The story of this land and these peoples is one that I have lived with all my life. My maternal grandfather, Ferry Carpenter, was a homesteader in Elkhead, and my two maternal grandmothers, Eunice Pleasant and Rosamond Underwood, were both teachers in the Rock School. Eunice was my grandfather's first wife. She died when I was a toddler. About a year later, Rosamond Underwood Perry became my grandmother when my grandfather re-married. My brothers and I, and many of our merged family cousins, did not realize we had a biological grandparents and by-marriage grandparents until we were well into adulthood. Our grandparents had been trusted friends since they were young adults and their strong bonds carried over to their collective grandchildren, whether related by blood or not. We were all beneficiaries of their love, generosity, and adventurous spirits.

I grew up feeling a strong and mysterious affinity with my grandmother Eunice. A photo and a small box of her tightly folded letters from Elkhead sat on my grandfather's bureau. He was a storyteller, a raconteur, but he rarely told stories about her; only occasionally he reminded us of her English skills and the column she wrote for the local paper through the 1930s. He would sometimes muse on her determination to complete college; she supported her younger brothers after her mother died and alternated teaching for a term to pay for a semester of college. Although there was little narrative of her life in a story-rich family, she remained a presence at my grandfather's ranch. The sheets were ironed on her mangle, in the way she had preferred. The butter was churned and formed into big round pats following her instructions. Her saddle hung in the tack room in the barn; my brothers and I artfully snitched caramels made with her recipe from the freezer on the back porch in the middle of the night.

I deeply longed to know her. I had a memory of being loved and cared for by her as a child. Whether this was direct experience or a memory that was given to me later, after she died, I do not know. When I was born—her daughter's first child, her first granddaughter after two grandsons—she knit me a blue-grey wool blanket with white kittens romping around on the corners.

Eunice grew up with six brothers in Lyndon, Kansas. Her mother, Katherine Seacat, died when she was ten. As the only girl in the family, convention dictated that she would serve as mother to her younger brothers. She was a stellar student and, like many of the ambitious women of her time, chose to be a teacher. She enrolled at the University of Kansas in Lawrence, about fifty miles from her home in Lyndon, and paid her way by teaching in various rural schools. After eight years, and after accumulating considerable experience as a teacher, she graduated with her bachelor's degree in English. A short while later, she got a job teaching high school in Tulsa, Oklahoma, where her older brother, Carl Pleasant, lived with his wife, Gertrude. To celebrate and to see her younger brothers who had moved to Craig and Maybell, Colorado, she took a train trip in August 1919 to visit them. There, she met my grandfather, Ferry Carpenter, at a community dance in Hayden, a small town next to the Yampa River in northwest Colorado. That night, he convinced her that she must visit the model rock school built by homesteaders in Elkhead; the next morning, he brought her there in a wagon and persuaded her to stay. She would teach the high school grades in the two-room school and guide the first group of seniors through their final preparations for college. Eunice telegraphed to Tulsa: "Wish release from contract. Find my health much improved here."[1]

She explained in a long letter to her sister-in-law, Gertrude, that she was swayed by the opportunity to teach in a model school in a community that placed so much value on education. The district had recently built a two-story stone teacherage with a kitchen, living room and dining area below and two bedrooms upstairs. She was thrilled to have a house of her own.

The school and the teacherage were in miserable condition when I was a child. The schoolhouse doors had been locked and the windows boarded up in the late 1930s; the Elkhead district had merged with the Hayden district in the 1950s. On our summer horseback rides and picnics to the schoolhouse in the 1950s and 1960s we found the teacherage abandoned; scavengers had pulled off the doors and windows, probably to reuse them elsewhere on a cabin or barn. We played in the solid rock structure, careful not to step through the weak spots in the floor upstairs. There was a bench seat built into a gabled window in the roof; the view inspired long moments of contemplation, even when I was a child. I sat and imagined my grandmother there, preparing to teach in the morning or reading on the weekends. My brothers and I cleaned the floors of the accumulated animal droppings and leaves, sweeping down the tight curving steps that dropped into the living room. The kitchen stove was long gone but there was a fridge box built into the window on the north wall. It would have been just large enough for a chunk of ice and the tomato aspic and salmon salad my mother recalled her cooking.[2]

Although my grandfather spoke sparingly of my grandmother, he had a rich reserve of stories about Elkhead and the community. When we asked for a story, he would begin: "Let me tell you about the time . . ." and then start in with his arrival in Hayden as a young man, followed by stories from his life as a homesteader, lawyer, and rancher. He was a prominent figure in Hayden and Routt County. I was always introduced as his granddaughter and those were the terms I used whenever I met a stranger. My name was not particularly relevant; my lineage was.

One morning in early spring, as I was leaving a freshman physics class at my college in western Massachusetts, I found myself on a slightly higher, drier stretch of sidewalk where I could see a bit more sky. I knew I wanted to spend the summer in Colorado and I decided at that moment to do an oral history project on the Elkhead School. It was a simple plan; interview everyone who had lived in the community and gone to school there. A college friend, Becky Fernald, and a Denver friend, Mary Palmer, agreed to join me.

We arrived in Colorado in June, hauled supplies up to my grandparents' homestead cabin north of town and looked for part-time work in Craig to support ourselves. We started interviewing with a short list of names that my grandparents gave us. After a call to set up a time, we would assemble the two-and-a-half-inch reel-to-reel tape recorder, drive into town and knock on doors. My entrée was that I was Ferry Carpenter's granddaughter, but the greeting I often received took me by surprise: people looked at me with a start and exclaimed, "Oh good golly, she looks just like Eunice! Look at her! She's the spitting image of Mrs. Carpenter." I felt a sensation of intense alertness and anticipation: here was someone who had known Eunice, been with her, spoken with her face-to-face. What did they know? What did they see in me? I wanted to be drawn inside that memory and have it for my own.

Yet, as I began to dig deeper, I found that the story I was uncovering was much bigger than myself, or that of my family. The story of Elkhead is about land, and people who attempted to inhabit the land, alone and together. First were the Ute with their inherited cultural sense of community, of shared lands, shared responsibilities and a common identity. Tight on their heels were homesteaders from all over the world; most of them strangers to each other, who did not initially intend to build a community, but only sought to own land and support themselves. Eventually they did, deliberately, and became citizens of a particular place. Eventually they also found communal values to be not just necessary for their survival, but central to their identity as well.

Elkhead was taken from the Ute; they were forced onto a reservation in Utah, hundreds of miles away. Their beloved Bears Ears country, as they referred to Elkhead, Colorado, was surveyed and sold or given away to homesteaders, mainly white men and women of European descent. Ute culture, characterized by communal values, jointly owned land, and strong traditions of collective and cooperative behavior, was systematically thwarted and all but eradicated. The Ute were forced to become farmers on individual plots of land. Their children were sent away to boarding schools to learn English and manual trades. Many Ute, particularly those who were from northwest Colorado, rebelled, fighting to maintain their traditions and customs, their language, and to regain the land that had supported their way of life.

I have attempted to weave the stories of the Ute and the homesteaders together, not to make them one but because there are so many parallels, so many ironies, so much to learn in seeing the two people's stories side-by-side. The Ute people began with knowledge of the good of the whole, shared values and strong connections to the land. A sense of community was integral to who they were. Elkheaders created a community. Both had a kind of community for which we have become nostalgic: a community where the common good was regularly placed above the advancement of the individual, where people were hospitable and trusting of strangers, and where the needs of the youngest and the oldest were attended to first and most generously.

For both the Ute, and those who became known as Elkheaders, I have attempted to find the history as it was spoken or written, in their own words.

To immerse in the broad stream of history (not just float down the middle where the current is strongest, where leaders and exemplars push forward their version of the future) is to gather and assemble the most inclusive story, the one that includes the edges and the eddies. For me it has meant slowing down to read and consider Nicaagat's experience at the White River Agency, or to hear and consider the testimony given by Ute who returned to Colorado to hunt. This history emerges from the truly local, from micro-events: when a visitor came to town, when a neighbor helped stack hay, when another put on the Valentine's party, or a third shot the coyote that was killing her chickens. Who were the people of the Bears Ears country? The Elkheaders? What held them together? What were they trying to accomplish? What was their vision of the world as it should be?

CHAPTER ONE

Beautiful, Beloved Land

(PRE-1879)

Ferry Carpenter first visited Elkhead as a young man. He grew up in Evanston, Illinois, the son of a moderately wealthy shoe manufacturer. In 1901, when he was fourteen, he was taken by his mother, Belle Reed Carpenter, to New Mexico to cure his asthma. Belle Carpenter was convinced that the air in Chicago was making her son sick and believed he would grow and thrive where the air was clean. Years later, Ferry Carpenter remembered his head was full of the romance of the West, an imagination fueled by cowboy-and-Indian movies and going to Buffalo Bill's Wild West Show in Chicago. He was overjoyed to leave Evanston and become a cowboy.

Ferry Carpenter began his journey as a boarder on the Whitney Ranch near Maxwell, New Mexico. His parents paid twenty-five dollars a month for his lodging, but within a few months Ferry learned to ride a horse and work on a ranch well enough to pay his own way. A year later, he moved to the neighboring Dawson Ranch, where he worked for the Texas cattleman and entrepreneur John B. Dawson.

Carpenter was a tall young man, thin and wiry, with short dark hair and dark blue eyes. Not many people considered him stakes where they could find section corners. Around noon, they stopped in a shady aspen grove to have lunch. A small stream flowed slowly but steadily down the nearby shale ravine. The source of the spring was obscured, tucked in a fold in the land, hidden by grass, aspen and Gambel oak brush. The water was cold, signifying that it was coming from somewhere deep underground, and it was sweet—not alkali like many of the nearby seeps. While Carpenter and the crew ate their lunch, the surveyor casually remarked that someone would soon claim the land: the spring was now on federal land. The new line they had found that morning shifted ownership from the state to the federal government.

That evening, Carpenter consulted his boss, Dawson, who advised him to claim the land quickly before someone else did. Carpenter, however, was not yet twenty-one and was thus ineligible for a homestead until his birthday on August 10. Excited and anxious that someone else might claim the land before he could, Carpenter returned to the spot that night and set up camp. The next morning, he pounded in wooden stakes roughly delineating his claim of 160 acres. Either no one became aware of Carpenter's age, or they did not find the land to be particularly valuable, because the claim went uncontested. Carpenter camped there for the rest of the summer. He loved the land, not just for the opportunity to get some property for almost free, but also for the beauty of the place. He camped where he could see a slice of the Yampa Valley, about ten miles away, and the Flat Top Mountains, still covered with a bit of snow about sixty miles to the south. In the mornings, he could ride up a nearby ridge and look down into the Dry Fork of Elkhead and in the distance to the north, the twin peaks known as Bears Ears. On the morning of his birthday, August 10, 1907, he woke up before dawn, saddled his horse, and made the long ride to the land office in Steamboat Springs to file on his homestead.[3]

Carpenter thought himself to be the first to claim the land, and one of the first to find the spring. Like his neighbors, he referred

Suriap, Yampa Ute, photographed by William Henry Jackson as part of the Hayden Survey, 1868. National Anthropological Archives, Smithsonian Institution 0157306694700.

to the land in Elkhead as newly opened; in truth, the land had been held and occupied in the summer and fall for centuries by the Yamparika, a band of the Ute tribe.

The Ute shared common language and culture. "We call ourselves Nuuchuu or Nuu'ciu, "the people."[4] Early explorers and government agents tended to drop the first consonant and typically referred to "Yutas," "Utacas" or "Uticas," and later to "Ute" in historic documents, reports, and testimonies.[5] Most contemporary references use the word Ute; currently the three tribes that comprise the Ute Nation refer to themselves as the Southern Ute Indian Tribe, the Ute Mountain Ute Tribe, and the Ute Indian Tribe of the

Yellow Flower (John), Yamparika Ute. Photograph by William Henry Jackson, Hayden Survey, circa 1872. National Anthropological Archives, Smithsonian Institution BAE GN 01572.

Uintah and Ouray Reservation.[6] The name Yamparika or Yapudttka refers to a band of Ute in northwest Colorado. The Yampa plant, with its sweet edible root, grows plentifully along rivers and streams in the West.[7]

Although many non-Native American people have written about the Ute, their history and culture, few Ute have had the opportunity to write about themselves. Recently the three tribes of the Ute worked together on an exhibit in the History Colorado Center in Denver and the Ute Museum in Montrose. The result is the most authentic and definitive history and interpretation of Ute experience to date. I have drawn extensively from the published materials available in the exhibit and use vocabulary, spellings and descriptive terms chosen for these exhibits. Wherever possible, I have sought out firsthand, primary sources, written or spoken by the Ute themselves.[8]

The Yamparika and other Utes say they belonged to the land, not the other way around. Whatever terms are used to express a connection to the land, the Ute lived in Elkhead many hundreds, if not thousands, of years before it was claimed by homesteaders.

Some archeologists and historians now posit that the Ute arrived sometime in the 1400s, having migrated east from the Pacific coast. The Ute do not have a migration myth. Their explanation of their past is that they have been on the western side of the Rockies and in the Great Basin forever. A prominent anthropologist who developed the first dictionary of the Ute language suggests that the earliest people lived around lakes in the Great Basin—lakes which no longer exist but were likely present at the end of the Pleistocene period—and that they gradually dispersed to the east and south.[9] This theory is compatible with Aztec lore that says their people came from lakes in the north. It also explains how so many languages, spoken in such diverse places, were found to have common roots. The Ute language is related to other Great Basin languages, collectively called Shoshonean or Numic. It is also part of a huge language family called Uto-Aztecan that extended as far south as Central America. The Uto-Aztecan language family includes the Hopi, Pima, Pagago and Yaqui in Arizona and northern New Mexico and the Mayo and Tarahumara in other parts of northern Mexico. It also includes Nahuatl, the language of the Aztecs and other groups in Mexico and El Salvador.[10]

For the tribe, the land in Elkhead was part of an area called Bears Ears country. A traditional story, told here by Andrew Frank, describes this land:

The Bear Ears' Country

> A Bear met some Indians. They asked, "Where are you going?" He said, "I'm going to the Bears-Ears country. I'm looking for the country. Back here, over there, is the best country, with bull-grass, strawberries, and good eating. That's what I am looking for."[11]

Bears Ears country derives its name from two volcanic stubs, one slightly behind the other, presiding over the northern boundary of Elkhead. They look precisely like a bear's ears—unmoving, noble, listening. Visible for many miles around, the northwestern ear stands at 10,577 feet and the southeastern ear at 10,494 feet; the bare rock knobs rise steeply above the talus slopes and columnar basalt cliffs of their common mountain. Today, they form part of Routt National Forest and the Elkhead Range, an extension of the Rocky Mountains. The peaks preside over a long stretch of the Yampa River and are visible from many parts of northwest Colorado.[12]

Bears Ears country was centrally located in the Yamparika Utes's summer and fall hunting ground. Elk, deer, pronghorn, buffalo and bighorn sheep were the big game. The land was also an important place to gather chokecherries, wild strawberries, seeds, and medicinal herbs and roots. Bears Ears, Sugar Loaf, Saddle, Meaden and Pilot Knob, all mountains over 10,000 feet high, were places of spiritual and healing power. Lower down, along the Yampa River, the Ute found healing and spiritual renewal in the warm mineral springs.

Bears are integral to Ute culture. One of the oldest dances, one still practiced today, derives from a story about a bear waking up in the spring after a long winter of hibernation. There are several versions of this story. This is the version told by Snake John, member of the Ute tribe and a descendant of White River Ute, who were earlier known as Yamparika and Parianuche Ute.

Ute Girl studio portrait circa 1870. Denver Public Library, Western History Collection Z2728.

Origin of the Bear Dance

> In the fall the snow comes, and the bear has a wickiup in a hole. He stays there all winter, perhaps six moons. In the spring the snow goes, and he comes out. The bear dances up to a big tree on his hind-feet. He dances up and back, back and forth, and sings, "UUm, um, um, umr!" He makes a path up to the tree, embraces it, and goes back again, singing "Um, um, um!" He dances very much, all the time. Now Indians do it and call it the "Bear Dance." It happens in the spring, and they do not dance in the winter. The bear understands the Bear Dance.[13]

The Ute territory, the land they inhabited for many centuries, was inconceivably vast: who today can know what it was like to move freely over 225,000 square miles, or 144 million acres? The Ute people resided in and drew their livelihood from western Colorado and much of eastern Utah. They were in parts of New Mexico and Wyoming. Their place on this land was undisputed for hundreds, if not thousands, of years.

There were no fences, no surveys, no titles: the Ute lived there because they got there first, not because they bought it, or had conquered some other people.

The Ute used the land collectively. From as far back as they could remember, they shared what they had and moved freely within their piece of the continent. Natural landmarks—mountains, lakes, and rivers—were the only boundaries. Looking at the land that way, before it was divided into states, the Ute inhabited the area between the Rocky Mountains and Great Salt Lake, most of which is now referred to as the Colorado Plateau and the Great Basin, and between Rawlins, Wyoming, and Abiquiu, New Mexico. Their territory included 14,000-foot peaks along the eastern edge and desert lands at an elevation of around 7,000 feet in the Great Basin on the western border.

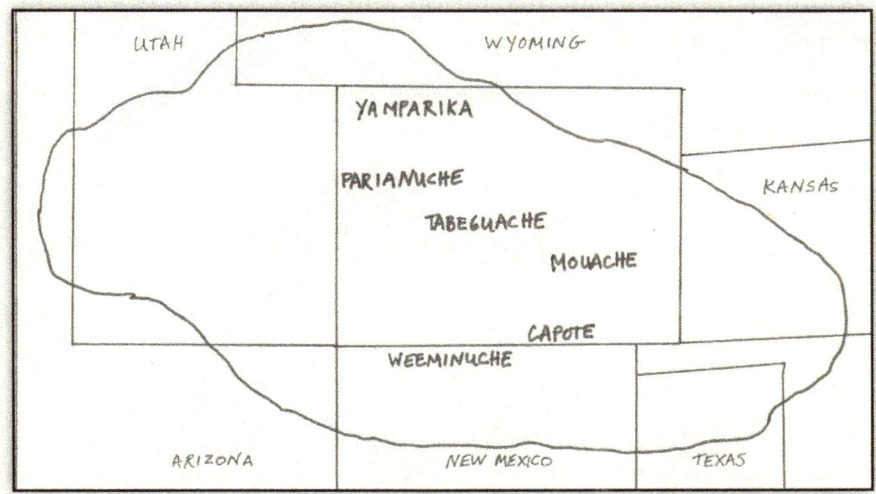

Colorado Ute bands and their approximate locations prior to 1879. The Cumumba, Uinta-ats, Tumpanawach, San Pitch, Pahvant, and Sheberetch bands lived in Utah.

Six bands, the Uinta-ats, Pahvant, Tumpanawach, San Pitch, Cumumba, and Sheberetch lived primarily in the desert lands of eastern Utah. In Colorado, each band was associated with a watershed and its principal river. The Yamparika were predominantly located along the Yampa River. Their neighbors to the south, the Parianuche, were connected to the upper Grand, later renamed the Colorado River. Both peoples frequented the White River before it joined the Green. Further south, in central Colorado, the Tabeguache band lived along the Gunnison, and the Mouache, Capote, and Weeminuche bands inhabited lands near the Arkansas, Conejos, Rio Grande, Animas and Delores rivers.[14]

Ute bands in Colorado typically oriented their seasonal circuit to a watershed and the course of their rivers. The headwaters of a river, at a high elevation, were inhabited in the summer and fall; the delta of the river, at lower elevation, served as winter and spring quarters. As one anthropologist described it, "they had the best watered area, they had the diverse environment from the mountain tops to the plains, the bottom of the front range and on into the Great Basin."[15]

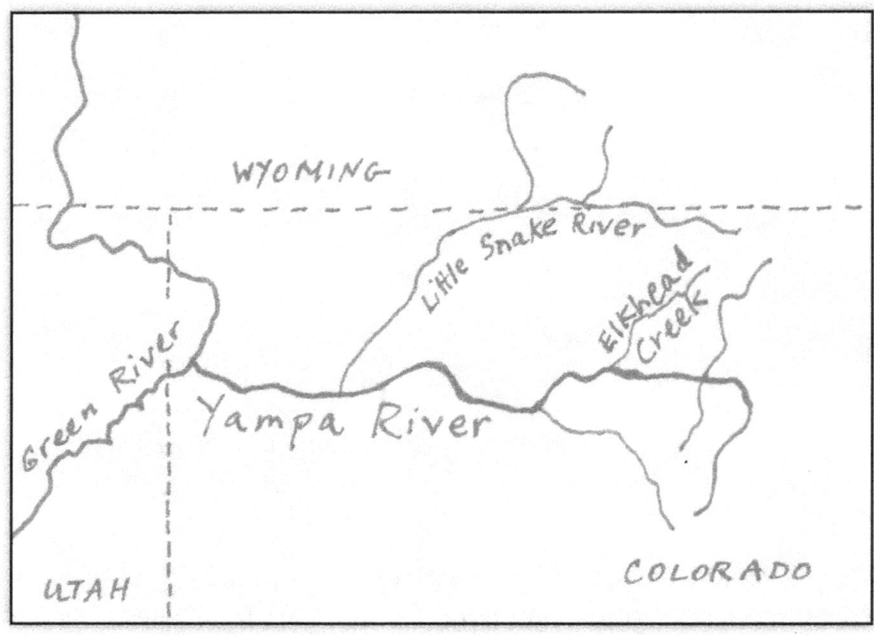

Yamparika lands in northwest Colorado were located along the Yampa River and its various tributaries. The Yampa joins the Green River in Colorado near the Utah border.

The Ute saw the world as oriented in a clockwise direction. Their perspective was based on the experience of standing on a peak facing south where the sun comes up on the left and goes down on the right. They believed that the sun passed through the underworld before emerging again on the left the next morning. To describe their environment, they had words for the sky and the underworld, words for high alpine areas, forested slopes on the sides of mountains, and a word for the flatter, drier areas in the basins and plains. Their worldview described three zones on the land, depending on elevation, climate, vegetation and animal life. It was an ecological model that also defined a way of life, based on an intimate knowledge of the land.

The Ute's seasonal circuit or seasonal migration was organized around resources they needed for their material and spiritual lives, timed to take advantage of what was available during each season and at different elevations and climatic zones.[16] Following well-established trails, they spent late spring, summer and early fall in the high mountains and late fall, winter, and early spring in the lower elevations. They moved up in elevation to fish and hunt big game, such as buffalo, elk, pronghorn, and bighorn sheep, and to harvest roots, seeds, and berries. Chokecherries, Yampa root and various grass seeds were vital additions to their diet. During the summer months they ground, sliced, dried and stored meat, vegetables, and nuts. They moved down to lower elevations in the winter where there was little or no snow and where they could gather another important part of their diet, the highly nutritious piñon nut.

Early observers described the tribe as nomadic and roaming, almost as if they wandered around with little purpose. In fact, the Ute used "systematic efficiency for the gathering of food and for the comfort of the season."[17] They had a complex, finely tuned relationship with the land, one they had honed over many hundreds of years.

The Yamparika, like other bands of the tribe, moved in small groups of around twenty families. The groups had leaders for various tasks—someone who decided when to hold important ceremonies, when to begin a hunt, where to go next to find an important food source, like chokecherries. But the bands, and the tribe itself, did not have chiefs, nor was there a tribal council. The bands for the most part co-existed peacefully; they traded, shared information, and met at various seasonal ceremonies such as at the annual Bear Dance. Although family groups identified as belonging to a particular band, intermarriage was common and membership in a particular band was fluid.

In a 1909 interview, John Duncan, a Ute, described life before contact with non-native Europeans and others:

The Indians of Long Ago

A long time ago the Nowintc [Ute] had little to eat. All the time they drank water. If anything grew on the ground, they would eat it, and they ate roots also. They had no woolen blankets but made blankets of cedar bark from the cedars on the mountains. They used sage brush for the blankets also, and somehow slipped them on themselves. Sometimes they used deer hide with the hair on and sometimes made deer hide leggings and moccasins. They were very poor. They had no guns—only bows and arrows—with which to kill deer. They took mud and made cups of it to drink water; they made kettles too, and cooked in them.[18]

Long line of women and girls at a Bear Dance near Ouray, circa 1920. Leo C. Thorne Collection. Used by permission, Uintah County Library Regional History Center, all rights reserved.

The Yamparika had a few essential possessions: parfleche and buckskin bags for their leather and fiber clothing, and baskets for carrying water, for gathering berries, seeds and plants, and for cooking. They made deerskin pouches for medicinal herbs and sacred objects.

Ute woman, Pootquas, making baskets. Leo C. Thorne Collection. Used by permission, Uintah County Library Regional History Center, all rights reserved.

A household group would also have wood and horn cups and ladles, a matate and mano for grinding and pounding, bows, arrows, an awl for stitching, cutting tools, light and small musical instruments, and hides—elk, deer, buffalo, rabbit—for clothing and shelter.

Everything they had they made by hand. Every tool or piece of clothing or household object had been found and crafted from some part of the Ute's natural environment. Sagebrush fibers were woven into mats and made into clothing; grasses became baskets; rocks became metate and manos; chokecherry limbs became bows and arrow shafts. Porcupine quills were fashioned into brushes, animal teeth into jewelry and ornaments. The Yamparika, and their neighboring Ute bands, were of the land, in the land, part of the land. "My flesh looks like the ground," John Star, a White River Ute, explained in 1903. "That's the reason I like this land; my flesh is like the land."[19]

There is very little record in the Ute's own words that describes their pre-contact lives. Until the 1950s, they did not have their own written language. Ute left pictographs and petroglyphs on rocky outcrops but they were little concerned about leaving a record of their time on the land and with each other. The early European people who encountered them on their land rarely spoke their language, and if they did, were primarily interested in what they could get from the Ute—food, land, or trade items like animal skins; these outsiders were absurdly incurious about who the Ute were and what their history had been. A few travelers and explorers were interested in how they could convert the Ute to Catholicism.

The first recorded encounter between the Northern Ute and a European seems to be that of Fray Silvestre Velez de Escalante on the Dominguez-Escalante expedition. On September 1, 1776, in what is now western Colorado, Escalante wrote that the explorers "encountered eighty Yutas all on good horses." The next day, he wrote . . .

> "We . . . came upon a sagebrush stretch where three Yuta women with a child were preparing the small fruits they had picked for their sustenance in the arroyos and rivulets thereabouts. We went over to talk to them, and right away they offered us their fruits, which were chokecherry, gooseberry, lemita [sumac], and some of this year's piñon nuts."[20]

Although Escalante's is the first known description of a specific encounter with the Ute, the Indians had already been in contact with the Spanish for at least 100 years. In the late 1500s the Ute obtained horses from the Spanish.[21] Early records describe trade with the Spanish: the Ute brought hides and slaves (typically Indian women and children they had captured) and traded them for horses. The northern or Colorado Ute bands very quickly became noted for their horsemanship and horse breeding. With horses, their range expanded, and they were able to more easily hunt big game like buffalo. By the 1860s, the Northern Ute had thousands of horses.

A Belgian Jesuit priest, Father Pierre-Jean De Smet, traveled through western Colorado in 1841 and 1842. Like others, he found the Ute very peaceable—both between members of their tribe and toward strangers.

> The country of the Utaws is situated to the east and south east of the Shoshones, at the sources of the Rio Colorado. The population consists of about 4,000 souls. Mildness, affability, simplicity of manners, hospitality toward strangers, constant union among themselves, form the happy traits in their character. They subsist by hunting and fishing, and on fruits and roots.[22]

John C. Fremont, a military officer and explorer from Savannah, Georgia, passed through Ute lands in 1844 and described in his journal camping along the Yampa River. On the night of June 10,

1844, he said his party "encamped in a fine grove of cottonwood trees on the banks of the Elk Head river, the principal fork of the Yampah river, commonly called by the trappers the Bear River."[23] Fremont's primary interest was to locate natural resources and routes between the Great Plains and the Pacific coast. He paid little attention to the Ute he encountered. When he did mention them, it was to denigrate or express fear. He called the Ute of central and eastern Utah "miserable Diggers" and wrote that "humanity here appeared in its lowest form, and in its most elementary state. Dispersed in single families; without fire-arms; eating seeds and insects; digging roots."[24] Although he did not meet any Yamparika Ute along the Yampa River, he expressed considerable fear of them and their neighbors. "We made here a very strong corral and fort and formed the camp into vigilant guards. The country we were now entering is constantly infested by war parties of the Sioux and other Indians, and is considered among the most dangerous war grounds in the Rocky Mountains . . ."[25]

The first person of European descent who took an interest in the Ute as a people with a language, culture and history was John Wesley Powell, a one-armed veteran of the Civil War who came to northwest Colorado on his way to explore the canyons of the Colorado River. In the winter of 1868–1869, he camped with his wife and several crew members in a valley of the White River, near what is now Meeker, Colorado. There was a band of Tabuat (sometimes referred to as Taveewach or Uncompaghre, now known as the Tabeguache) Ute camped nearby under the leadership of Quinkent or Douglas. The group was spending the winter on the more southern, lower altitude, and warmer lands of their seasonal circuit.

Powell and his crew pastured their horses in the sheltered valley and built simple log cabins for shelter. He spent four winter months along the White River learning the Ute language, asking questions and taking notes on what he saw and experienced.

> I tell the Indians that I wish to spend some months in their country during the coming year and that I would like them to treat me as a friend. I do not wish to trade; do not want their lands . . . I tell them that all the great and good white men are anxious to know very many things, that they spend much time in learning, and that the greatest man is he who knows the most; that the white men want to know all about the mountains and the valleys, the rivers and the canyons, the beasts and birds and snakes . . . I tell them I wish to learn about their canyons and mountains, and about themselves, to tell other men at home; and that I want to take pictures of everything and show them to my friends.[26]

After his daring adventure taking rafts down the Green and Colorado Rivers through the Grand Canyon, Powell returned to the West many times and continued his studies of the Ute, whom he referred to as the Southern Numic people. In 1873, Powell hired Ai-poup (Richard Komas), who was attending Lincoln College in Pennsylvania, and brought him to Washington, D.C., as a translator and informant. Ai-poup helped Powell expand his vocabulary and knowledge of Ute customs and folklore. Together they did the first line-by-line translation from Ute to English of the Story of the Eagle. Ai-poup died a year or so later of tuberculosis and for many decades no one took his place as a translator of Ute language and culture.

For several centuries after European colonialization of the Americas began, the Ute in western Colorado were able to continue their way of life mostly undisturbed. They lived in a relatively high mountainous enclave that explorer after explorer, hurrying through on their way to California or Oregon, declared "worthless." Outside observers enumerated the land's many problems: rough terrain, little water, and long distances from a railroad or navigable river. The U.S. government and investors noted the presence of coal in outcrops, but its value was considered too low for development. From these developers' perspective, there was plenty of land on the other side of the Great Desert, along the Pacific coast, and little incentive to displace the Ute.

Well into the nineteenth century and after the Civil War, the Ute were living a life little influenced by the huge changes in the nation around them. At least until the early to mid-1800s, the Colorado Ute were a small tribe, just a few thousand people, in a large, remote, mountainous region. Soon their isolation, and relative peace and security, would end. And soon the U.S. government would inflict multiple transgressions: forced removal, confinement, and severalty, against their land and sovereignty.

CHAPTER TWO

Displacement and Dislocation

(1849–1881)

The Spanish held all of southern and western Colorado until after the Mexican-American War (1846–1848). Mexican territorial claims—including what is now California, Nevada, Arizona, Utah, New Mexico, Texas, a sliver of Wyoming and much of Colorado—were all relinquished or sold in the Treaty of Hidalgo. The Spanish had never settled or controlled northern Colorado; their resources were overextended in attempting to maintain their base in Mexico, New Mexico and southern Colorado. The new border between Mexico and the United States was now the Rio Grande River.

After the U.S. government acquired this huge chunk of the Colorado Plateau, the Bureau of Indian Affairs (BIA) sent an agent to Abiquiu to negotiate a treaty with the Ute. On December 30, 1849, Quixiachigiate, who was described as the Principal Chief of the Utah [Ute] Indians, and twenty-eight "principal and subordinate chiefs," first signed away their independence and gave up their sovereignty. The so-called treaty of "perpetual peace and amity" was actually a document of submission:

> Article 1: The Utah tribe of Indians do hereby acknowledge and declare they are lawfully and exclusively under the jurisdiction of the Government of said States: and to its power and authority they now unconditionally submit.[27]

Fremont had made a rough map of the area between the Rockies and the Sierras but few non-Native people had any knowledge of the lands included in the purchase. Many people still assumed there was a river flowing west from somewhere in the Midwest that connected directly to the Pacific. No one had mapped the mighty Colorado River's course from the Rockies to the Gulf of Mexico, much less its many tributaries. The Mormons had trudged from Illinois to the Great Salt Lake in Utah in 1847, crossing the Rockies at South Pass in Wyoming, but the land north of Abiquiu and south of Bears Ears in Elkhead, between the Chama River and the Yampa River, was unmapped.

The 1849 treaty was not at all specific about where the Utah Indians lived, although it did state that a reservation would be created and that, in the meantime, the Ute were to stay put: "to cease the roving and rambling habits which have hitherto marked them as a people; to confine themselves strictly to the limits which may be assigned them."[28]

What really irritated the people of European descent at this time was the common Indian practice of raiding. Horse-mounted Indians raided pueblos for their corn and other crops. They raided neighboring tribes for horses, hides and meat. And stronger tribes raided weaker tribes for captives; they sometimes raised the children as slaves, sold and traded slaves, or adopted women and children into their tribes as their own wives and children. Emigrant families, bachelor miners and prospectors of all sorts seeking their fortunes on the main trails through Santa Fe and across South Pass were vulnerable. It was relatively easy for mounted Indians to swoop in and take supplies, domestic livestock, horses, or even people. Early on, Indian agents were the receivers of endless complaints about stolen goods on the various routes west. The military was constantly being called in to escort and protect non-Native settlers, miners and wanderers who were pushing west to the gold in California or some other mirage of wealth and prosperity.

Official documents described the raids as "depredations." The Ute in 1849 agreed to "deliberately and considerately, pledge their existence as a distinct tribe, to abstain, for all time to come, from depredations."[29] Representatives of the government and many faith groups believed that agriculture was the path to civilization. Planting and tending crops, it was thought, would create Christians and lift the Indians from "depravity." A future was possible, if only the Indians would settle down, live in a house, plant a garden, milk a cow and send their children to school to learn English and proper table manners.

From their brief meeting in Abiquiu, the Ute returned to their winter camps, some along the Chama, others to the north along the San Juan and other sheltered river valleys. Pen and paper were not part of the culture. Nor did they have much use for money. Even if they had a word for submission, it was not a state they had ever collectively experienced. There are no recorded stories in the Ute tradition that speak of a conquered people. Although they had signed an acceptance of their new place as subjects of a foreign government, they had a few years of freedom left.

After the Civil War, Colorado changed rapidly. The discovery of gold and other minerals set in motion the rapid development of mines and mining towns. These were not typically "one man with a pick or pan" operations; they were corporate enterprises that included heavy investments in machinery, dependence on roads and coordination with railroads. Mines brought in permanent settlements to the Colorado Rockies. Towns were planted in the middle of Ute hunting grounds and roads took the place of their well-worn trails.

The first Ute reservation and the first delineation of Ute territory in Colorado occurred in 1863, as part of the Tabeguache Treaty signed at Conejos. Non-Native Coloradans wanted the Ute confined to the western half of the state so that they could open mines "without interference or protestation" in the central Rockies. The treaty at Conejos established a reservation in central western Colorado for the Tabeguache but did not directly affect the northern bands. The Yamparika and Parianuche did not sign this treaty.[30]

During this time, the Ute successfully avoided confrontation with the U.S. military or the Colorado Territorial militia. Conflicts were happening all around them. The closest, and in many ways the worst, was the Sand Creek massacre: in November 1864, the Colorado militia under the leadership of John Chivington attacked a friendly Cheyenne-Arapaho village on the eastern side of the Rockies and killed and mutilated many Indians, mostly women and children.

The Ute were fortunate in being out of the way, nestled among the mountains. They also volunteered to assist the military and served as guides and soldiers in various campaigns against other tribes. Fifty Ute accompanied Christopher (Kit) Carson in his 1863 campaign against the Navajo that resulted in a prolonged battle in Canyon De Chelly and the subsequent Long Walk to Bosque Redondo, where the majority of the Navajo people were incarcerated at Fort Sumner in New Mexico. Ute also participated in attacks on the Sioux, the Arapaho, and Comanche. Their horsemanship and marksmanship were much admired. Nicaagat, a northern Colorado Ute who later became a leader of the Yamparika and Parinuche bands, was a well-known soldier and guide who worked under General George R. Crook in the Dakotas. It was not uncommon for the military to send a request to an Indian agent on a reservation for Indian fighters; often, Ute men would temporarily enlist.

Despite friendly relations on many fronts, and perhaps because officials considered the Ute malleable, the incursions into Ute lands continued unabated.

The next treaty the Ute signed was written farther north, in Hot Sulphur Springs, in what was by then the Territory of Colorado. Hot Sulphur Springs is named for the thermal springs that flow into the Colorado River on the edge of Middle Park. In 1866, a group of investors came up with a plan to build an overland road through Hot Sulphur Springs, connecting Denver with Salt Lake City. The idea was far-fetched, but the potential profits were enormous. The road was supposed to leave Denver, climb over the Continental Divide (at around 11,000 feet), cross Middle Park, climb over the Continental Divide again at what is now Rabbit Ears Pass (9,400 feet), follow the Yampa west to the Green River, and continue across the eastern Utah desert to Salt Lake City.

A small group of Ute representatives were on hand to negotiate this treaty of "perpetual peace and friendship," which acknowledged the tribe's claim to the land and essentially asked the group not to raid builders, travelers or settlers along the road. In return, the treaty promised livestock and provisions both immediately and in the future for the "Uintah and Yampa or Grand River [Yamparika and Parianuche] bands of Utah Indians," as the northern Colorado Ute were then called.[31]

There were eleven Ute signers at Hot Sulphur Springs:

Sa-ga-wich or Buzzard
Jack, or One Name (this was likely Nicaagat, who was called Jack or Captain Jack after his time in the military)
Pa-end or High
Sa-Pach or White
Un-ca-chep or Red Lodge Pole
Nevada or Snow
Sach-wa-tschwhich or Blue River

Pa-ha-pitch or Swimmer
Ya-ha-me-na, Prickly Pear
Pan-qii-to, or Minnow
Ta-ha-ken, Washington

Why did the Yamparika and Parianuche sign this treaty? It was their first treaty and the gains they made appear insignificant. Their losses at that time were only on paper—a proposed road—so perhaps they were willing to take the gamble and did not think the road would disrupt their lives. A more likely reason was hunger. The winters in the early 1860s had been long and harsh and game was scarce. The buffalo were fewer in the mountains and the Ute faced growing competition for hunting on the eastern plains of Colorado. All of the Plains Indians were facing food shortages as the buffalo were slaughtered for meat and, more commonly, for hides.

The 1866 treaty provided twenty-five head of cattle, unspecified provisions, blankets and clothing at the signing and promised "annually thereafter blankets and stock either horses, cattle or sheep, to the value of five thousand ($5000) dollars, and provisions to the value of three thousand ($3000) dollars."[32] In addition, in recognition of the northern Ute's prominent herds of horses, the treaty promised twenty-five horses "with saddles, bridles, and blankets for each complete" upon ratification.[33]

Even though it established no official reservation, the treaty brought reservation culture to northwest Colorado. Non-Native pressure to occupy and develop the land had crossed the Rockies. The northern Ute were now selling land and access in return for rations and horses. Although the 1866 Hot Sulphur Treaty was never ratified by the U.S. Congress, attempts at subjugation were well underway.

Sometime between 1866 and 1868 a group of reformers, including Kit Carson and Alexander C. Hunt, the Territorial Governor of Colorado, drafted a letter on behalf of the Ute. This letter is unique

Ta-ha-ken (Washington) one of the Yamparika signers of the 1866 treaty, circa 1900. L. Tom Perry Special Collections, Harold B. Lee Library, Brigham Young University, Provo, Utah. P16, Item 207.

for its time in its advocacy for the tribe. Powell did not camp with the Ute until the winter of 1868 and few people of European descent seem to have had the Ute's interests in mind in their rush to take all they could from Colorado. In this letter, the writers attempt to persuade policymakers, presumably the BIA and Congress, to address the needs of the Ute and avoid conflict. Instead of agriculture, they advocated raising livestock: cattle and sheep instead of corn and beans. "Farming proper cannot be carried on in the region of their new reservation on account of the scarcity of arable land" but, the writers continue, "stock can be raised to good advantage by wintering it low down on the large rivers, and driving it to the upper waters during the summer."[34] The suggestion recognized the Ute's traditional seasonal circuit, which was so well-adapted to the range of elevation on their lands. The writers also seem to recognize the Indian's long history of animal husbandry. They point out that "some of these Indians have already from ten to fifty head of sheep and goats, raised from a small stock obtained from the settlers in exchange for skins; thus proving conclusively that they will care diligently for such domestic animals."[35] Furthermore, "as shepherds they will excel even the Mexican who is deemed the best known."[36] They painted a dire picture of the alternative:

> Either this must be done or they must be permitted to roam as heretofore, through settlements, where, when pinched by hunger they will satisfy their cravings by forced contributions from the unlucky farmer or ranchers whose herd lies near their line of travel. Such depredations are, if not actual war, at least its seeds, and we feel safe in saying that nine out of every ten of all Indian outbreaks, originate in this sort of aggression on their hunt, caused by their necessities for food and transportation.[37]

The vision Kit Carson and the others had is remarkably pluralistic. It is also pragmatic. The authors had deep respect for the

Ute warriors and felt that the United States would waste enormous resources fighting them, and would likely lose. "War," they assert, "with these Indians would be a most disastrous issue, and would certainly result in the entire destruction of the Mountain Settlements of Colorado and New Mexico. We give it as our belief that fifty Ute Warriors could keep a whole regiment of soldiers fighting for months, and then unless one should die from exposure or starvation, they (the Indians) would not lose a man."[38] Far better to give them sufficient land, cattle and sheep, as well as guns and ammunition for their hunts, so that they could live alongside their neighbors of European descent in peace.

Needless to say, this wise advice went largely unheeded. There was a general sense, however, that the treaty at Conejos was insufficient and that another treaty would be necessary to create a reservation and a system of annuities and rations for all the Colorado Ute.

In late 1867, Kit Carson personally escorted several Ute chiefs to Washington, D.C., to visit President Andrew Johnson and discuss treaty terms. Representatives of nearly all the Colorado bands joined Carson. The treaty at Conejos had proved nearly worthless because it had been completed and signed by only one of the seven Colorado bands. Carson and others wanted to correct that mistake and create a treaty that would serve all of the Colorado Ute. Consequently, Ouray (Uncompaghre), Kaniache (Mouache), An-ko-tash (Uncompaghre), Jose-Maria (unknown affiliation), Nicaagat (Yamparika/Parianuche), Guero (Uncompaghre), Pa-ant (Yamparika), Pi-ah (Parianuche), Su-vi-ap (Yamparika), and Pa-busat (Capote) were in Washington to sign.

Ouray was the most well-known member of the delegation; the U.S. government designated him the chief. The Ute did not formally designate chiefs; they had leaders who served in various capacities. The government, on the other hand, wanted a chief who would speak for the entire tribe. Ouray was chosen because he spoke English and Spanish, and because he was regularly described as reasonable and farsighted. Ouray's wife, Chipeta, was the only woman to accompany the group to Washington. She charmed the press, who referred to her as an "Indian princess." That Ouray could neither speak for all Ute, nor had any authority over all the bands, or even over the Uncompaghre, did not matter to the government.

Delegation to Washington, 1868. Photo taken by Matthew Brady. Left to right: An-ko-tash, Pe-ah, Su-ru-ipe, Uriah M. Curtis, George M. Chilcott, Sa-wa-ich, Albert C. Boone, Alexander C. Hunt, Nicaagat, Hiram Bennett, Lafayette Head, Wa-ro, Daniel Oakes, Chief Ouray, Edward Kellogg, Severo, William Godfrey. National Portrait Gallery.

The final treaty was signed at the Washington Hotel on March 2, 1868. The following summer, various government officials carried the treaty to all seven Colorado bands and added thirty-three signatures; in the end, there were at least five Ute signers representing each band. The 1868 treaty established all the Colorado bands as the "Consolidated Ute Tribe" and set aside 15 million acres for their reservation. The Ute got all of western Colorado, west of the 107th parallel, from the Rockies to the Utah border for their "absolute and undisturbed use." There were several curious and discordant sections. Instead of livestock, the Ute were to receive one hundred dollars worth of seed and implements every year for three years. An amendment took away $45,000 to promote livestock and one "good bull for every twenty-five cows." The Ute were to be farmers, not ranchers. And instead of guns and ammunition for hunting, they were allotted up to $30,000 worth of food rations "until they are able to sustain themselves."[39] The BIA's earlier iteration, the Office of Indian Affairs, established two agencies: one on the White River, near the present-day town of Meeker, for the most northern Colorado bands including the Yamparika, and one called Los Piños, south of the present-day small city of Gunnison, for the southern bands. The White River Agency and surrounding reservation was about seventy miles south and west of Bears Ears and the Elkhead lands.

The March 1868 Treaty contained one strange omission. Without any explanation, the northern border of Ute land in Colorado shifted approximately fifty-four miles south. The 1868 treaty made no mention of the Wyoming/Colorado border at the 41st parallel north, the natural line for the Colorado Ute; the line in the treaty is "a point fifteen miles due north of where said meridian intersects the fortieth parallel of north latitude."[40] There was no mention of the lands along the Yampa River, Elkhead, the confluence of the Yampa and the Green or North and Middle Park; nor did the document take note of Rabbit Ears, the landmark which signaled the northern boundary in the 1863 Conejos Treaty.

Seemingly unknown to the Yamparika, and the Ute tribe, the first Fort Bridger Treaty in 1863 had already assigned all lands north of the Yampa, encompassing the Elkhead mountain range including Bears Ears, Rabbit Ears and California Park, to the Eastern Shoshone. A few years later, in the second Fort Bridger Treaty signed in July 1868, the federal government took all those lands back. The Shoshone were left with severely diminished lands on Wyoming's Wind River Reservation. The two Fort Bridger treaties never mentioned the Yamparika band or the Ute tribe. In one maneuver, the 1863 Fort Bridger Treaty completed the sale and transfer of millions of acres of Ute land without their knowledge or consent.[41]

Those lands legally disappeared for the Ute. When the government prepared a treaty with Colorado Ute in 1868, there was no description of these lands or mention of their transfer to the Shoshone. It was little wonder that for at least the next 45 years Yamparika, and later White River Ute, would continue to ask about lands along the Bear River, as the Yampa was often referred to, refusing to admit they no longer held those lands, and expressing disbelief at their loss. The Yamparika Ute became nearly invisible, their long claim to the lands surrounding the Yampa River extinguished.

The Yamparika also lost their name. After 1868, the Yamparika were bureaucratically merged with Parianuche and called White River Ute after the name of the agency that governed the northern half of the reservation. The Mouache, Capote, and Weeminuche who drew their rations from the Los Piños Agency did not become Los Piños Indians; but for some reason the Yamparika and Parianuche, or Grand River Ute, became simply the White River Ute.

Dependence on rations, submission to an agent, and confinement on a defined reservation did not suit the Ute and especially not the northern Colorado bands. Frustrated Indian Agents came and went, filing reports of plowing undertaken and crops sowed that yielded little or no harvest.

The agents perennially complained about the failure of the government to provide schools, and later, when there were schools on the reservations, about the Ute's failure to send their children to school. At that time, the government operated a three-tier system of schools for the Ute and most Native American Indians. At the top of the system were elite boarding schools: Carlisle, Hampton and Forest Grove. Students who were sent to these schools were "chosen for their intelligence, force of character and soundness of constitution."[42] Very few Ute children ever attended these schools. At the next level were reservation boarding schools typically overseen by a Christian church. Ute children attended boarding schools at White Rocks, Utah, Grand Junction and later Ignacio, Colorado, and in Santa Fe, New Mexico. On the bottom tier were reservation day-schools sometimes taught by missionaries and usually very poorly funded and barely staffed. For most of the Ute, all of these schools were abhorrent and parents did everything possible to keep their children away.[43] Instruction was in English; Ute language was forbidden. Boys were taught to tend to livestock and farm. Girls were instructed in homemaking. There was no attempt to connect the curriculum to the tribe's culture or customs, much less to the place where they were to grow up. Diseases coursed through the schools, especially the boarding schools. Hundreds of students died of tuberculosis and many were blinded by trachoma.

Schoolboys line up in uniform at White Rocks boarding school. No date. Leo C. Thorne Collection, used by permission, Uintah County Library Regional History Center, all rights reserved.

Schoolgirls line up in uniform at the White Rocks boarding school No date. Leo C. Thorne Collection, used by permission, Uintah County Library Regional History Center, all rights reserved.

The insistence on inculcating traditional Christian culture permeated nearly every decision by the government and its agents. The Colorado Ute, and especially the Yamparika Ute, were resolutely uninterested in agriculture. They held to their customs and reputation as horse people—horse breeders, trainers and traders. Every White River agent complained about the Ute's herd of horses.

To study this section of history is to feel a terrible sense of impending doom. The story does not end well. Whatever accomplishments were to be had on the land, or glories to be celebrated, were thereafter drawn on a dark background of violence, betrayal, and stolen property.

The crisis for the Ute had been delayed because other than miners, few people outside the Ute tribe had found much of value in the lands of western Colorado. But in 1879, the end came swiftly. Nathaniel Meeker, a journalist and wanderer, was struggling financially in the utopian Union Colony he and others founded on the eastern plains of Colorado. Needing to repay a debt to his benefactor, Horace Greeley, he applied for a job as an Indian Agent.

Meeker and his family traveled to northwest Colorado in March 1878 to take charge of a remote outpost on what Indians called the Smoking Earth River, and those of European descent called the White River, near what is now the town of Meeker. Along with

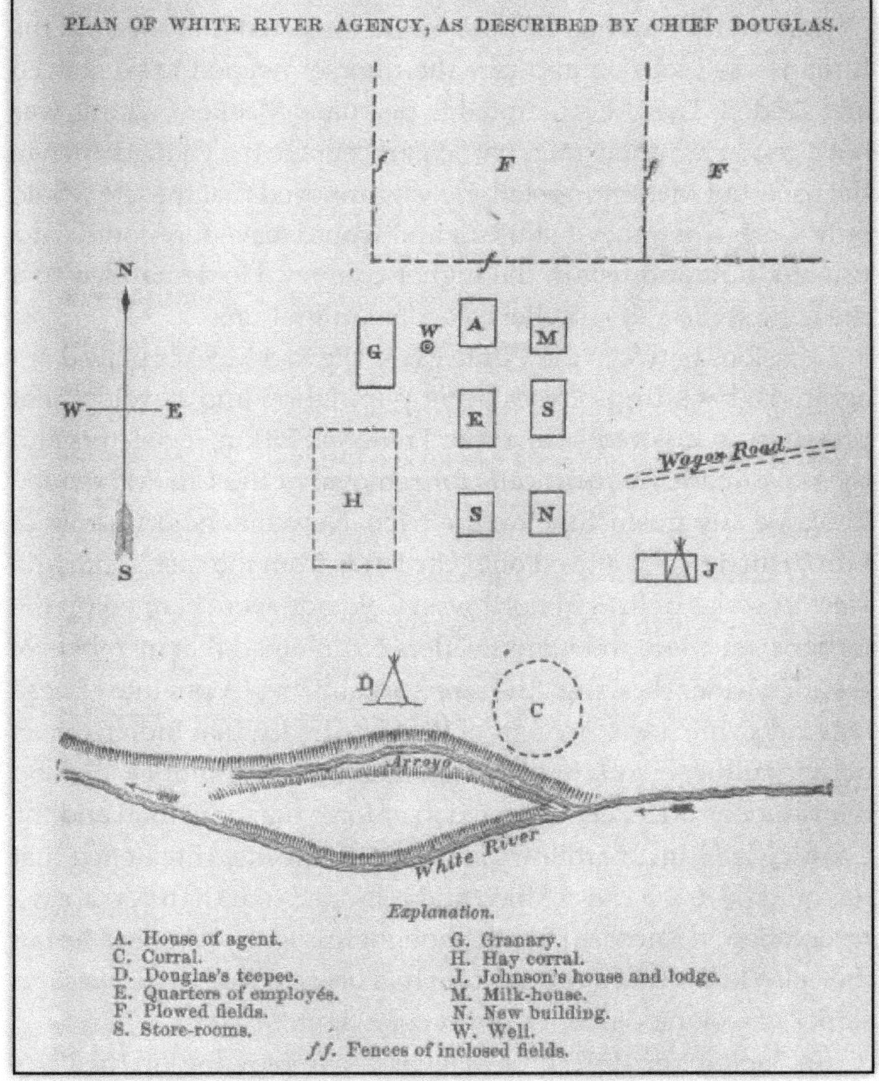

Plan of the White River Agency as described by Quinkent (Chief Douglas). From testimony before the 1879 White River Commission.

his wife and daughter, Meeker, sixty years old and, by then, an elderly man, began an effort to civilize the Ute by turning them into farmers. He told the Ute they could not get their government rations unless they contributed to cultivating the reserve. They dug miles of ditches and turned ground for cultivation.

Late in the summer of 1879, Meeker insisted that the land the Indians used to train and race their horses needed to be plowed and seeded. The Ute attempted to persuade Meeker that this was not a good plan and would particularly enrage the younger men in the tribe, but Meeker insisted. He was annoyed that the Ute would only work when they felt like it and would leave for months at a time to hunt and fish in the higher country. He demanded that the tribe settle and end their seasonal migrations.

Tensions between the White River Ute and Meeker played out against a backdrop of escalating population and development pressures in Colorado. Governor Frederick Pitkin, legislators and the press made frequent calls for removal of the Ute and tended to blame any misfortune on the tribe. Newcomers, primarily of European descent, moved onto Ute lands from the east, south and west. A series of fires in northwest Colorado were blamed on the Indians; ranchers and homesteaders complained that members of the tribe were "escaping" the reservation. The BIA put into effect a new rule, which was not part of the Ute's treaty, that Indians must do agricultural work in order to receive their annuities, or food distributions. Meeker attempted to enforce the regulation and the Ute accused him of arbitrary restrictions. Meeker threatened that he could have the Ute chained and relocated to Indian Territory, a reservation in Kansas. The Ute thought this was probably a lie but they also knew that a cavalry unit had been moved to the western slopes of Colorado in anticipation of a fight.[44]

In September 1879, after Meeker began plowing up the Ute's racetrack, a Ute chief, Canella (also known as Johnson), may have shoved Meeker during an argument about the racetrack;

Meeker allegedly fell backwards over a hitching rail. According to Canella,

> I told the agent that it was not right that he should order the men to plow my land. The agent told me I was always a troublesome man, and that it was likely I might come to the calaboose. I told him that I did not know why I should go to prison. I told the agent that it would be better for another agent to come, who was a good man, and was not talking such things. I then took the agent by the shoulder and told him that it was better that he should go. Without doing anything else to him—striking him or anything else—I just took him by the shoulder.[45]

Meeker immediately wrote to Colorado Governor Pitkin and sent a telegram to the Commissioner of Indian Affairs:

> I have been assaulted by a leading chief, Johnson, forced out of my own house and injured badly, but was rescued by employees . . . the opposition to plowing is wide; plowing stops; life of self, family, and employees not safe; want protection immediately; have asked Governor Pitkin to confer with General Pope.[46]

Governor Pitkin was eager to confront the Ute and requested troops. At the same time, the War Department dispatched 153 soldiers from Rawlins, Wyoming, to investigate. Disaster was imminent. Messages sent were not received, and people who assumed they were in a peaceful situation ended up in the middle of a conflict; others, eager for violence, prevailed. It is unknown who fired the first shot along Milk Creek near the White River Agency. At the end of the battle, thirty-seven Ute men, ten soldiers, and eight male agency staff, including Meeker, were dead. Three women and two children, including Meeker's wife, Arvilla, and his daughter, Josephine, either were taken hostage or were escorted away from the conflict into the mountains south of the agency.

There was no subtlety in the response. The Denver newspaper immediately renewed calls for the removal of the Ute and the opening of the 12 million acres they owned. U.S. Senator Nathaniel Hill began a campaign, "Utes Must Go." The Buffalo Soldiers, an all-Black cavalry unit, and an additional 450 troops, were sent to end the confrontation. Three weeks after the initial confrontation, and after Secretary of Interior Carl Schurz intervened to call off the military, the conflict subsided and the Ute released Meeker's and agency employees' family members. Chief Ouray and others relinquished most of northwest Colorado and agreed to move to a reservation in Utah. Ouray died a few months later before the U.S. military forcibly marched members of his band, the remaining 300 Tabeguache Ute, onto a reservation. By early 1880 the Ouray and Consolidated Ute Tribes had no rights to land in northern and central Colorado.[47]

Nicaagat, one of the leaders of the White River Ute, rode horseback to the Los Piños Agency in southern Colorado in early December 1879 to testify before the Special Commission assigned to investigate the incidents at the White River Agency. His testimony reveals the arc of Ute history up until that time and is the most authentic account of what happened to the tribe between September 29 and October 21, 1879. Nicaagat was an eyewitness and a participant. He could speak of the tensions and paradoxes that had led to the fight on Milk Creek, the deaths of the Indian agent and his staff, and the capture of three agency women and two children. It is worth going back over the story to hear it from his perspective.

Nicaagat was a Goshute who was taken as a child by Spanish slave traders, then purchased by Mormons. He was abused and later escaped to join the Ute.[48] By the 1860s, he was being called Captain Jack or John and was working for General Crook in the Dakotas. After he left the military, he became well known as one of the principal leaders of the Yamparika and Parianuche bands. He left no record of his personal history; as his reputation grew, the myths around him became more fantastic. His name first appears on paper in 1866 when he, along with other members of the Yamparika and Parianuche bands, signed the treaty at Hot Sulphur Springs, Colorado. Two years later, at another treaty signing, his name is translated as Greenleaf. In a photo taken at the time, he appears to be a young man, between twenty-five and thirty, of medium build. His hair is pulled back behind his ears, his eyes are set far apart. He is dressed in deer skins, with a very intent, unafraid gaze.

Nicaagat as a young man. Photo taken by A. Zeno Shindler during Nicaagat's stay in Washington, D.C., 1868. National Anthropological Archives, Smithsonian Institution 01573106694500.

In 1873 Nicaagat was photographed for a stereoscopic series and identified as a Ute chief.

Nicaagat, 1873. National Anthropological Archives, Smithsonian Institution 09831600.

Nicaagat was called as a witness before the Los Piños Commission on December 3 and 4, 1879. General Hatch, the presiding officer, opened the day's testimony by saying to Nicaagat, "I want Jack to tell his story; how the agent treated him, and all about the troubles at White River."[49] Nicaagat (Jack) began:

> One time I was on Bear [Yampa] River; I had returned from a buffalo hunt; this was the first time I knew anything of Meeker. I heard at this time that the agent wished to move Sow-er-wick's house from the old agency, where he lived, down to the new agency; Sow-er-wick did not wish it moved. It was then that I was called for by Sow-er-wick . . . When I arrived at the old agency I found nothing left standing except Sow-er-wick's house; the agent had taken down and moved everything else . . . I there met the agent, who had come up from below; he told me that we must all move down to the new site, and I answered him, "you had better wait a little

> before doing this, as we want to understand the reason for moving; I don't understand it." I told him that the site of the old agency had been settled by treaty, and that I knew no law or treaty that made mention of the new site. Then the agent told me that we had better all move down below, and that if we did not we should be obliged to; that for that they had soldiers.[50]

This account of an opening confrontation between Meeker and the Ute centers around a sheltered, grassy valley where John Wesley Powell spent the winter in 1868-1869. Powell camped near Ute leader Quinkent, who became known as Douglas or Douglass. The area was a Ute winter camp where many horses could find feed under the light snows. Meeker saw the land as irrigable farmland and felt the Ute needed to get rid of their horses. As Quinkent testified, "the agent told me that we should not have so many horses, because they were eating up all the grass, and that we had better kill a part of our horses and only save a few, so as to save the grass."[51] Meeker moved the agency and all the buildings that were nearby. He then focused on plowing and planting the valley land where the Ute had traditionally wintered their horses.

Nicaagat described troubles with Agent Meeker and what the Ute saw as double-dealing: Meeker kept giving the Ute something and then taking it back. Pushing them one way, and then another: dividing the land into house plots, and even assisting in building log cabins, and then insisting the houses be moved and the plots turned over for cultivation. After telling a story of promised government wagons, Nicaagat continued:

> The great trouble with the agent was that he would tell one story one day and another the next, so that we did not know how to take him or when to believe him.

> Sow-er-wick used the wagon for a month and took it back to the agent. At this time an employee came from the agency to my house and called me to see the agent, who wanted to talk to me. When I went to see him he told me that he had received information that some Indians had set fire to houses, and that he had received notice that some soldiers were coming to where we were. He said, not only one but several houses had been burned by the Indians. I then told the agent I thought we had better, he and I, go and see these houses that had been burned, that we might understand something about it. He answered me that it was none of his business to talk about these things, and I asked him how that could be, as he, being Indian agent, he was the man who should regulate such matters. He said the Utes were very bad men and that they should get out the best way they could; that he had no business to be worrying himself in talking for them. I then said, "How is this? It is not well for you to talk in this way. If you take it in hand and show how it is, all would be right." The agent said, "I am not going to talk about that; I am going home." I told the agent he had better do or say something about this, and then he could go away; but he said it was the business of the Commissioner, and he (Meeker) would have nothing to do with it. I told him he was the man placed there by the Commissioner to look after and speak about these things. He then said tomorrow he should leave.[52]

Nicaagat describes quite accurately the contradictory charges of the agents. They were to defend the Indians against those who maligned or threatened them; but they were also supposed to change them into another type of people, with a different culture, different way of life, with an identity based in individualism rather than as a member of a tribe. Meeker was not alone in being awkwardly suspended between being an advocate and defender and an assimilator and oppressor. Unfortunately, he was less willing than most agents to straddle the conflicting demands, and he believed the military could solve his problems. He sought the attention of anyone he could appeal to in power. He longed for a show of force that would bend the Ute to his will. Nicaagat continued his testimony:

> On the second day after this the agent left, and two days afterward I went on a trip to Bear [Yampa] River. While there, I came to the house of a friend, a white man (Peck), who asked me what news there was from my agency. I told him I knew of none, and he asked me, "How about this notice here from your agent," showing me a written paper. I asked him to let me see the notice. He told me, "This letter says that the Indians wish to fight." I told him that perhaps he understood a good deal in Ute, and could understand what they said. The man answered that it was not the first letter that had been sent out this way; that ever since spring letters and notices had been sent out. The man (Peck) then told me that it would be a good idea for he and I to go to Denver and see Governor Pitkin, who could advise us regarding these matters. On the road Peck told me about the house that was burned; and I told him we had better, in passing, take a look at the place, which was Thompson's house. We passed by there, and we saw Thompson's house standing; it was not burned.[53]

Peck's store, operated by Hannibal Erskine Peck and his wife Mary Frances, was near the present site of Craig, Colorado, along the Yampa River.[54] Although many miles northeast of the reservation, the store was a busy place that sold guns and ammunition to the Ute, as well as other supplies. It appears that Peck was much more inclined to believe Nicaagat over Meeker when it came to the intentions of the White River Ute. Together they rode horseback the over 200 miles to Denver in hopes of meeting with the governor.

> On arriving in Middle Park we found the same reports that I had heard at Bear River, and we were told of notices having been distributed the same as at Bear River. I then told Peck we better hurry up and get to Denver to see how things were working there. In two days we were in Denver. Upon arriving I was very anxious to see the governor before going anywhere else. Several men told me they could not bring me to where the governor was, but that it took men of influence to do so; and some told me that Mr. Byers, of Middle Park, could take me to the governor.
>
> I went to Byers, and with him we went to the governor. The governor asked me how things were in my country, on White River, saying that the papers were saying a great deal about us. I told him I thought so myself, and for that reason I had come to Denver. I said I did not understand why this business was in such a state. Then the governor said he was not saying this to be talking; that here was a letter, and he showed me the letter. I told the governor I was very much astonished at all this; that I was always wishing and striving for peace; and was much surprised at what was going on. He then said, "Here is a letter from your Indian agent." I told him that, as the Indian agent could write, he had written that letter; but that I, not being able to write, had come to see him in person and answer it. That much we talked; and then I told him I did not wish him to believe what was written in that letter.[55]

Nicaagat was called back to the governor's office the following day.

> Afterwards I was in the governor's office again, and he asked me if it was true that Thompson's house was burned. I told

> him that I had seen the house—that it was not burned. I then talked to the governor about the Indian agent, and told him it would be well for him to write to Washington and recommend that some other agent be put in his place, and he promised to write the next day.[56]

Pitkin did not hold to his promise. He was more likely to stoke the antagonism against the Ute as he was keenly aware of the value of their land in western Colorado. However courteously he treated Nicaagat as an individual, he had no interest in keeping the Ute in Colorado.

Nicaagat rode home to northwest Colorado. Along the way, near present-day Kremmling, he encountered an African-American regiment known as the Buffalo Soldiers. Nicaagat tried to correct the misinformation that Meeker was spreading. He felt he had been heard by the Buffalo Soldiers.

> After leaving Denver, when I arrived in Middle Park I met some soldiers. The officer asked me how things were going on at White River; that he had heard that there was trouble there. I told him, as far as I knew, everything was quiet; the soldiers were colored. I told him what he had heard were lies. He pulled out a paper and showed me, saying that it was information received from the agent regarding the trouble. He told me that what I had told him was all right, that he believed it. He told me there was no use his going any further toward White River.[57]

When Nicaagat returned to the White River Reservation after his trip to Denver he encountered a suspicious and stubborn Meeker. Meeker questioned why Nicaagat had gone to Denver. He was not in the mood to negotiate or even listen to the Ute. He dismissed Nicaagat and his efforts and resolutely continued to wait for military assistance.

> I then passed on and came to White River. When I arrived, the Indian Agent was again at the agency. The day after I arrived I went down to the agency, and the agent received me by asking me what business I had running around, and what business took me to Denver. I informed him that I had seen papers in which he had given information about things that were not happening. He answered, "Is it your business to go around finding out what I had written?" Then I told the agent that it was not right that he should be always talking that way; that he was an Indian agent and should not talk roughly to his Indians, and it would be better for him to keep quiet. At that time he did not answer me, but a little while after, while I was still seated, he told me that these were orders from the Commissioner. I then went back to my camp, and an American employee came to call me again. I found I was called on account of the business regarding the plowing of the land where the houses stood; that I should have the houses moved further down. The houses were fenced in, corrals were built there, and yet he wanted them moved. So he told me that all that site which he had given to the Utes for their houses, he now wanted for himself for the agency.[58]

Tensions continued to escalate. According to Nicaagat, Meeker was insistent that the Ute move their homes and corrals so that the land underneath the homes could be plowed and planted. The Ute continued to resist but did not directly confront Meeker. Nicaagat appears to have been caught in the middle. Meeker complained to him and wanted him to act like a chief and convey his orders to the Ute; Nicaagat did not agree with Meeker but could not convince him that he was courting danger by displacing Ute homes. Nicaagat knew that Meeker was provoking the Ute into a conflict, but he could not find a way to stop him. Their conversation became very personal—Nicaagat addressed Meeker as an equal, to no avail.

Henry Jim, 1878. National Anthropological Archives, Smithsonian Institution 06685600.

> The next day, he [Meeker] sent another employee to call me, and I again went. On my arrival, the agent told me that a shot had been fired at one of the employees, which went very near him. [The agency employee had been plowing on the disputed ground.] I then asked Henry Jim if that was true,

> and Henry Jim said, "Tah-titz was firing at a mark." I told the agent that they said they were firing at a mark, and he said, no; that they were threatening by firing. I told him to not get angry about this; to let it pass by. I told him that he was an employee of the government, and that his business was to keep the peace. I told him he was getting old, and consequently got mad quickly.[59]

Problems continued to compound. Meeker moved agency buildings closer to land more suitable for farming and, in so doing, forced many Ute to move their homes. He requisitioned their horse pasture for cultivation and sent his employees to plow the meadow. To induce cooperation from the Ute, he withheld rations from tribe members who did not comply—it was a strategy that Indian agents often used, at the suggestion of the Bureau. According to other testimony at Los Piños, Meeker had never given rations to Nicaagat or members of his band.[60] Meeker apparently received an order from the Commissioner not to issue rations to Ute who were not part of his agency.

> He then said that he would tell me the whole truth of it, which was, that if we wished him to give rations to the whole Ute Nation, he thought it best not to issue any; that such was the order of the Commissioner; that if they did not choose to have him do as he was ordered, and wished him to give rations to all the Utes who came, that he would force them to obey orders by bringing the soldiers there. I told him that I stood in the light of a son to him, and for that reason had come to advise with him, but I could not see why he should talk about bringing the soldiers here to enforce orders. "Anyhow, your tongue does not amount to anything," says the agent. "You don't know how to write, and I do; what you say amounts to nothing." The agent continuing, "The words you say don't

> go very far; my papers and what I say travels far and wide." I then asked him, "Why, then, do you send for me and get me to talk to you if it amounts to nothing except to have me abused in this manner?" I said, "I supposed you think you have beaten me now with those words that you have spoken." I told him that for my part the poorest and lowest American in the country would make a better agent, so far as I was concerned than he did. I asked him if he would not take back what he had said; that he had talked very badly, and in a way to cause trouble; and that we do not wish to have any trouble with our American neighbors on Bear [Yampa] River and elsewhere, and I hoped he would think better of what he had said. I told him I thought it would be better if he talked in some other way in this matter. He said, "You can stay there and talk," and walked off. I then went to my camp.[61]

Meeker accused the Ute of stealing rations and supplies from the agency warehouse. Nicaagat again decided to travel to speak directly with outside authorities.

> I then thought it best for me to go to Fort Steele, as I could not forget what the agent had said about my trip to Denver. I told my squaw she had better go and buy sugar for the camp; and then we started out for Bear River. I arrived there the same day. While we were at the store buying sugar, one of us went out to water the horses, and turning the corner saw two soldiers coming. The woman [Mary Frances Peck] belonging to the store then came out with her child in her arms. It was then I knew that one of them was a sheriff, from Snake River, and the other a soldier. The woman of the store then burst out crying, but the civilian said, "You need not have any fear."[62]

> I then asked them where they were camped. They told me about two miles above . . . We went over to the commanding officer's tent, and he offered us tobacco, and asked us to smoke . . . I then told him he had started out on account of things that were not true; that now I was there and could talk to him. He answered that he had started in the war under what he had heard, and that he had received a notice that the Indians had the agent besieged. I told him that the agent himself had ordered the Indians to stay around him, and that was all the besieging I knew anything about. I told him heretofore the agents had always allowed the Indians some range, but that now they wanted to collect them around them . . . I told them that I never expected to see the soldiers here. I told him we were all under one government, Indians and soldiers, and that the government at Washington ordered us both; that we were brothers, and why had they come? We had always been friends and used one another well, and what had been settled by government had not yet been abolished; that everything was yet peaceable.
>
> A soldier at this time rode up. I said: "Look how lean the government horses are; they go backwards and forward carrying lies." I said it would not make so much difference the horses getting in such bad condition if they were only ridden in a good cause. I told them that I had been a great friend of and traveled considerably with General Crook, and that I did not like to see the soldier come in on my land.[63]

Nicaagat attempted to identify and confront the rumors that he felt Meeker was circulating. When the officer (presumably Major Thornburg, who had been dispatched from Fort Steele) said "that he understood the Indians wished to go on the war path," Nicaagat reminded him that Meeker did not understand Ute and unless he used an interpreter he could not possibly know the Ute's intentions regarding a confrontation or war.[64]

> The officer told me he had received two telegrams, and for that reason he had put himself *en route*. I told him I knew of no difficulty having occurred at the agency. Nothing like anybody being killed or hurt, nothing of that kind, whatsoever.
>
> The officer told me, at all times even brothers by blood fought and quarreled, and that it made no difference. I told him, "but when they were good brothers both of them would give way." I told him I thought Ouray would not want the two brothers to fight, and I think so, too, and that by good kind talking blood never would be shed in this country, and that all could be settled by peaceable talk. He told me he supposed what I said was all right; but under his orders he could not pay attention to what I told him. I asked him to tell me how many men he had found killed on the road since he left the fort. I said this out of friendship, because when all is friendly, whites as well as Indians can travel the road without fear of molestation. The officer said, "that is true, I understand all that very well." I said I did not like the way things were turning out; that I did not want to have the blood of my friends upon me.
>
> The officer then told me that the report was out that we had beaten our Indian agent, and that the poor old man was lying in bed bruised and bleeding from the beating we had given him. I told him that perhaps the spirits of the dead men had done this to the agent. That all the Utes that were alive had already left the agency and were coming toward Milk River on a hunt. The officer then said to me that he understood from the letter he had seen that the Indians had beaten the white family, the girl, the old woman, and the agent. I told the officer he had better leave his people where

> they were and go and see for himself whether the agent had been beaten or not.[65]

Nicaagat and his fellow Ute had a deep distrust of written messages. They were accustomed to face-to-face meetings and information gathered firsthand. Over and over, they advised Meeker, soldiers, and officers, and other officials, to check for rumors before they acted. Nicaagat and others asked Meeker to go to Thompson's house and see for himself if it was burned, just as he asked Thornburg to visit the agency and see for himself if Meeker and his family had been injured. That preparations for war could be made based on a written message baffled the Ute. As far as they were concerned, the truth could only be known face-to-face, by direct experience.

> The officer then said that where we were then was a long way from the agency, but that if he found good grass when nearer the agency he might perhaps go as I said . . . He told me he was a friend to the Indians, but in obeying his orders he might kill the Indians or they might kill him; it was all the same. I answered that I did not think it was good that any of us should kill one another; then I left . . .
>
> The next day I went to the agency to talk with the agent about the arrival of the soldiers. I told the agent that the soldiers were coming, and that I hoped he would do something to stop their coming to the agency. He said it was none of his business; he would have nothing to do with it. I then said to the agent I would like he and I to go where the soldiers were, to meet them. The agent said I was all the time molesting him; he would not go. This he told me in his office; and after finishing speaking he got up and went into another room, and shut and locked his door. That was the last time I ever saw him.[66]

Nicaagat was not alone in warning Meeker that bringing soldiers onto the Ute reservation would provoke violence. Quinkent (Douglas), Colorow, and others tried to arrange for peaceful negotiations and offered to go with Meeker, or one of his employees, to meet the soldiers before they entered the reservation.[67] The following day, September 29, 1879, was one of confusion and tragedy. Nicaagat rode to "where the Utes were assembled, near a small stream running into Milk River" on the northern boundary of the reservation. From the hill above the river, Bears Ears Peaks and the Elkhead range are plainly visible to the north.

> I talked to the Indians and told them they had better retire from the road and go toward a little lake some distance from the road. I told them I expected the soldiers would camp on Milk River, and then I would go to where they were. The soldiers came on toward Milk River, and we saw them looking out in that direction; and a little while after they came on at a gallop, and stopped awhile at Milk Creek before starting on.
>
> After they had passed the trail I went down toward the road and told the Indians to wait awhile. I told the Indians to halt and make no demonstrations, so that I might go down to the soldiers. The Indians, as I had told them, assembled, and by the time the soldiers had come pretty near them the former deployed on one side up the mountains and down on the other. The little creek was about the center, and the troops were on one side of it along a hill without brush. When the Indians saw the troops deploy they also deployed down toward the lower end.
>
> At this time we heard from where we were the firing commence at the lower end of the line. I called out to them, "Hold on! hold on!" and repeated it several times, but in spite of my orders, the Indians commenced firing too. I then sat

> down to look at it, and then I took my pipe and, smoking, started off for camp.[68]

Words of resignation: "I then sat down to look at it, and then I took my pipe and, smoking, started off for camp." All of Nicaagat's efforts had not prevented a disastrous confrontation. He had gone to Denver to speak with the Colorado governor. He had spoken directly with the commanding officer. He had tried to reason with the agent. He had interceded with his fellow Ute who were armed and waiting on the reservation line to see if the troops entered. After the shooting began, and no one ever was sure who fired the first shot, he used the last bit of his authority and reputation to yell "Hold on." Major Thornburg, several other members of the military, and over a dozen Ute men died in the fight.

Not one of the Ute who testified was willing to give the name of any other Ute who had been involved either in the battle or in the incident at the agency. They resolutely held together and, like Nicaagat, if less eloquently, spoke of the whole story without assigning blame or honor to any single individual. Over and over the government agents asked for names and again and again the Ute refused to give names. At one point early in the testimony, General Hatch asked Ouray point blank, "Do you know who were in it." Ouray answered, "I do not; I cannot say." The recorder, Gustavus Valois, interjected, "No Indian would be safe from his own people, whether implicated or not, who testified against those who were guilty." Ouray added, "Show me any act of law by which a man is compelled to [in]criminate himself."[69]

The only witnesses who named names were the three agency women who had been held captive. The women had been preparing the midday meal and later were washing dishes at the agency during the Milk Creek battle. Afterwards, when the confrontation moved to the agency compound, they witnessed only a very small slice of the action. They wisely spent most of

Quinkent (Douglas) and Canella or Shevano (Johnson), two of the Ute deemed by whites as primarily responsible for the fight at Milk Creek and the devastation of the White River Agency that followed. Staged photographs, with Ute men holding rifles, guns, and in some cases wigs presented as scalps, were typical of the time. Studio photographers, most often in located in Denver, took photographs of Utes to sell to tourists. The photos were created and marketed to portray their subjects as fearsome, well-armed warriors. Original Photograph Collection, image 95.200.279. History Colorado.

their time under a bed and hidden. The names they gave were those of their so-called captors and those they assumed had been part of the incident. Nevertheless General Hatch demanded that the following Indians be "turned over for trial": Chief Douglas [Quinkent], Chief Johnson [Canella], Wausitz (Antelope), Ebenezer, Pasone (Big Belly), Ahu-u-tu-pu-wit, Johnny (son-in-law of Douglas), Serio, Cre-pah, Tim Johnson, Thomas (a Uintah), and Paruitz.[70]

Ouray brought in one young man, Quinkent's son-in-law, Johnny, who was placed under arrest. He was the only tribe member ever turned over by the Ute. Quinkent, Powell's informant, was arrested on his way to Washington, D.C., and incarcerated at Fort Leavenworth. Quinkent eventually returned from prison a broken man and was killed on the Uintah reservation. Nicaagat was not on the list of suspects, was never arrested and apparently never made the move to Utah. But his name was constantly associated with the incident as someone who had led Ute "warriors" into action against Thornburg. A few years after his appearance before the Los Piños Commission, he was charged with violating game laws and soon after was killed by soldiers during a confrontation in Wyoming.

Speaking before the commission at Los Piños, another chief of the White River Ute band, Colorado or Colorow, reflected on the Milk Creek incident and the ensuing devastation of the White River Agency:

> Many said that it was very much like a fight between two drunken men, who, when someone came and parted them, found they had been fighting for nothing but foolishness.[71]

At the close of his testimony, Colorow enumerated the killed and the missing. "Killed.—Tah-titz, Wah-cha-pe-gatz, Chu-ca-watz, Uah-pa-chatz, Ca-tol-sen, Cat-su-atz, Wa-wa-gutz, Tet-putz-sin-rah,

Yan-cap, Pa-ger, Wa-pa-qua, Pou-shun-lo, Sou-ie-er-atz, Tu-rah, Pah-wintz, Tu-wu-ick, Poh-ne-atz. Missing.—Pou-witz, Pat-soock."[72]

The consequences of the skirmish would be much greater for the Ute. The tribe lost many members. They also lost almost all of their beloved and beautiful home in Colorado.

CHAPTER THREE

Pre-Emption and Pressure for Land

(1880–)

Even while the Ute held western Colorado, before they were removed to the reservation in Utah, speculators and land seekers claimed land in Elkhead and in the nearby Yampa Valley. The best land, and the best water, were taken by a process later called pre-emption. Pre-emption and later, homesteading, were not supposed to happen before the U.S. government owned the land and government surveyors had established corners and drawn plots, sections, townships and ranges—a grid overlay—that gave a number to every acre of land and created order and an address for every parcel. Enforcing boundaries and waiting for the lands to be surveyed and "opened" was unpopular among settlers. The government was also aware that having settlers claiming and defending land made it harder for Native Americans to return to their homelands. Many policymakers, including John Wesley Powell, thought the Indians needed to be prevented from returning to their hunting grounds. Closing them out of their lands was a way, as Powell put it, to "compel" the Indians to give up hunting and become farmers.

Native Americans generally were not eligible to homestead because they were not legally U.S. citizens. It was not until June 2,

1924, when Congress enacted the Indian Citizenship Act, that all U.S.-born Native Americans became citizens.[73]

In Elkhead—the Ute's prized, cherished hunting ground—this quiet policy meant that the government essentially looked the other way as settlers and developers primarily of European descent trespassed, grabbed and held the choicest lands.

Sometime before 1888, and long before good records were kept, probably before a county clerk's office had been established, seven men—August Aigner, Charles Daniels, Cyrus Hartzell, Albert Hazeltine, Henry Huber, William McKinlay and John Ruth—claimed the most valuable lands along Elkhead and Calf Creeks. The land transactions are recorded as "Pre 160" to acknowledge that none of the parcels conformed to the 1862 Homestead Act; they were pre-emption claims. Under the General Pre-Emption Act of 1841 settlers could purchase up to 160 acres of surveyed public lands where the "Indian title has been extinguished" for $1.25/acre. In 1862, the pre-emption laws were extended to include unsurveyed lands, and in particular, lands in the newly established Colorado Territory. Pre-emption allowed speculators, prospectors and a few home seekers to claim the most valuable agricultural lands many years before the land was surveyed and "opened" for homesteading. Even after the pre-emption law was repealed in 1891, claims by existing residents were still recognized and patents, or titles, were issued for pre-emption claims.[74]

Little trace remains of these names. An exception is Aigner, now the name of a rocky volcanic ridge that sits between Calf Creek and Elkhead Creek to the north of their confluence. Were these men partners or competitors? They neatly divided up the meadowland so that all seven got about an equal share. Or was the neatness the hand of a recorder, perhaps a way to justify conveying all the land in the next transaction? In 1889, all seven parcels, totaling 1,080 acres, or just under two square miles, were combined and transferred to William and Mary McKinlay, who promptly named their place the Elkhead Ranch.

The McKinlay Ranch, as it became known, was the dominant property in Elkhead. Whoever owned the parcel always had so much more than their neighbors: more hay, more livestock, more farm equipment. Unlike the homesteading families that aspired to establish a ranch, the owners of the McKinlay Ranch were usually able to hire labor to do much of the work.

The property changed hands rapidly after the McKinlays successfully merged so many small claims into one ranch. Ten years after that feat, they sold it to Henry Van Kleeck, who sold it in the same year to George Marshall. Three years later, in 1902, Marshall sold it to John Adair and Dr. John V. Solandt, in whose hands it remained until 1930.

John Adair was part of a large family that moved to Routt County from near Athens, Tennessee, in 1882. He had three brothers and five sisters living in the Steamboat area. One brother, James, moved on to Alberta, Canada, but the rest of the siblings stayed. In 1902, John Adair formed a partnership with Canadian-born Dr. John Solandt. Solandt had trained as a veterinarian but shifted his attention and applied his knowledge to humans. He opened up a practice in Hayden in 1897 and became a beloved doctor who spent much of his career on horseback or later, in a Model-A, tending to patients in the far corners of the county.

Following in the footsteps of the seven speculators on Elkhead and Calf Creeks, Charles Clapp and Charles Daniels claimed land to the south along Elkhead Creek in 1891. Whether these land claims became residences is hard to know. They were not filed as homesteads; they were probably pre-emption claims sold by the government for $1.25 per acre. These men were likely investors who leased out the land for summer pasture while they waited for an opportunity to sell for a profit. They were gone in a few years and no trace of their time in Elkhead remains.

Pre-emption land seekers and later, homesteaders, participated in a highly individualistic process of acquiring land that invariably created certain rivalries and discontents among neighbors. Though the process was slow, eventually everyone who established a residence and actually settled down to live on the land would experience a struggle between their individual needs and rights, and the realities of living in a community that needed

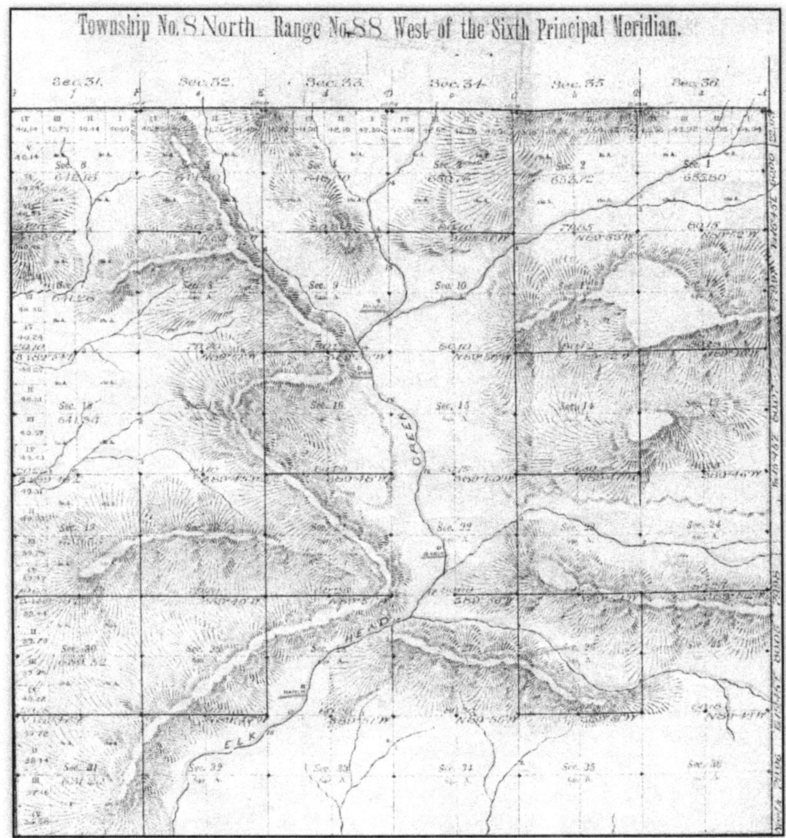

Survey map of central Elkhead area created by Thos. W. Halliday, Survey Generals Office, Denver, Colorado, in 1881, using field work done in 1880. Map shows four ranches dotted along Elkhead Creek. These were pre-emption claims, noted as ranches, which were combined to form the Elkhead Ranch in 1888. Calf Creek and Dry Fork are not named and no other settlement is recorded. Bears Ears Peaks, an important landmark and spiritual home for the Ute, is six miles north of Section 3 at the top of the map.

to be formed, nourished and protected. The Ute had never known such divisions, but they also had not had the challenge of building a community out of a bunch of disparate, dislocated individuals, each seeking personal fortune. Elkheaders arrived from all over the United States; a few came directly from other parts of the

Five Ute women. No names, place or date given. Library of Congress.

world. They left behind families, homes and neighborhoods. Part of their work in Elkhead was to forge bonds and find ways to make decisions together for the betterment of the whole—raising and educating children, the caring for the sick and elderly—surviving, if not thriving, together, from birth through death.

The land, its plants and animals, streams and mountains, sustained the Ute. They belonged and were connected to both their territory and to each other. For the most part, there wasn't anyone else around, nor did another people contest their possession of the land for hundreds, thousands, of years. Perhaps because there was such abundance all around them, and no tradition of private ownership, the relatively small bands lived collectively, with little or no competition among them. When they sought wisdom and power, they climbed up the highest peaks, like Bears Ears, and waited alone. When they were injured or sick, they sought cures in mineral springs and among the plants they knew. They organized their lives inside the group they belonged to and around the seasons and the elevation and climate of their vast lands.

These were skills that Elkheaders, unknowingly for the most part, would aspire to obtain. The homesteaders would try to find a balanced way of life best suited to the land and the climate, essentially attempting to replicate what the Ute had created and adhered to for so long: interdependence—with the land, with each other—Elkheaders would gradually discover as they attempted to survive in the same conditions.

"Bears Ears country" and "Elkhead" are names for overlapping geographical places, but they also refer to the people who resided there and to the communities they formed. Communities are mysterious and often ephemeral. They can be part of a culture or deliberately built. Their existence often remains unrecognized and unheralded, and a community seemingly can easily be broken and dispersed. Do we know we have been part of a community only in retrospect? Nostalgically? Or perhaps, to turn this idea around another few degrees, are we always part of some community, as human beings, and only infrequently recognize what we are in the midst of, and appreciate the connections that are deeply nourishing and vital? We say a community came together. And we say a community fell apart. Like breathing, in and out, is community an inherent part of the human experience? Or does forming and maintaining a community take determination, effort, hard work?

For the Ute, community was inextricably part of their culture, their social structure, their sense of who they were. They were individuals with distinct names, but they were always members of a group that functioned as a community.

The homesteaders, on the other hand, were typically from a much more individualistic culture. By their nature, and as a product of their time, they had broken bonds with family and perhaps communities to set out on their own. They were ambitious, desperate and excited by a new opportunity to reside and claim a new place.

Research on communities summarizes the essential elements of community as: a group of people become a community, in the relational sense, when they are apt to set aside individual needs for the betterment of the whole; communities form when people share common ideals and a common vision for the future; residence and permanence, long-term membership and rootedness, are vital to forming the bonds necessary for community. People need to trust one another, act like neighbors and participate in each other's affairs over long periods of time to form a community.[75]

For people who have grown up in an individualistic culture where self-actualization is a top priority, a shift can happen. We are social animals; we like to talk and get to know people. We feel safer around people we know and trust. Most individuals will turn to friends, neighbors, acquaintances, and seek connection, especially in times of great joy, loss, or a threat from outside their group or place of safety. Especially in times of shared hardship, people tend to set aside their immediate needs and wants in order to attend to others, share resources, lend a hand, and by those responses, bits of altruism, they will begin build community. Sometimes quickly, but more often gradually, people will adopt the habit of thinking and acting for the common good.

Nicaagat's tremendous efforts to lead Meeker, the governor, and the military away from confrontation with the Ute is testament to his ability to place the good of the whole above all else. As David Hill, a theologian, explains, "our civil society depends . . . on linking an ethic of the common good with the uses of power."[76] It would take many years and living in tough conditions before the homesteaders would find their way to this kind of thinking and action. It would be decades before individuals who defined themselves as land seekers and opportunists would undergo a transformation to become citizens of a place and eventually members of a community.

CHAPTER FOUR

The Ute Return to Hunt

(1897)

In the fall of 1897, before the snow fell, and after the elk calves and fawns had matured, a small group of Ute families left the reservation they had been forced onto in 1880, crossed the Green River and camped west of Maybell along the Little Snake River near Lily Park. They were approximately seventy miles downriver from the Bears Ears country and Elkhead, in an area that had been part of their winter seasonal circuit. They were off the Ute reservation to hunt for mule deer meat and hides.

Lily Park is big and open—about five square miles of grassland. Encircling the park are bluffs, mesas, and peaks that rise a thousand or so feet above the valley floor. The Little Snake River enters from the north there to join the east-to-west, swift and wide Yampa River. Just beyond the confluence of the two rivers, the enlarged Yampa enters a deep canyon and disappears around a corner. For the Ute, Lily Park was a perfect place to camp, hunt, and process meat: long vistas, two rivers, wide, open grassy meadows, shade from the narrow strip of cottonwoods, plenty of firewood, and surrounding hills usually full of wild game. It was also secluded and quiet, over twenty miles away from the nearest town of Maybell.

A small encampment along a river circa 1885-1895. It is unlikely that this was taken in Lily Park but it shows what a Yamparika and Parianuche camp would have looked like along the Yampa and Little Snake rivers in 1897. Denver Public Library, Western History Collection Z-186.

The Ute who returned to Colorado in the fall of 1897 were members of the Yamparika and Parianuche bands which the government arbitrarily combined and called the White River. The land along the Little Snake and Yampa rivers was well known to them as their hunting ground. As far as they were concerned their hunting rights had never been lost and were guaranteed to them by treaty forever.

In Steamboat Springs, a hundred miles away, a county game warden, W.K. Wilcox, heard the news and decided to take action. He had no authority over Indians, nor did he get permission to intervene. He got on his horse, rounded up some local cowboys with plenty of guns, and together they set off for Maybell, and from there to the camp in Lily Park. Along the way the spontaneous posse was joined by local ranchers and cowboys until the riders numbered at least fifteen. Wilcox deputized the men and said he had been sent by his superior to arrest the Indians if they did not leave Colorado.

The game warden's posse found the Ute on the north side of Little Snake River not far from where the Snake joins the Yampa.

The posse arrived at ten in the morning on Sunday, October 24, 1897. Pit-she-shook, an older Ute woman who had stayed behind in the camp that morning, said, "Some of the Indians cried out, 'The cowboys are coming.'" Cowboys clearly meant trouble, especially in a large group. "When I heard this I ran to the wickeyup and got a rope and my saddle. [I] caught one . . . and saddled him and got a little granddaughter and put her on the horse and told her to go which she did."[77]

In the camp, the Ute said, there were four men and three women. Wilcox said they found six men and eight or ten women and a few children. Wilcox also said there were "two deer, still undressed, many deer hides, with some beef hides, and a quantity of deer hair" in the camp.[78] Other witnesses did not mention beef hides. Everyone agreed that the Ute were in the middle of butchering several deer. The women were cutting and laying meat out to dry. All of the men who were old enough and able to hunt were out hunting. The Ute usually dried their meat before they transported it so that it was lighter and would not spoil on the journey. They cleaned and stacked hides that they would use for clothing, bedding and shelter. Some of the hides they would trade for household goods, food and ammunition. After a few days' work everything that could possibly be used would be hauled behind horses on travois or carried in bags tied to the Ute's saddles. As the 1898 report later stated, "This was the old hunting ground of the Utes before they were removed from Colorado and they have always depended on game for no small part of their food and clothing."[79]

Warden Wilcox and his posse stayed on horseback and kept their guns drawn when they rode into the Ute camp. "The cowboys came into the camp with their guns in their hands pointed and were riding in a line," Nannatchaav testified; "they all had their belts full of cartridges."[80] Wilcox demanded that the Ute leave immediately or he would arrest everyone. He and the posse tried to arrest two men, Shimaraff and Coo-a-munche, but they managed to get away. Wilcox seems to have realized that no one spoke English, noting that no one appeared to understand. He repeated his demand and used gestures to make himself clear.

After sending her granddaughter away on horseback, Pit-she-shook hid for a while and then returned to the camp. "I said to a cowboy, 'You scare me; what are you going to do?'" She tried to tell the posse that the Ute were leaving. "'Here are our horses,'" she told the cowboy, "and we are ready to go and we are going home.'" Either no one understood her or they were unwilling to let the Ute simply leave. "The cowboy said 'No,' shaking his head."[81] Hours passed while the posse attempted to arrest the Ute. At one point, Wilcox and his deputies picked up one of the men and put him on a horse but he was able to get off the other side and sat down on the ground.

Captain William Beck, a member of the U.S. Army acting as an Indian Agent on the Uintah reservation, had a sense the summer before that conflict was coming. In July, he wrote to his superiors in Washington expressing his confusion about state game laws versus treaty rights. In his letter he quotes from Utes who spoke at a Council in June 1897:

> "We want to hunt because our rations are not sufficient, and we can sell buck-skins and buy things with it."
>
> "There are no brands on the deer and to whom do they belong? We were raised to hunt them for their meat and skins. The Indians do not say to the Cow-boy, whom they see shoot a deer 'why do you kill our deer?' They say nothing about it."

> "The Indian can travel on the road like a white man and make no trouble, why should he not go the same as a white man?"[82]

In the letter Beck expresses uncertainty: "I do not know the decision of the Department relative to this matter, i.e. whether or not the State Game Laws of the states mentioned [Colorado and Utah] govern in the cases of the Indians or the provision of the ratified treaty by the Indians with the United States in that regard."[83] Conflicts around the Ute returning to hunt in Colorado had been festering since they had been removed to the reservation in Utah. Various agents issued hunting and travel passes but they were consistently disregarded by state authorities. Un-gut-she-one-Starr mentioned in his testimony that he showed Wilcox his pass but was told it was worthless. "The leader of the squad of the men came up to me and took hold of my horse's bridle . . . They said he was the Game Warden, or Deer policeman. I showed them a piece of paper which they said was no good."[84] Did the Ute have a right to hunt, or not?

The stalemate in Lily Park went on for hours. Sir-e-outs, who later identified herself as a sixty-six-year-old White River Ute and Sow-er-a-muche-kent's mother, stayed close to her son. "I was so excited for fear they would harm my son," she stated. "I was watching my son fearing they might get him."[85] The wardens became more and more frustrated. No one was responding to their demands and a few of the Ute had slipped away. In the afternoon, three or four hours after they had arrived, the government report states that "the wardens commenced firing on the Indians, and, after killing two men and wounding two of the women, left the camp."[86] Nannatchaav, who was in the middle of the fracas, gave a detailed account:

> I was standing on right hand side of Sow-er-a-muche-kent and the old woman Sir-e-outs was standing in front of us.

A group of Ute in Colorado 1893. Library of Congress.

One of the cowboys walked toward them and opened his coat saying I am a Deer Policeman. Starr was standing on my right and the Deer policeman made a grab at him. Starr dodged behind Sow-er-a-muche-kent. The Deer policeman finding he could not catch Starr then grab Sow-er-a-muche-kent by the left arm. Another Deer policeman grab him at the same time on the other arm. Just at the time these two Deer policemen had grabbed Sow-er-a-muche-kent two other Deer policemen grab Shimaraff by each arm, while he Shimaraff were sitting down. Yum-butz was sitting near and one Deer policeman grabbed him by the arm. Another Deer policeman pointed his pistol at me. I grab it and struck

> it up with my bare hand. He then walk away from me. The firing then began immediately, as I remember nothing until recognized Sow-er-a-muche-kent lying on the ground. I next saw Sir-e-outs, and Shimaraff all on ground. I found that I was shot in the head. I was shot from the back and fell on my face.[87]

Yum-butz and Un-gut-she-one-Starr tell essentially the same story but Starr adds that when he saw two of his companions being held by Wilcox and members of the posse, he fled. "I ran toward my horse and got on him and by this time they were firing at me; the bullets falling all around me."[88]

Sir-e-outs, who had been standing next to or in front of her son, tried to protect him. She testified:

> I do not know how I got shot. I saw the men start toward my son and shoved one of the men away with my bare hands, begging them not to hurt my son. Talking to them in Indian.

The next thing she knew she was in the middle of gunfire.

> All the white men shooting. When they commence shooting my son fell on his face and started to run away and fell under a cedar tree. [I] did not know I was wounded until I came to, and then I found that I was shot in the arm.[89]

Who fired first will never be known. Some members of the posse spoke to the press and testified that in the middle of the confrontation, while they were forcibly mounting Indians onto horses and attempting to make arrests, a Ute woman ducked into her shelter and emerged with a pistol in her hand. Kimberly, a posse member standing beside her, struck the gun to the side and in so doing it fired and hit a second Ute woman. At that point the posse members

A young Yamparika or Parianuche woman with her child in a cradle board. 1916. Library of Congress.

opened fire on all the Ute. One of the white men, Al Shaw, fell or was knocked to the ground and was presumed dead.

After their shooting (all accounts concur that the dead were "riddled" with bullets) the posse left and went to J.B. Thompson's ranch about three miles away. Not one member of the posse was injured in any way. Even Shaw reappeared unharmed several days later.

The Ute remained in the camp only long enough for the men out hunting to return. They then buried their dead according to their customs, in crevices and between boulders. They traveled through the night and camped at dawn on the top of Blue Mountain. Several days later they completed their journey to the reservation, where the injured got medical care and where they told their outraged story to the Indian agent. According to their testimony six people were killed, including a boy.

News of this incident, called a cruel massacre by some and fair warning by others, traveled in distorted versions all over the U.S. Al Shaw was reported as killed. Thompson's ranch was supposedly burned to the ground. Numbers of Ute involved ranged from 12 to 200 and wardens from 14 to 25. Almost all newspaper accounts portrayed Wilcox as a hero and the Indians as stubborn and defiant, in need of a stern lesson. *The New York Times* wrote three days after the incident that the "White River Ute are exceptionally ugly, and have been apparently anxious to pick trouble with parties of whites with whom they have come in contact."[90] But there were a few responses, notably from people who lived in and around Lily Park, who felt that Wilcox had needlessly endangered everyone in northwest Colorado. The residents were quoted by the military as saying that the incident was "not an Indian outbreak but a white man's outbreak."[91] In Rio Blanco County, the neighboring county to the south, a paper reported, "Much feeling is shown against Wilcox here for his indiscretion in attempting to arrest a camp of forty Indians, as it is almost certain to result in the killing of settlers in the western part of this and Routt counties."[92]

White Crow. Photograph taken in Meeker, Colorado, 1902. Library of Congress.

The U.S. Special Indian Agent who investigated, Elisha B. Reynolds, was careful to avoid assigning any blame. He got statements from Un-gut-she-one Starr, Sir-e-outs, Nannatchaav, Yam-butz and Pit-she-shook. All said a version of the same thing: at no time had they seen any guns or pistols in the hands of the Indians. He did confirm the Ute story that six, not two, Indians were killed though he held with Wilcox's simplified version that the Ute had fired the first shot, thus enabling the wardens to claim they were acting in self-defense. Reynolds's strongest statement was that Wilcox should not have tried to arrest anyone and should have given the Ute three days to leave.[93]

Ute on horseback, 1899. Denver Public Library, Western History Collection, P-70.

The Commissioner of Indian Affairs' annual report on the Ute concluded with this acknowledgment of the tangled legal and moral situation between Ute and whites:

> They cannot understand why they should be shut out from [hunting] during certain seasons of the year by State laws, especially when the right to hunt game in this region was guaranteed to them by a treaty with the Government, which provided that such right should be inviolable and continue so long as game existed there.[94]

The Ute were in a limbo. Could they hunt in Colorado? Could they survive life on the reservation in Utah?

CHAPTER FIVE

Resistance and Refusal: The Ute Depart for South Dakota

(1906)

> What these Indians demand is a big hunting ground—not farming country. They do not wish to farm and do not care to have settled homes; but their appeal to the President last spring, and to the soldiers since, has been for a game country which they could inhabit and where the white man would leave them alone.[95]

If the Ute were to cease being hunters, what were they to become? Forced onto reservations, held on unfamiliar desert lands, they looked for ways to escape and, if not return to their mountains, at least to their former way of life, the crux of their identity.

In 1906, at the annual spring Bear Dance on the Duchesne River in Utah, Ungacochoop or Red Cap, a White River (formerly known as Yamparika) Ute, got up on a box and began addressing the crowd with anger in his voice. A local resident who provided testimony to the Vernal, Utah, newspaper described the scene:

> About once every hour he would get up on a box and deliver himself of a harangue. "The white men," said he, "have robbed

> us of our cattle, our pony grass and our hunting ground," and then seeing that others approved his words, he grew bolder in his fiery tirade. He called upon all the Indians who were willing to fight for their rights to shave their heads in token. Shortly after, thirty or forty young bucks were seen among the crowd with their hair so cut that it stood straight up all over the top of their heads, and with their painted faces looked positively wild.[96]

Red Cap's grievances resonated with other Ute at their most important annual gathering. They had lost a large portion of their reservation land.

The Ute were in the middle of what was called severalty, mandated by the Dawes Act of 1887 and implemented tribe-by-tribe across the country. In 1906 it was the Ute's turn. The government wanted the Ute people to live on small plots of land as farmers. Under the Dawes Act, each adult tribe member chose a parcel on the reservation: eighty acres for the head of the family, forty acres for each additional family member. If they refused to choose, they would be designated a plot. The rest would be sold for $1.25/acre to white settlers and speculators. Surveyors arrived at the reservation to parcel out the land, followed by an Allotment Commission.

Members of the Tabeguache band reacted to this new policy by selecting the most remote, dry and rocky areas, presumably to sabotage the regulations and to make a clear statement that they would never be farmers. Most of the White River band refused to cooperate in any way, and in their absence were hastily assigned lands that the agent associated with them, or, if none could be found, random undesirable lands that no one else wanted.

As Red Cap mentioned in his fiery address, the land was only the most recent loss inflicted upon his people. They had lost

Ungacochopp or Red Cap portrait taken in Washington D.C., 1905. National Anthropological Archives, Smithsonian Institution, NA INV 00883606.

western Colorado, their home, and their hunting ground. On their reservation they had steadily lost land, water and grass as settlers claimed parcels long before the severalty process began. Now, their forsaken reservation was being officially opened to white settlers. President Theodore Roosevelt signed a proclamation opening the "unreserved and unallotted lands" of the reservation on August 28, 1905. A surge of homesteaders entered, claiming whatever lands they could find. A group of Ute went to Washington, D.C. to plead with the president, to no avail. By late 1905, the allotment process was complete.

1905 Delegation to Washington. Left to right (front row): Appah and Arrike; (center row) Ungacochoop (Red Cap), Kochootch, Charlie Shavaroux and Witchito; (back row) unidentified white man, Siats (interpreter), Ungatowinorokant, Soccioff, unidentified white man, Boco White (interpreter) and unidentified white man. National Anthropological Archives, Smithsonian Institution, NAA 066686300.

In May 1906 the flight began. Around 400 Yamparika and Parianuche (referred to at that time as White River Ute), accompanied by a few Tabeguache and Uintah Ute, gathered together on Dry Fork, near Vernal, Utah. They told everyone they were going to South Dakota to join the Sioux. They would not return to the reservation by choice or by force. The local paper noted, "The Indians are well armed and had ammunition in abundance . . . They express freely their determination to fight rather than return."[97]

The Ute left the reservation on horseback, dragging all their belongings on pole travois. They took with them a herd of around 1,000 to 2,000 horses. One report said they had 500 head of cattle.

Group of Ute leaving for South Dakota to join the Sioux, 1906. Left to right: Willie Willie, Arapo, Dewey (son of Arapo), Duchesne George (rear), Slim Jim and Ungacochoop (Red Cap).[98] *Used by permission, Utah State Historical Society.*

It was not the first time the Ute had fled the reservation. In 1899, White River leader Sowawick declared, "We have put our hand on that [Colorado] land, and it belongs to us; our relatives are all buried there. Washington agreed to buy the land from us; but they never paid us for it, and it is still ours."[99] Sowawick led a group back to Colorado who were eventually pushed back onto the reservation.[100] In 1903, another small group of around twenty-five left, heading for the Black Hills of South Dakota, but they were quickly returned to the reservation, escorted by BIA's Indian Police.

In early 1905, as the allotment process was underway, a group of Ute went to Washington where they met with officials and the President. They asked for a reservation in Colorado and to be left alone. "They made an urgent plea for permission for their band to remove from the Uintah Reservation to some reservation where no white people would disturb them, or to find homes in the forest reserve."[101] The answer was no. The Ute returned to the Utah reservation and turned their energy into pulling up survey stakes "and did all they could, short of actual violence, to embarrass the work of the allotting commission."[102]

In June 1905, the government sent Lieutenant Colonel Frank West to Utah to investigate sales of guns and ammunition to the Ute in anticipation of a "threatened uprising on the part of the White River Utes at the coming opening of the Uintah Indian Reservation, Utah." After detailing the various rifles and types of ammunition that had been sold to the tribe in White Rocks and Vernal, he conveyed what he had been told by the Acting Indian Agent, Captain C.G. Hall.

> . . . that the White River Utes were discontented on account of the opening of the reservation; that they desire to return to their old reservation at Bear [Yampa] River, Colorado; that the prime movers toward this discontent were two White River Indians named "Eggleston" and "Tim Johnson"; that

> they had been agitators for a long time; that the former is said to have been one of the leaders in the Meeker massacre; also that there were some 75 to 90 able bodied men of the White River Utes, and that in case of trouble 5 or 7 Uintah Utes would probably join them.[103]

By May 1906, under the leadership of Red Cap and a fellow White River Ute, Appah, the group of discontents grew to include about a third of the reservation's residents. Almost all of the Yamparika and Parianuche joined, as well as quite a few Tabeguache and Uintah. They left the reservation en masse around May 20. They refused to turn around; no one could force them to return. Confusion arose as to whether the tribe members should be considered U.S. citizens; if they were, they would possess the right to leave the reservation, and if not, their rights were unclear. The question helped to slow a military response. At the time, a person who owned land was a citizen of the United States and, as they were landowners, some contended, the Ute possessed the right to move, as would any citizen. Despite these arguments, the Indian Agent Hall (who proudly signed his correspondence Captain, U.S. Army) received urgent orders from the Commission of Indian Affairs to bring the tribe members back to the reservation. Hall rode to Wyoming. The Commissioner of Indian Affairs report described his efforts vividly: "Their agent followed them into Wyoming, intercepted them in their journey across that State, and for several days counseled with them, urging and admonishing them to return to their own country."[104] When Hall realized his futility and told the Commissioner "the Indians were deaf to all reasoning" the Commissioner ordered him back to the agency.[105]

Many pundits, including Hall, thought the Indians could never make the journey to South Dakota. They would not have enough food; they did not have sufficient determination. Hall, who by this time was aware of the massive changes foisted on the Ute, still thought they would return. "It is believed," he wrote in an August 1906 letter, "that practically all of them will return to their homes in the fall and early winter, and, while their departure cannot be considered but unfortunate, it is thought that upon their return they will be more contented than before leaving."[106]

In Wyoming the reaction was panic. Ranchers and farmers claimed the Ute were killing their stock and stealing their ponies. The Wyoming governor requested troops be sent immediately to control the Ute. President Roosevelt ordered "a suitable force of cavalry to proceed to the scene of disturbance to secure the peaceful and lawful return of the Indians to the lands allotted to them at the Uintah Reservation in Utah."[107]

The War Department moved swiftly. Cavalry troops were dispatched from every direction to converge on the Ute in Wyoming. Fortunately, heavy snows and bad weather created delays and allowed time for War Department negotiators to reach the Ute first. Captain Carter P. Johnson and Robert G. Paxton of the 10th Cavalry rushed from Fort Robinson in the northwest corner of Nebraska to Gillette, Wyoming, arriving on October 21. "Despite the heavy snow and bad weather," the War Department reported, "they started northward on the morning of October 22 and a forty-mile ride that day brought them to the Indian camp."[108] The men called a council with the Ute but made no progress convincing them to turn around. Nor would the Ute wait or go to Gillette for another conference. The tribal leaders stated that they were going to Cherry Creek on the Sioux Reservation or to the Big Horn Mountains.

More troops were deployed but the tenor of what had come to be called the "Ute Campaign" changed. New troops from Nebraska were to move to Gillette and stay there, "as it was not desired to press the Indians nor cause them to continue their movement northward."[109] The remaining troops in Fort Robinson were sent by rail to Sheridan, Wyoming, to be posted in Ashland, Montana, in case the Ute veered north. Finally, the military sent a Signal Corp detachment from Omaha and infantry from Fort Mackenzie to Arvada, Wyoming, to create a supply depot.

While all these troops were getting into place, Captain Johnson traveled with the Ute on horseback through the snow, continuing negotiations along the way. He reported, "there was much talk regarding grievances and wishes."[110] Johnson was joined on the trek by Sioux Indians and interpreters who helped him to realize "that it was practically certain the Utes would fight and break up into small bands, burning and murdering, rather than go back."[111] When the Ute asked to go to Washington to get permission to settle on some part of the Sioux reservation, Johnson agreed and the War Department "acceded." In return, the government persuaded the Ute to go to Fort Meade, very close to the Sioux reservation in South Dakota, where they could spend the winter.

Group of White River Utes taken prisoner at Fort Meade, S.D. 1906. Left to right: Ben Tabbysheetz, unidentified, Ta-taw-wee Chegup, Mocha, Quien, J. Scott Apputnora, Quip, Tse-uts (brother of Red Cap).[112] *Used by permission, Utah State Historical Society.*

The military considered them prisoners, claiming that they were "held and provided for" at Fort Meade. But those terms meant little to the Ute. They camped near the fort on Alkali Creek and somehow survived the rough winter. They had made the 1,000-mile journey and they were at least close to the Sioux reservation. How the Sioux greeted them is an unknown piece of the story. The dominant interpretation is that the Sioux were not happy to see this tired group arriving from Utah with 1,000 ponies needing feed, surrounded by military escorts, and intending to move onto their reservation. What is certain is that the Special Indian Agent in charge at the Cheyenne River Agency, Thomas Downs, was in the mold of Nathaniel Meeker. Downs took an immediate dislike to the Ute and worried incessantly that they would stir up trouble with his charges. When met with defiance, his instinct was to press harder, threaten louder and withdraw rations. He did not get good advice from his superiors in Washington. The Commissioner of Indian Affairs was confused at best. He knew that the allotment process on the Ute reservation had caused the exodus and admitted that the process had been haphazard and rushed. Still, he longed for some way to force the Ute back to their reservation. He proposed that the Department of Interior could "order their expulsion from any foreign reservation they may have penetrated and impose a fine of $1,000 upon any one of them who returns without permission." But, coming to his senses, he immediately added, "But as they have no money, the fine would be for all practical purposes a nullity."[113]

In the Commissioner's 1907 report, numbers spoke plainly of what had happened to the Ute reservation.

> Uintah Valley: President's proclamations of July 14, 1905, setting aside 1,010,000 acres as a forest reserve, 2,100 acres as townsites, 1,004,285 acres opened to homestead entry, 2,140 acres in mining claims; 103,265.35 acres allotted to 1,283

Indians and 60,160 acres under reclamation, the residue, 179,194.65 acres, unallotted and unreserved.[114]

Red Cap (seated) and family camped in South Dakota. National Anthropological Archives, Smithsonian Institution. NAA Photo Lot 24.

Resistance to severalty and the application of the Dawes Act had been growing across the country and among Indian tribes since its inception in 1887. The process of taking away pieces of the reservation, and then removing the outside boundaries and "opening" the reservation to white settlers, began as soon as the Uintah Ute were first removed, and only intensified after the Uncompaghre and White River Ute arrived from Colorado. The incursions came from many sources and under many guises, not just through the Dawes Act, until every nearly every resource—land, minerals, grass, water and timber—was under siege.

Free land and resources held in common in the public domain became more scarce as the nineteenth century drew to a close. But demands did not abate. Grazing and farmland, water and minerals on the reservation became more attractive to the government, investors and settlers. Reservations, once set aside for Indians, were redefined as public domain, in the control of the government. White people seeking free land applied continuous pressure; homesteading became almost an entitlement. These people were looking for something for free: for money, for land, for a way to get ahead. As land, timber, minerals and water across the Midwest and West were surveyed, cut up into little chunks, claimed, bought and sold, reservations felt the pressure of outsiders who desired more and more so-called public resources. Suddenly, speculators and homesteaders claimed to have found paradise in narrow river valleys in the middle of thousands of acres of rough, rocky, dry land. What had once been seen as unneeded and unwanted scraps of land, and therefore a suitable place for the Indians, became desirable and lucrative to whites.

Gilsonite, a natural form of asphalt, was discovered on the Ute reservation in 1886. By a series of maneuvers, investors claimed the land; Congress approved the sale of 7,040 acres of the reservation.

As sheep became popular and remunerative, livestock owners moved enormous bands of the animals onto the reservation for grazing. In November 1899, Agent Myton collected $545 in fines from ten owners who had grazed a total of 28,600 sheep on the reservation.[115]

Water was needed to grow nearly anything in Utah. Even though supposedly only a few white farmers were living on the reservation—holdovers from pre-reservation days—there were miles and miles of ditches irrigating their land. In 1902, the U.S. Geological Service noted this illegal capture of water and requested clarification from the Department of Interior. Agent Myton wrote, "While those people have no legal right to the water, I would recommend if it is at all possible that you permit them to continue to use the water." He sided with the eighty white farms dependent on the Ute's water and noted that "there is only one Indian family within fifty miles of any of the ditches."[116]

Forest lands in the Uintah Mountains were coveted grazing areas. The timber itself was desirable and needed for construction and fuel.

In 1902, continuing the process of severalty, Congress passed a law "opening" the Uintah reservation. There were essentially three interlocking parts to the plan: survey and carve the land on the reservation into little plots; allocate a plot to each adult Ute, individually; and sever the rest from the reservation so that it could be homesteaded and sold to whites. Congress added one stipulation: the Ute must agree to the land's allotment and sale.

In May 1903, James McLaughlin, a special Indian Agent who claimed to have visited most tribes in the United States and to have overseen the process of severalty for a number of tribes, arrived in White Rocks, Utah. He called for a six-day council. His charge was to persuade the men on the Ute reservation to sign a letter allowing the land to be opened.

McLaughlin was determined and diligent. He hired translators and scribes. The record of these six days of meetings is transfixing: nearly all the Ute leaders spoke, many of them several times. While there is no record of the names of those in attendance, at least 120 out of the 280 adult men were present each day. McLaughlin pleaded, cajoled, mocked, explained, apologized and used all his persuasive powers. The Ute responded in plain language. They did not want to lose land again.

Many spoke of the ground inside the reservation as being heavy:

> Capt. Joe: The Indian reservation was not put down for nothing. It is held down by something heavy. We don't want this reservation opened, and we do not want White people coming in among us . . . We have these mountains, and streams and don't want anybody coming on this reservation.[117]

> Warren: Here in this land are our relatives and children covered over with earth. That is what makes this land so heavy.[118]

> Red Cap: The reservation is heavy, the Indians have grown here and their bones are in the ground, covered over with earth. That is the reason it is so heavy.[119]

Several spoke of their children, who would follow tradition and live on the land:

> Sowsonocutt: They did not put us here on this reservation for nothing. They put us here a long time ago. That's the reason we like this land here and we are holding it tight. All this land belongs to us and this reservation here belongs to little children growing up.[120]

> George Washington (Uintah): Washington says "When your boys grow up, this land will belong to them." But what you tell me scares me. I want to die without having blood on me.[121]

> Appah: My boy is living on this reservation. I don't want people coming here to settle this land . . . They cannot steal it by a lie.[122]

Every Ute who testified objected to severalty was aware that their collective and personal lives would be diminished by the loss of lands held in common, and the irreversible change to private ownership of plots:

> Sockive: You are not going to cut out this reservation into little pieces.[123]

> Happy Jack: The Indians do not want to be shut in.[124]

Little Jim: We do not want this land cut up in small pieces.[125]

Wapsack: The Indians do not understand anything about being put on a little farm.[126]

Grant: Where are my horses going to do when I have only a little piece of land? Must I tie my horses in that little field?[127]

"Must I tie my horses in that little field?" Ute on horseback in Colorado or Utah, 1905. Library of Congress.

Over and over, the Ute spoke eloquently and directly. They objected to opening the reservation with a clear "no" and reminded McLaughlin of the treaty that hung on the wall of the agency; they expressed dismay, disbelief and anger at the government's treachery.

Sockive: This land belongs to the Indians and we are not going to give it to you. I have not two hearts, I have but one; I have not two mouths, I have but one.[128]

> Red Cap: These people in Washington, they shake my hand, but they do not want me to throw my hands away. My heart is straight.[129]

Each speaker tried to explain their connection to the land:

> John Star: You see me and I see you. My flesh is black; you have good flesh, you are white like this paper here. My flesh looks like the ground. That's the reason I like this land; my flesh is like the land. That's the reason I'm going to keep it. Why should I give it away?[130]

Over the course of the six days, a few became resigned to the loss, or at least attempted to put the change into a known context:

> Appah: You are just like a storm coming down from the mountains when the flood is coming down the stream and we can't stop it.[131]

> John Star: I am pretty well acquainted with the White Man. I know him. White Men want something all the time. They want everything. They are after this land and are troubling me all the time.[132]

They called McLaughlin's papers, his copy of the Act of Congress, his various letters from his superiors, "the same as if it came out of a hole in the ground."[133] Red Cap, who would soon become one of the two leaders of the flight to South Dakota, said, "Your talk is like dark night. My talk to you I want to be like the daylight."[134]

McLaughlin forged ahead, his patience frayed. On the sixth day, he presented a letter for the Ute to sign agreeing to the allotment process and the loss of most of the reservation. Only 82 men signed out of 134 in attendance that day and the 280 eligible. Only seven of the eighty-two White River band members from Colorado signed. McLaughlin in his report recommended giving the better irrigable lands to those who had assented. There was no hint that the order would be reversed.

Two days after the conclusion of the council and after the letter had sat in the agent's office for days, awaiting additional signatures, White River Ute Tim Johnson approached McLaughlin with a proposal. He said he was acting as a representative of all the White River Ute. He offered that the band "would give up all claim to the Uintah lands and leave the reservation if the government would permit them to remove to the Bear [Yampa] River Valley in Colorado."[135]

What would have happened if the Ute had been allowed to return to Colorado? Would they have resumed much of their old lives along the Yampa, in Elkhead, California Park, Lily Park? What if they had been able to return for healing in the Medicine Springs (which by then had already been renamed Steamboat Springs)? Would they have been able to climb Bears Ears, Sugar Loaf and Pilot Knob to seek guidance and power? Ferry Carpenter and Eunice Pleasant were in high school in 1903; Elkhead had only been claimed by a few early settlers. What if those few pre-empters had been encouraged to leave and the entire six townships, connected by a few more to the Yampa River, had been reserved for the Ute?

In a way, it is useless to speculate—the Ute were never going to be allowed to return to Colorado. As McLaughlin explained in his letter, "I told them the proposition was untenable and could not be entertained, but he [White River Ute, Tim Johnson] insisted upon me submitting his request in my report, hence my mentioning it."[136] Still, to imagine their return is, in a way, a form of acknowledging that they never left. Their straight hearts remained there; their yearning was a different kind of claim to the land, one that could not be erased or forgotten.

Belle Forche, South Dakota, Ute encampment, 1906-1907. The military was instructed to arrest all of the Absentee Ute, Library of Congress.

The pain of a constricted life on a reservation, the loss of Colorado, and now, of a corner of Utah, did not subside for the Ute in South Dakota. Likewise, white people, especially local settlers, remained fearful of what the Ute might do if they were pushed too hard or cornered. The Sioux were apparently preoccupied and not inclined to join with the Ute in any rebellion. In fact, some Sioux expressed fear of what the dislocated Ute might stir up, or how they might be drawn into conflict. Reports from Agent Downs claimed that the Sioux were bringing in hundreds of thousands of dollars in grazing lease money for their lands. In 1907, the 2,500 Sioux were generally clustered in a few townships on the northern border of their reservation. Their land was not suitable for farming. Many were working on roads and bridges for wages. Word traveled back to Utah that the Ute in South Dakota did not even have enough land to graze their ponies.

In January 1907, as promised, a delegation of Ute leaders went to Washington. President Theodore Roosevelt, according to the

War Department report, "gave them an audience and particularly interested himself in the situation."[137] Theodore Roosevelt, himself a hunter, perhaps understood a little of what the Ute were asking for. They explained that all they wanted was a place where they could hunt and where they would be left alone.

> What these Indians demand is a big hunting ground—not farming country. They do not wish to farm and do not care to have settled homes; but their appeal to the President last spring, and to the soldiers since, has been for a game country which they could inhabit and where the white man would leave them alone.[138]

Roosevelt directed the Indian Bureau to find land on the Sioux reservation for the Ute at the junction of the Moreau River and Thunder Butte Creek. Captain Carter Johnson negotiated a lease of lands from the Sioux. He found four townships, or 9,200 acres, that formerly had been leased to local stockmen, and arranged for the Ute to pay four-and-a-half cents an acre per year for five years. At least now there was pasture for their ponies. The group of 393 Ute, with their herd of at least 600 horses, moved to their new home in June.

In August, word got to Special Agent Thomas Downs that Tim Johnson was planning to bring 130 more Ute to South Dakota, but no one else left Utah to join the group on the Moreau River.

A few months later, Roosevelt, the Secretary of the Interior, the Assistant Secretary of War and the Commissioner of Indian Affairs met to discuss what had become known as the problem of the "Absentee Ute." On November 1, 1907, they held an unusual press conference to announce their decision that the Ute 'must work.' The *New York Times* summed up the message: "belligerent Ute Indians must work or starve."[139] Another special agent, Charles Dagenett, supervisor of Indian employment, was dispatched to

South Dakota to find wage work for the Ute. A few Ute relocated to Rapid City where a number labored on a railroad. Not long after, the railroad went into receivership without paying the Ute all their wages. The government doled out the eighteen dollars annual annuity and waited. As winter set in, most of the band was eking out a living on the prairie lands of South Dakota. Surrounding their camp that winter were a few hundred troops, camped in makeshift dugouts, "as a police precaution to preserve order," according to the *Times*. Agents and the military anticipated a crisis once the group ran out of food.

Instead, as the spring of 1908 approached, the Ute decided to return to the Uintah reservation. No record exists as to how or why the group made the decision to leave South Dakota. The previous August, the same Agent McLaughlin who had convened the council in 1903 visited the Ute in South Dakota. He reported 370 Absentees—approximately 50 Uintah, 145 Uncompahgre [Tabeguache] and 175 White River. McLaughlin wrote on August 1, 1907, that all were "undergoing great hardship," were very poor and subsisting on three-quarters rations. He also said that the Sioux were helping the group survive. "Were it not for the generosity of the Sioux, who have made them many presents of clothing, tepees and even money upon their arrival here, they would be quite destitute."[140] McLaughlin predicted that the Ute would leave the next summer because of the lack of game, which meant they could not supplement their meager rations with wild meat. He also drew attention to the harshness of the winter at that latitude. "I feel quite confident," he concluded in his letter to the Indian agent in Utah, "that after being here a year and experiencing the rigors of a severe Dakota winter, that many of the Absentees will return to their reservation next spring."[141]

Captain Carter Johnson, who had negotiated with the Ute when they arrived, and had finessed the lease of Sioux lands to sustain them, went to battle with Downs about the reduced rations. He spoke to the press and criticized Agent Downs for constantly calling for more troops while at the same time pressuring the Ute with harsh and coercive methods. "One hundred pounds of flour," Johnson told the *New York Times*, "and a little patience are more potent factors in the solution of this problem than one hundred soldiers."[142]

Bernia Cesspooch carries her granddaughter, Bernice McKewan, 1918. Buildings at Fort Duchesne in the background. Leo C. Thorne Collection. Used by permission, Uintah County Library Regional History Center, all rights reserved.

Johnson was in South Dakota in the spring of 1908 to help the Ute prepare for the long trek back to Utah. The War Department, relieved to have avoided bloodshed, granted Johnson $10,000 for supplies, harnesses, wagons and "rent of camping grounds en route."[143] The returning Ute had wagons and mules instead of horses and travois. And ample provisions. Henry Harris, a Ute from the Uintah reservation, was sent north to serve as an interpreter on the journey. In late June or early July 1908, 350 Indians in 80 wagons left the Cheyenne River Reservation in South Dakota with Captain Johnson and a small troop of cavalry as escorts. After traveling all summer, crossing Wyoming diagonally, they arrived at the Uintah reservation on October 24. Along the way the Absentees seem to have gathered up ten more members; when they arrived Agent Hall counted 360 Ute.

The Ute were back to live with, as best they could, the haphazard allotments, the chopped-up reservation, the incursion of whites, and the probability of more losses in the future. What they returned to was their group, language and customs. Their People. The People.

Waiting for rations at White Rocks on the Uintah reservation, summer 1909. Special Collections, J. Willard Marriott Library, University of Utah.

CHAPTER SIX

The Rush: Homesteaders Claim Ownership

(1900-1910)

June 11, 1909

George Murphy has been helping Sam Lighthizer and Mr. Frink with the Roberds fence.

William Kleckner cut his knee with an axe, but the wound is healing first rate.

Mr. and Mrs. Day have a tent upon their homestead on Elkhead and are beginning to make things look like home in that vicinity.

September 3, 1909

Mrs. Murphy and Mrs. Sam Lighthizer were berrying on the John Adair Bear River ranch the first of the week. They spent the latter part of the week putting up chokecherry, sarvis berry and currant jams and jellies.

AD Galloway has set out a fine strawberry patch on his Dry Fork place.

George Murphy has been haying all week.

The wind and rain knocked down a lot of Sam Lighthizer's prize oats.

Routt County Republican, Hayden's newspaper.

The wide fertile valleys next to Elkhead Creek had already been taken by 1900, but very few people, if any, actually lived there. Cattlemen grazed their herds on the unfenced lands; speculators searched for coal and other minerals. It was not until the land was surveyed and homesteaders were assured that the Ute were confined on the reservation that settlement began in earnest. In 1900, James W. Oldham filed the first legitimate homestead claim on a section of upper Dry Fork, closely followed by Almon Galloway and his wife Nina, Sam Lighthizer, Hugh McBride and Charles and Cliff Fulton. They each staked out 160 acres in forty-acre parcels. Along Dry Fork they arranged their four, forty-acre squares to claim as much creek and flat meadow land as possible. Together they captured four miles of the meandering, intermittent creek.

Dry Fork is a very different watershed than Elkhead Creek in several respects. Elkhead Creek is a year-round stream, often becoming slow or even "pooling up" in the late summer but it is never entirely dry. Elkhead Creek drains the southern side of Bears Ears Peak, and together with the North Fork and Calf Creek captures the runoff from over twenty-eight square miles. Dry Fork is modest by comparison. By mid-July, it typically runs dry; the creek's rounded black basalt rocks turn a bluish grey, the algae that covers them dries a bleached white. Some water sits in a few pools that have springs nearby, but by August even these pools are very small or disappear altogether.

Dry Fork begins where Cottonwood and Mill creeks join, a leafy section of huge cottonwoods and horsemint-smelling earth. The Dry Fork watershed includes Quaker Mountain and the west side of Pilot Knob, but the stream never has the volume found in Elkhead Creek. Once the snow has melted only a few springs keep it flowing. Dry Fork also meanders more than Elkhead Creek; it cuts a huge but nearly perfect 'S' through the Elkhead area. Elkhead Creek, by contrast, seems to speed more directly to the Yampa

Valley, as though it has more urgent business and need to join the main river.[144]

James Oldham, known as Jim, was one of Elkhead's more quixotic and unpredictable homesteaders. He was both typical and extremely different. His neighbors later recalled that he could

Almon and Nina Galloway, early homesteaders on Dry Fork, circa 1910.

be reasonable and sane one minute and delusional and paranoid the next. His story encapsulates one of the central paradoxes for homesteaders. Can individuals who necessarily need to be self-reliant, independent and strong-willed, and where those traits are cultural norms, also express compassion, cooperation and submission to the good of the whole?

Oldham was the first homesteader on Dry Fork. For his first three years he had the place to himself. In 1903, the Fulton brothers, Charles and Cliff, homesteaded on either side of him along the intermittent creek. Within a few years, Oldham had many neighbors; an area that was once open and unclaimed by whites became filled, if not crowded. Almost immediately, there were conflicts between Oldham and the Fultons over a ditch, a carcass in the drinking water, a "scrub" stallion (an ungelded male horse of poor lineage), property lines and accusations of trespassing.

Oldham was born in Illinois in 1868 to farming parents who later settled in Butler, Missouri, a small community south of Kansas City, near the Kansas-Missouri line. He had two younger brothers, Frank and Henry. In the late 1890s, when he was about thirty, a family dispute propelled him out of the family home in search of his own life and property. He traveled west working various jobs: to Arkansas, Texas and finally to Capital City near Ouray, Colorado, to work in a mine as a silver ore sorter. There, he lived in the Sneffels boarding house with a bunch of single men from Austria, Germany and Slovenia. Known as a glum, downcast person, and never a very adept worker, he was teased by his fellow ore sorters and eventually discharged. In Ouray, he was befriended by an older man, George Vaile, who persuaded him to leave the area and join him in Routt County, where he could claim land of his own. In the summer of 1900, he staked out and filed for a homestead on 160 acres along Dry Fork. His friend, Vaile, had a ranch several miles to the east on the other side of Wolf Mountain, in an area known as Deep Creek.

Oldham was the first to file a legitimate claim on Dry Fork and he was most likely the first to file in Elkhead under the Homestead Act. Under the 1862 law, anyone who was over twenty-one or a head of a family and had not fought against the United States could claim 160 acres of surveyed public land. Unmarried women, freed slaves and immigrants were all eligible. After paying a filing fee of eighteen dollars (or ten dollars for a temporary claim), a homesteader had to live on the land for five years, build a residence and make other improvements. Civil War veterans could deduct the time they had served in the Union Army from the five-year residency requirement. A cash option allowed a homesteader to get a deed to the land by living on the land only six months and paying $1.25/acre. The law had no provision for determining legitimacy of claims other than presenting affidavits from neighbors and friends declaring the homesteader had held to the terms of the act.

Elkhead did not experience a land rush in part because the surveys in northwest Colorado were slow and piecemeal. From 1900, when Oldham established his claim on Dry Fork, until 1920, corners and lines were constantly being contested and moved. The terrain was so rough and the equipment so imprecise that most homesteaders simply paced off their parcel by starting from where they thought the nearest neighbor had established a line. It was not uncommon for lines to change hundreds of feet, even half a mile, when a new survey came through. Private surveyors advertised their services in the county but they were beyond the means of most homesteaders and they, too, were hardly better than pacing with a compass.

The problem was trying to lay a grid system, a pattern of square mile boxes, over hilly, if not mountainous terrain. In the western United States, beginning from what was then considered the West in Ohio, government surveyors established "initial points." The first initial point, a large nail or pin, was set in 1785 on the north shore of the Ohio River in western Pennsylvania followed by thirty-six initial points around the West. Each pin established a meridian running north and south and a base line running east and west from which all survey lines were drawn. Elkhead was surveyed from the Sixth Principal initial point in central Kansas. The base line from that point passed through the southern edge of Routt County.

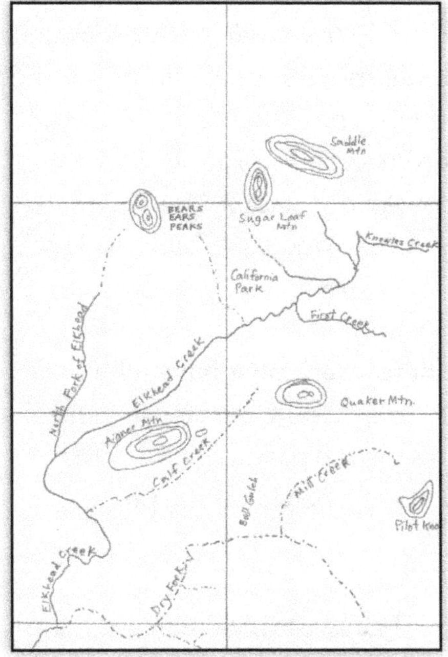

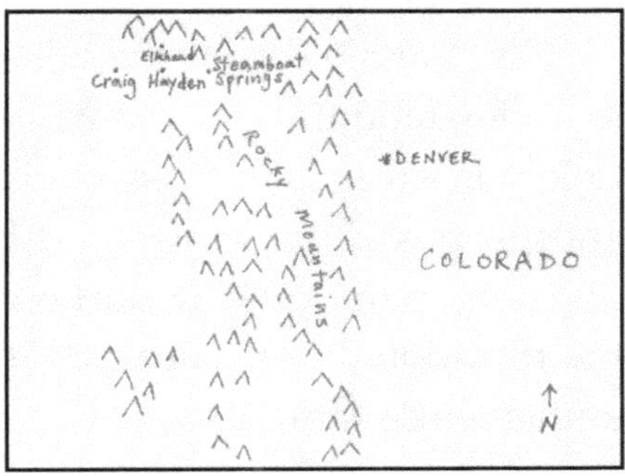

Scale: Each box equals a township: 6 miles north to south and 6 miles east to west. A township is comprised of 36 sections. Each section is a square mile or 640 acres.
Creeks – year-round flow ---
Creeks – Intermittent /seasonal flow -.-.-
Mountains and Peaks –

Natural features and boundaries of Elkhead, Colorado, a portion of the lands the Ute people referred to as Bears Ears country. Bears Ears peaks, part of the Elkhead Range (northwest ear 10,577; southeast ear 10,497 feet above sea level), are visible from most parts of the area. The Elkhead school district included Bears Ears peaks. The district encompassed 222 square miles: eighteen miles north to south (with an additional mile on the southwestern edge) and twelve miles east to west.

Water, and its absence, are the defining elements of the Elkhead landscape. Very little rain falls and though heavy snows are common in winter, the total precipitation is very low, often less than seventeen inches a year. Snow blankets the land for months. When it melts in the spring, the water becomes runoff and quickly leaves the saturated muddy ground in thousands of small gullies and streams. A few weeks later, the soil will be dry and dusty again.

None of this would have much significance if there was enough rain or snow to sustain crops, or to provide drinking water for humans and domestic animals, and if the water were distributed evenly over the countryside.

John Wesley Powell, the same Civil War veteran who attempted to understand the Ute and who made the first boat trip down the Colorado River, intensively studied what he called "the Arid West" and proposed a completely different system of land and water division. In his 1878 "Report on the Arid Regions," he wrote that the traditional homestead of 160 acres was unsuitable to lands with so little rainfall.

> The grass is so scanty that the herdsman must have a large area for the support of his stock. In general a quarter section [160 acres] alone is of no value to him; the pasturage it affords is entirely inadequate to the wants of a herd that the poorest man needs for his support.[145]

Powell suggested homesteads of at least 2,560 acres, or four square miles. He also noted that the system of surveying and dividing land into townships and square-mile sections, in place since the Land Ordinance of 1785, was unsuited to rough terrain and dry lands in the West. The problem of who got there first and grabbed all the water was well understood by Powell:

> Many a brook which runs but a short distance will afford sufficient water for a number of pasturage farms; but if the lands are surveyed in regular tracts as square miles or townships, all the water sufficient for a number of pasturage farms may fall entirely within one division. If the lands are thus surveyed, only the divisions having water will be taken, and

> the farmer obtaining title to such a division or farm could practically occupy all the country adjacent by owning the water necessary to its use.[146]

Powell anticipated a time when a few people would hold all the best water and the government would be left with thousands of acres of unclaimed land. He described a scenario where, in place of ten small farms that shared water for livestock and irrigation, there was one farm controlling the same acreage. "But if the water was owned by one man, nine would be excluded from its benefits and nine-tenths of the land remain in the hands of the government."[147]

Powell advocated for clusters of triangular-shaped plots where one point would connect to a water source. In that way, every landholder would have access to water, no one person would dominate or exclude others, and with a minimum of four square miles, farms might have a chance to be self-sustaining.

Powell offered many far-reaching ideas in his "Arid Regions" report but probably the most radical was one he tucked into a paragraph casually titled "Pasturage Lands Cannot be Fenced." Powell suggested that livestock and lands be held communally, a method of proprietorship that, interestingly, would have resembled the Ute's traditional patterns of communal ownership. Gone were the little plots with the private herds tended inside fences: "The great areas over which stock must roam to obtain subsistence usually prevents the practicality of fencing the lands," Powell wrote. "It will not pay to fence the pasturage fields, hence in many cases the lands must be occupied by herds roaming in common; for poor men, cooperative pasturage is necessary, or communal regulations for the occupancy of the ground and for the division of the increase of the herds. Such communal regulations have already been devised in many parts of the country."[148]

Few in the West listened to Powell. Most legislators had never been in such a dry climate and, moreover, the process of severalty was charged and unique. Free land, cut from "virgin" territory, free to anyone willing to stake a claim and fence it off, was a powerful, romantic idea. Over the next decades, there were revisions made to the Homestead Act. The Desert Land Act of 1877 allowed settlers to claim an additional 160 acres adjoining their original homestead or 320 acres if they would bring water to the land and irrigate. The Stock Raising Homestead Act of 1916 allowed settlers to claim 640 acres—one square mile—for grazing. Even the opportunity to get a square mile represented only a quarter of the acreage that Powell thought was necessary for survival. As Powell predicted, the 160-acre section township system of squares was unfair to most. It would eventually contribute to the doom of the homesteading enterprise in places like Elkhead.[149]

James Oldham, in full compliance with, but also constrained by the Homesteading Act, claimed four forty-acre squares, strung in a line. His plot sought to capture as much as possible of Dry Fork's intermittent water. He rode to Glenwood Springs in the fall of 1900, recorded his claim and returned to his isolated sagebrush hills to "prove up" by living there and making improvements for five years.

Oldham stayed with his friend and mentor, George Vaile, during his first long winter in Routt County. Together, they tried to find a wife for Oldham. An acquaintance of Oldham's, a young woman known as Rose from his hometown in Missouri, wrote to him seeking advice on how to get a job teaching in Colorado. Vaile interpreted the letter as a tease and encouraged Oldham to start a correspondence. "I jollied him a little," Vaile said; "during the winter I composed some of his letters for him that he wrote to her."[150] After a few letters back and forth, Oldham, with Vaile's assistance, wrote Rose and proposed marriage. Spring came and Oldham returned to his homestead cabin on Dry Fork. When Rose finally replied to his proposal, Oldham returned to Vaile's house to show him the letter. According to Vaile, Oldham "was apparently very angry, and he began to abuse this girl a good deal and say disagreeable things about her, and so I presumed at the first off that she had refused him."[151] Vaile asked to see the letter and when Oldham finally showed it to him, "I told him it was a very nice letter which, if I had received it I would have thought it was a formal acceptance, but it was worded in such a way that it was not quite straight out. She said she had prayed on the subject and did not know what to do, and so forth, and so on, and I laughed about it at the time and told him all she needed was a little coaxing." But Oldham had already written a reply. Rose found his letter offensive and insulting; the courtship was over.[152]

Men like Oldham, the Fultons, Adair and Carpenter shared a common aspiration to have a wife and children—but the immediate and urgent dream was to have a cattle ranch. Not a farm, a ranch. Farmers worked in the dirt; ranchers worked with cattle and horses. Farmers wore lace-up boots with a flat heel; ranchers wore high boots that were difficult to walk in because they had a higher heel, designed to fit into a stirrup while riding horseback. Farmers tended a crop; ranchers tended livestock. Ranchers had money and status in this culture; farmers were the poor ones, called "dirt farmers" or "sod busters," dismissive terms in the western Colorado lexicon.

The ideal cattle ranch was a shifting vision, a western mirage. The dreams began in earnest during the time of the great cattle barons. During the 1870s and until the early 1900s, a fairly small group of wealthy men in the United States and Europe invested in cattle. With relatively small landholdings, they figured out how they could run their cattle on the "open range" and their cattle could consume the "free" grass. These operations, so mythologized in the lore of the cowboy, were essentially large mowing operations: the herd of cattle munched their way across the landscape, their jaws chewing up all the vegetation, turning cellulose into beef.

Primarily people of European descent, sanctioned and aided by the government, exterminated buffalo from the western states as part of an effort to extinguish American Plains Indian culture, which depended on buffalo for food and lodging. They were also removed so that the native grasses would be available to cattle. Buffalo were as central to the Plains Indians, and later the Ute, as corn was to the Mayan. During the Great Slaughter, up to 75 million buffalo were killed and replaced by millions of cattle on the range.

A typical cattle operation started with a herd in South Texas, which would be driven, at a pace of a few miles per day, north to a railway depot in the West or Midwest. By chewing and walking slowly across the grasslands, a steer could double its weight in a few months. Cattle barons, as they were known, like J.B. Dawson of Maxwell, New Mexico, would buy 30,000 head in Texas and drive them to Colorado, where they were sold to another cattleman for an enormous profit. Charles Goodnight, Dawson, John Iliff, and many others pioneered the great cattle drives and amassed fortunes for themselves and their investors.

The dream of such easy money, like the dreams that fueled the mining rushes in the West, never really went away in Colorado. Many small-time homesteaders, struggling to make a living on a patch of ground with uncertain water, thought the day might come when they would be running a ranch with a herd of cattle. Their ideal was simply a scaled-down version of the cattle baron plan: they would have summer ground and winter ground, a "shove up" into the mountains, a roundup in the fall and then sell off their fattened cattle for a large profit.

In Routt County at the turn of the century, there were several large cattle operations with tens of thousands of cattle. In the late spring they moved the animals into the public "open" sagebrush and forest lands to fatten up on the free grasses and sold them in the fall. Some of these large cattle ranches were assembled by buying up homesteads along the Yampa River. Others derived from the pre-emption law, a law that allowed portions of so-called "public domain" to be purchased.

When J.B. Dawson sold his land in New Mexico for coal development in 1905, he relocated and amassed a large ranch along the Yampa River, near Hayden. It was through Dawson that Ferry Carpenter came to Hayden. Much later, when Carpenter left Elkhead, he moved back to the Dawson Ranch. The other large "outfits" in the area were the Sevens, Two Bars, Two Circle Bar and the OVO.[153] Their zenith was between 1860 and 1900, before homesteading closed off much of the open range and before the government attempted to control grazing in the national forests.

Northern Elkhead is an approximately million-acre, 1,500-square-mile forest interspersed with park-like grasslands. The area was designated as the Park Range Forest Reserve by President Teddy Roosevelt in 1905 and became the Routt National Forest in 1908.[154] Before the government decided to manage the area, lumbermen, cattlemen and later a few sheepmen used the forest as they chose. Each summer they left behind a trampled, dusty pasture. One forest supervisor described the cattle business as he found it in 1908:

> On the west slopes of the Park Range Forest Preserve, that bordered the intermediate zone separating the desert range from the summer range and almost exclusively within the Forest, was the dumping ground for steers imported as yearlings to stock the open grazing land in northwestern Colorado. The customs of the range followed the habits of the wild game. The stockmen moved the herds, from the desert where they had wintered, slowly toward the distant mountains to the east for summer pasturage. The cattle of beef age, that is, three or four-year-old steers, were allowed to drop in the intermediate zone where the sage brush sheltered the blue stem grass and

> put fat on these cattle almost equal to corn. The younger and lighter steers were moved on to the higher ranges entirely within the Forest. This process of range management was called the "shove up." And when the fall storms came the process was reversed and it became the "shove down." [155]

According to another member of the forest service at the time, "The open portions of the range were grubbed out to such an extent that the dust from the cattle drives could be seen for miles and looked like forest fires. California Park and the North Fork country were very heavily grazed . . ."[156]

Practices changed slowly. In 1908, a local homesteader, Harry (J.H.) Ratliff, took the job of overseeing the Routt National Forest. He decided to end the freestyle grazing bonanza in the Bears Ears part of the Park Range, the area immediately north of the fledgling Elkhead neighborhood. In mid-summer 1908 he made a count of the cattle in the forest. "It was astonishing," he recalled, "even to me, that we counted 46,000 head of cattle on range supposed to be pasturing around 20,000 head."[157] He was particularly concerned about California Park, a large, high bowl of lush, diverse grasses encircled by Bears Ears, Sugar Loaf, Meaden Peak and Pilot Knob. Ratliff enforced limits on the number of cattle that could enter the forest in the spring and, after many years of lawsuits,[158] fences, and disputed roundups, the forest and the livestock that grazed there came under the control of the government.[159]

The timber on these lands—dense forests of pine, fir and aspen—were technically part of the forest reserve but in practice seemed to fall more under the general rubric of the commons. Any homesteader could take a wagon into the forest and cut trees for firewood, a corral, fence posts or cabin logs. Cutting timber for personal use was an unquestioned right and the rules around grazing that Ratliff heroically enforced applied mostly to grass, not trees. The first business in the Elkhead area, besides raising and selling cattle, was a sawmill on the forest reserve. Early in the 1900s, Erasmus Darwin (known as E.D. or Ed) Smith and Frank Lazarus began cutting trees and sawing rough-cut lumber on Pilot Knob.

Smith grew up in East Salem, Pennsylvania, on his parent's farm. When he was twenty-one he left for Colorado and worked as a miner in the famous gold camps of Central City, Black Hawk and Leadville. While in Leadville, he learned of open land in Routt County and homesteaded in the Yampa Valley in 1884. On a trip back to Leadville in 1889 he met and married Hannah Lauver who was from Mifflintown, Pennsylvania. They spent several years ranching along the Yampa, where their eight children were born. Then Smith met Frank Lazarus, a sawyer and carpenter from Michigan; together they opened the first sawmill on Pilot Knob. They logged and cut timber, hauling the finished lumber by wagon and sled eighteen miles to Hayden. Smith opened a second mill on Bears Ears in 1908 or 1909.[160] Smith also built a planing mill and for a while made finished lumber, wainscoting and flooring, but his planing mill was destroyed by fire about a year after it opened.

Smith family on the Ed and Hannah Smith homestead on lower Dry Fork.

For over twenty years the sawmills in the Elkhead forests supplied lumber for homesteaders' cabins, and later, the wood to build the first schools. The sawmills were also a source of jobs. Cutting trees, working in the sawmill and hauling cut lumber to Hayden was wage labor that provided occasional income to early settlers. The Pilot Knob sawmill became something of a social center. Smith, Lazarus and the crew lived in tents and simple cabins next to the mill. Hannah Smith was a well-regarded cook and most of the time Smith's children worked at the mill. During the summer and fall Hannah cooked the midday meal for all the workers; anyone coming to buy lumber was also welcome to eat.

One of Oldham's first ventures was to grow vegetables that he sold to the sawmill. Before long, his primary enterprise was growing timothy grass and selling the seed. Oldham's home on Dry Fork was a simple shack; his efforts to improve the land went into fencing and digging a ditch to bring water to his meadows along the creek. In his first year on his homestead, he borrowed money from George Vaile and invested in seed and horses. When he had a little extra money, he hired single men like Ed Knowles and Frank Corbin to help him with ranch work. He was on friendly terms with other men in the area like John Kitchens, who, with his brother-in-law and partner William Kleckner, claimed several hundred acres on the northern part of Elkhead Creek. Oldham appears to have made ends meet by returning to mining during the winter, trading a few horses, and selling vegetables and seed he cultivated on his ranch.

Ferry Carpenter lived about two miles south on his homestead and saw Oldham fairly regularly. Carpenter would stop at Oldham's cabin when he was riding through Dry Fork. He described their first meeting in 1907:

> I was working, making a small reservoir near my house and he rode up and introduced himself, wanted to know if I was

> the fellow that had taken up that claim, and I said yes, and I think he asked me at the time if I would come over and look at a ditch, or something on his place, relative to a lawsuit. I did not know the man at the time, even by reputation, when I said I was a newcomer and I did not care to mix in anything like that.[161]

Carpenter also remembered Oldham stopping by his cabin on his way to and from town.

> He would come and talk a little while with me and sometimes bring my mail out from town and talk about crops, come down in the field and told me where I was making a mistake in the way I was plowing my land and cultivating, or something in that way.[162]

While visiting Oldham's place, which he described as "a batch outfit like any homesteader's," Carpenter noticed that Oldham had "several very nice books there to read." He was intrigued: "I remember looking them over one time I was there and being surprised that a man living as he did should have books like that. There was a book of astrology . . . and I remember a book on Lincoln. You generally just see a Montgomery Ward catalog and something else in a place like that."[163]

Carpenter was intensely social; he loved a good party, loved to dance and play music, loved to tell stories. As early as 1909, he hosted an annual dance and party to celebrate his birthday and to mark the end of the summer and his return to school "back east." Typically an announcement in the paper welcomed everyone to the all-night dance. A week or so later the paper would include a full report of the music and dancing, the food, and how many horses were tied to the hitch rail in front of Carpenter's cabin. The 1909 dance drew over fifty people, including two wagons of young people from Hayden, and nearly every homesteader in

Elkhead. The party only ended after sunrise, at around seven in the morning, and after a dance contest to see who could last the longest. Bruce Dawson, Bill Rider and Art Horton, bachelors in Elkhead, played the banjo, fiddle and guitar, and Hal, the brother of a Dry Fork homesteader, called the square dances. At around five in the morning, Rider announced a "dance down waltz" and three couples, including Carpenter and a young woman named Anna (Annie) Elmer, entered the dance floor. The men who'd been outside around a fire smoking and talking horses and crops crowded into the doorway and porch to see the fun.

> It was the fastest music I've ever stepped to but I had the prize hay pitcher of Morgan Bottom for a pardner and felt like I could see it thru to a hard boiled finish. Round and Round we tore—it was fine with the floor all to ourselves—an occasional whoop or yell of encouragement as "Stay with 'em Tex" or "Go to it Ferry" and soon we all had our coats off and the sweat a rolling off of us—well there were no quitters and after nearly an hour the musicians gave it up and slowed down to a slow step and quit amid much shouting and clapping.[164]

Annie Elmer, whom Carpenter described as the "prize hay pitcher of Morgan Bottom," was the same age as Carpenter, and the daughter of a Swiss immigrant rancher along the Yampa River. Her father died when she was fifteen. Being the eldest of her siblings, she took control of the ranch, not only running the business but making sure all of her younger siblings finished the eighth grade. Carpenter had enormous admiration for Annie, the one woman he acknowledged was stronger and more determined than he. She was also petite and pretty.[165]

After about an hour of nonstop dancing, the musicians were exhausted; the dancing finally slowed to a stop. The contest was over without a winner, and daylight reminded the dancers that a full day of work was ahead. After the crowd dispersed, Carpenter was so wound up he cleaned up his cabin and then played his fiddle for an hour before he went to bed. He slept until noon the next day.[166]

Carpenter believed it was his duty to include everyone; part of his charm was that he saw each individual as a potential community member and fellow enthusiast. Oldham, with his tendency to a sour disposition, was a challenge for the sociable Carpenter. The following winter, while Carpenter was in his first year of law school, he wrote Oldham a letter and sent him a little book on Lincoln's boyhood for Christmas.

My dear Jim,

I ran into a little book that I thot was exceptionally good on Abraham Lincoln's boyhood.

I thot you might enjoy reading it and so send it under separate cover.

I was very much interested in the books of your library that I saw one Sunday I was there when Jack was staying on your place.

I remember you said you liked History and as Biography is closely related to it and both are great favorites of mine, I always like to talk to anyone interested in them.

I have not much time this winter for anything outside of Law and find that subject the most invigorating mental subject I ever tackled and I am situated in a very remarkable and inspiring place to study and work.

Wishing you a very Merry Christmas and A Happy New Year.

I remain your friend
Ferry Carpenter
1751 Massachusetts Ave.
N. Cambridge, Mass.[167]

Oldham replied the day he received Carpenter's letter and before the book arrived. "I would certainly enjoy reading it," he quipped, "but say if you try too [*sic*] make an Abraham Lincoln of me you will try a greater task than mastering Law.[168] Oldham goes on to refer obliquely to his troubles in Elkhead, "but I do not differ from that once mastermind in that I try too adapt my self to the comparative trying conditions as best I can and never give up. And when things seems going too wreck reform them and fite [*sic*] myself into a new position as best I can."[169]

Oldham's letter then turned to the beneficial influences of the law over religion before ending with a personal request:

> I suppose there are some remarkably bright and intelegent [*sic*] young women studying Law at Cambridge you did not say anything in your letter about it, as they are now taking up most all kinds of work—there is a very great variety of work on the Oldham Ranch it comprises law, gardening berry culture, grain and Hay, besides breaking Horses, cooking and general Housekeeping. Now I think all this is too much for any one man, now if you are acquainted with anyone of this who is studying Law that you can recommend and wants a permanent Position of this kind you tell her this is only one place of 1000 so it will be but one chance in a 1000 and that this opportunity can remain open but a very short time I would like for her to play good on organ but never mind the music. We will have the music later on if all goes well.[170]

While Oldham's egging for Carpenter to find a him a wife at Harvard Law School might seem a joke, it appears to have been a serious request. He was often counseled that his troubles, what one acquaintance described as a "plain case of sheep-herders' melancholy," would be solved by marriage.[171] Nor was the request necessarily a strange one: many men at the time expected to find a wife by mail order, or to catch a young teacher as she cycled through a local rural school.

But Oldham did not find a wife, nor did he ever seem to have kept a close friend. His two brothers married and stayed in Missouri on the family farm, or nearby. Later, his brother Frank moved to Ouray, but neither he, nor other members of his family visited Oldham in Elkhead, nor apparently did Oldham visit his parents or his brothers. As time went by, he became less and less friendly with people who had considered themselves friends, or at least acquaintances.

Oldham's real troubles, however, began in 1903, the year the Fultons became his neighbors on Dry Fork. The Fultons were from Yellow Springs, Ohio. Cliff and Charles also grew up in a family of boys, but unlike Oldham, they were a tightly-knit crew: a number of the brothers moved west together. Cliff and Charles were immediately popular in Hayden and Elkhead. The first mention of them in the *Routt County Republican* is on April 3, 1908: "The Fulton boys took in the dance Friday night." That year, Charles began to court Paroda Bailey, a twenty-one-year-old schoolteacher from Mt. Ayre, Iowa, who was teaching south of Hayden. The newspaper followed the couple's trajectory in short, innuendo-laden snippets. Charles married Paroda in late August 1908 at Hahn's Peak. After a short honeymoon in California Park they began ranching together on the Fulton homestead on Dry Fork.

The Fulton brothers were gifted horsemen, with a specialty in breaking and training draft horses. Like their neighbors, they had a dream of ranching, but it was always horses that brought them cash and helped them survive Elkhead's conditions. They were industrious and friendly; they soon had employment hauling wagonloads of goods or logs, and their homes became part of the social circuit.

Paroda Fulton had taken courses at Drake University in Des Moines before traveling west to teach. As one of the few women living in Elkhead in the earlier days of homesteading, she became known for her intelligence and good sense. Her first son, Ben, was born in the summer of 1909 and over the next nine years she gave birth to four more sons in the homestead cabin on Dry Fork. She was a community builder by nature, holding picnics for the Fourth of July, helping form the school district, loaning books to the school teachers, and regularly gathering the single men into social occasions.

Charles and Paroda Fulton family with the schoolteacher, Mary McDowell and a neighbor, Charles Pizor, on the front stoop of their cabin on upper Dry Fork circa 1916. Front row l to r: Bill and John Fulton and their uncle, Ed Fulton. Back row l to r: Mary McDowell, Charles Fulton, baby Cliff, Paroda Fulton, Ben Fulton, and Charles Pizor.

Oldham took an immediate dislike to the Fultons, and particularly to Charles. In his first accusations, using the newspaper as his mouthpiece, he claimed that Charles Fulton deliberately let a scrub stallion loose on the range. His concern was for several fillies he had on fenced pasture; he wanted Fulton to keep the stallion in a barn or stable. There is no suggestion that the stallion broke the fence or impregnated his mares, but Oldham began a campaign against the Fultons. He published a series of notices in the paper. The first began:

> Jas. W. Oldham has secured the following legal advice on mustang stallions running large: 'No mustang or other inferior stallion over the age of one year shall be permitted to run at large in this state.'[172]

Several months later the warnings escalated.

> Third and Last Warning. I have been damaged not less than $60, sixty dollars, by range studs. Keep your two-year old stallions off this range or I will shoot them. You have your choice in the matter. I mean it. James W. Oldham.[173]

Sam and Pearl Lighthizer homestead on lower Dry Fork. Circa 1908.

When Sam Lighthizer bought a section of land south of Oldham in 1904, he became another neighbor that Oldham immediately distrusted. Lighthizer and his brother, Hal, and sister, Florence, came to Elkhead in 1904 from Ida Grove, Iowa. On their initial trip to Colorado their father had a heart attack and the family turned back. Delayed but not deterred, the siblings took their father back to Iowa and set off again for Colorado. Sam settled on Dry Fork and Florence became the superintendent of county schools until she married John Adair and took up residence on the Adair-Solandt Ranch. Like the Fultons, the Lighthizers would be swept up in a drama brewing around Oldham.

Ed Knowles, a bachelor who homesteaded in California Park, worked for the sawmill and at various ranches when he needed cash. Oldham hired him during the stallion troubles. Knowles cleared the brush around Oldham's cabin so that he could monitor his fence line and see who was approaching his land. Knowles also noted that Oldham bought a gun and a shotgun, recalling later, "I told him, I says, 'you won't have no neighbors at all after a while,' and he says, 'I would rather not have any than to have people that stand in with the bunch, with the Fultons.'"[174]

On April 20, 1908, the neighborly conflicts escalated. Several men, including Charles Fulton, met Oldham near his property line. Oldham again accused Fulton of deliberately leaving his scrub stallion loose on the range. Fulton argued that the two-year-old stallion was "blooded" or bred and not a mustang or wild horse. Insulting someone's horse was akin to insulting a family member, especially if the horse owner was someone who took pride in their horsemanship and horse breeding. A verbal row escalated into a fistfight; Oldham ended up with both eyes blackened and his face badly bruised. Charles Fulton summoned a deputy sheriff and charged Oldham with lunacy. Oldham was arrested and taken to Steamboat, about twenty miles away, and from there north to the county seat, Hahn's Peak. Along the way, Oldham gave an interview to the Steamboat paper and claimed he was simply trying to protect his mares from the stallion. He garnered additional sympathy by suggesting that Cliff aided his brother, Charles, in beating him up. A simple rule governed a fair fight: a man shouldn't be outnumbered. Soon after, Oldham charged the Fulton brothers with assault. The paper ignored the incident except to comment that Cliff Fulton had a bad case of measles the week of April 24. Later, Charles would swear in court that Cliff had no part in the fight.

Oldham was held overnight in jail at Hahn's Peak. The next day, the county court judge acquitted him of the insanity charge. A few years later, Oldham sued Charles Fulton for malicious prosecution and a jury awarded him $1,500 in damages against Fulton.

Oldham had asked for $2,000 in damages, or roughly $50,000 in current dollars; the $1,500 he was granted represented more than all the assets owned by Charles and Paroda Fulton. Oldham tried to arrange a sale of Fulton's homestead, to have the sheriff seize his farm implements, his bobsled, his livestock, and auction them to pay the debt.

Oldham continued to fuss over the Fultons crossing his land, impeding his ditch, and just two years after the Fultons arrived, Oldham claimed that they had purposefully laid a calf carcass in his ditch, blocking the flow and poisoning his drinking water.

As Oldham's problems grew, various people offered to help. Single men like Ferry Carpenter and Dave Sellers cultivated friendship and offered to mediate between him and his neighbors. At one point, Sellers got the Fultons to agree to a meeting to resolve their differences. Charles Fulton said he "would get straight with him any way I can." Oldham initially agreed to the negotiations, but as the date approached, he backed out.

George Smith, the editor of the *Routt County Republican*, had printed many of Oldham's statements for the paper and followed the various conflicts among the neighbors. When the judge dismissed the assault charges against the Fultons, Smith wrote a short opinion piece disguised as a news item. "A neighborhood row is to be regretted always, and we never knew any good to come from one. Let it drop, boys."[175]

But apparently Oldham couldn't stop. He purchased Fulton's share in his ditch, moved his fence line, and then sued Fulton again for damage to the ditch. He asked another neighbor, Herbert Jones, to repair the ditch, but then refused to pay Jones for the work. Then he got in another fistfight, this time with John Adair; he sued Adair for $500 in damages. He publicly accused his long-time friend and supporter, George Vaile, of selling him stolen horses. He posted signs around his property telling his former friend to keep out.

Oldham's problems with his neighbors were extreme, but they serve as a reminder that there was not a lot of cohesion among the Elkhead settlers in those years. Many men were single and the distances between homes was typically measured in miles, not feet. The homesteading system set up competition among them: for the best land and water, for access to public, unclaimed land. The policy of severalty, dividing land that had never been divided, transferring public land into private ownership, broke up and destroyed the commons. The practice was considered elemental to progress, to the formation of society, to capitalism. In Elkhead, the division of land created a place with no center or gathering place, no common ground and no structure that inspired cooperation. Until the school district was formed in 1910, residents had no reason beyond necessity to even see each other; the norm was self-reliance, determination, the power of will over adversity.

People like James Oldham exemplified those characteristics; he genuinely felt that his neighbors were an impediment to advancement. As the community began to slowly form, in small clumps and clots of families and friends, Oldham became known as a crank. The more a center formed, the more defined the margins became. At the same time, the prospect of new land—a space where this ideal independence might still be possible—was diminishing. Northwest Colorado, where the Ute hung on for so long into the 1800s, was one of the last places opened for homesteading in the forty-eight states.[176] For people like the Fultons, Carpenter and Lighthizer, Elkhead was a place of opportunity where they could settle down and own land. Paradoxically, for people like Oldham, Elkhead quickly became crowded and confining: there was nowhere else to go, no more West to beckon.

CHAPTER SEVEN

Claiming, Building and Striving

(1910–)

July 8, 1910

July 1910 finds the East Elkhead country better fixed as regards transportation and communication facilities with Hayden than ever before. The new road under the bluff, put there by the Citizen's Club has brought us half an hour nearer town and several hard pulls.

The post office at Elkhead, with its tri-weekly delivery, has been a boon to the ranchmen—who have never been certain when they could get or send mail. And, too, the Elkhead telephone company has begun to overhaul and remake its line so as to furnish phone service unsurpassed by any other mutual line in the county.

Quite a bit of building has been done in this section the last few weeks. Ernest George, who has taken up the land between the Murphy and Galloway place, has put up a good 16x24 log house. Jack White has completed a new log chicken house. Fred Schaefermeyer has put up a log house for Lou Segur on his homestead adjoining Fred's place. J. Pierie Prevo has the logs cut for his new house.

There is a larger variety of growing stuff on Dry Fork than ever attempted before. A.D. Galloway has tomato plants in bloom. He started them in cold frames. He also has some pumpkin plants in bloom. Ferry

Carpenter has set out two dozen apple trees which came from Brandon, Manitoba Canada and are of a stock that bears fruit in a hardier climate than this. They are all doing finely.

George Murphy returned Sunday from Snake River.

A.D. Galloway brought a new milk cow of Dave Sellers.

Mrs. Charles Fulton gave a picnic party in Hayden on the evening of the 5th and the bachelors of this section came in for a good time and a fine meal.

July 29, 1910 East Elkhead

This week the old adage, "Make hay while the sun shines," has been guiding most of the Elkhead ranchmen. Stacks have been going up every day on the Adair-Solandt place. Reece Horton has been at it all week with a crew and expects to finish by Tuesday.

Ernest George has been helping George Murphy hay on the latter's place.

The Fulton boys have started work in their fields.

Jack White is getting out house logs for a new residence.

Willie Carson of Chicago, who has been visiting on the White Place, went over on the South fork Monday to visit his aunt, Mrs. Denton.

The George Honnold family has been visiting at the Fultons. Both families went up to California Park for a camping trip over Sunday.

Mr. Glandon was repairing the telephone line Saturday.

The squirrels and chipmunks have destroyed more grain than ever before in this region, and plans are being discussed to devise a co-operative plan against them.

Mr. Bingham of Texline, Okla., who has been visiting his brother-in-law, C. T. Roberds, has been up to survey ditches and a reservoir for his desert claim adjoining the Roberds claim.

We had a slight frost Saturday night, but not enough to hurt tomatoes on the Galloway place.

"East Elkhead," *Routt County Republican.*

Herbert M. Jones, his wife, Minnie Mae, and nine of their eleven children moved from Quincy, Michigan, to Elkhead in July 1910. Jones had been a cement worker; he and Minnie Mae owned a small piece of property in Quincy. The Jones's older children, Susie and Kathleen, had moved away, but Bessie, Frank, Paul, Helen, Florence, Yoleta, Tommy, Herbie and Minnie were still at home. The family moved from Quincy to California and back to Quincy several times while their children were young. In the summer of 1909, the family was living in Quincy near Herbert's parents when Herbert made a trip to California alone.

On his way back to the Midwest in late summer, Jones stopped in Hayden and by chance met Ferry Carpenter at the livery barn. He asked Carpenter about land open for homesteading. Carpenter had just graduated from Princeton and was working for J.B. Dawson before he began law school in the fall. He described the encounter:

> I rode into town one day and put my horse in the livery barn (that was the civic center in those days) and I threw my saddle in the saddle room and as I came out, there was a little fella sitting on the bench by the saddle room door. Had on a kind of engineer's hat with a green visor. I knew who he was. I knew he was a homeseeker and I didn't like to be impolite, so I said, "Howdy" to him and he said, "Howdy," and then as I got a little way off he said, "You live on the north side of the river?" Well, he could see I came in over the bridge that way. I said, "Yes, sir." He said, "Is there any good open land out there?" "Good open land?" I said, "Isn't a patch of open land there you could whip a dog on. Rocks and brush. Terrible."
>
> "Oh" he said, "that's too bad. I was closed out in Michigan; I got a big family, and . . ."
>
> "Pardon me," I said. "Did you say you had a big family?"
>
> "Yeah" he said. He did.
>
> I said, "How many?"

He said, "Eleven." [177]

Carpenter made a sudden reversal and offered to take Jones up to Elkhead so that he could see the various parcels still available to homesteaders.

> I said, "Partner, I'm buying you your supper. Come right over to Shorty's now." And he kind of backed off and put his hand here. I think he had his wallet there; he thought I was some kind of con man. Then I went to the mutual telephone that had one wire strung on the top of the barbed wire fence, you know, to get out, and I called up my partner. I said, "Jack, the Lord's heard our prayer. I've got a feller with eleven head." So I explained to him that we've been holding out on a little piece of land over on Calf Creek, with a nice little creek running through it and I said, "Aigner mountain is where the elk hole up in the wintertime and you can have all the fresh meat you want. We don't have any game wardens here and we don't aim to let them come in." And I told him we'd get him out a little irrigating ditch and we'd set him up the pen for his cabin. Now the pen is ten logs on four sides and I said, "We'll set that up and get you ready and what's more we'll pay your filing fee, $4.75.[178]

According to Carpenter, Jones chose his land, sight unseen. After the second or third flip of the spring wagon on their way to Calf Creek in Elkhead, Jones told Carpenter, "I'm willing to swear that I've seen it," and they returned to town where Jones filed on his homestead.

Calf Creek, like Dry Fork, is an intermittent creek—running full with snow melt in late spring, diminishing to a trickle in early summer and drying up by August. Unlike Dry Fork, Calf Creek begins in the aspen, high up on Quaker Mountain.

The stream collects water from several small gullies and moves quickly downhill until it gets to the flatter land closer to where it joins Elkhead Creek at the Adair-Solandt or old McKinlay Ranch. Along the way it is fed by small springs on the slopes of Aigner Mountain. Where Dry Fork makes wide meanders that create small flat meadows, Calf Creek tends to cut into the hills and stay tight in a narrow draw until it gets to the bottomlands. Consequently, the drainage has a more sheltered, secluded feel, more small spaces with smaller vistas, more of a neighborly aspect, cozier. Along the banks of Calf Creek grow short willows and tall thick-barked cottonwood trees. In a few places where the creek meets an obstacle it makes several tight turns, creating little pockets of grassy meadow, rarely wide enough to cultivate or to turn a piece of equipment.

Herbert and Minnie Mae Jones family, Calf Creek, circa 1910. Back L to R: Susan, Frank or Paul, and Herbert. Middle L to R: Helen and Minne Mae. Front L to R: Yoleta, Florence, Minnie and Tommy.

The Jones family homesteaded about 100 feet above Calf Creek, near one of the many springs that form small dips and shelves on the hillsides of Aigner Mountain. The cabin was in an attractive draw where aspen flourished, and under the trees in summer, thick green timothy grass grew. Outside this narrow thicket of aspen, the vegetation changed to the more typical sagebrush and short grasses, like blue stem and red top.

After filing on 160 acres, Jones went home to Quincy and brought his family out to Elkhead the following spring. The Denver and Salt Lake Railroad had reached Steamboat in January 1909 and homesteaders could reserve a box car, load it with their farm equipment and household supplies, and ride west to claim their free land.[179]

Originally named the Denver Northwestern and Pacific Railroad, the line began in Denver, climbed over Rollins Pass—also known as Corona Pass—at an altitude of 11,680 feet. It descended into Middle Park, and followed the Yampa River north and then west to Steamboat, Hayden and Craig. The plan was eventually to shorten the route by building a tunnel under the Rocky Mountains and connect Denver with Salt Lake City by way of the many coal mines in northwest Colorado. Although the tracks reached Steamboat in 1909, they did not get to Hayden, twenty-four miles away, until October 1913. The railroad's principal investor, David Moffat, was a millionaire railroad magnate, banker and mine owner in Denver. After he died in 1911, the renamed Denver and Salt Lake Railroad was reorganized, sold, and in and out of bankruptcy. It never reached Salt Lake; the terminus was, and still is, Craig, just seventeen miles west of Hayden. And it was not until 1928 that the company was able to realize Moffat's dream, a six-mile tunnel under the Continental Divide that cut hours off the trip from Denver. Nevertheless, the railroad had a huge influence on the development of northwest Colorado. In 1909, the Hayden paper reported that Moffat had spent $50,000 advertising the wonders of Routt County and promoting the area to homesteaders, miners and speculators.[180]

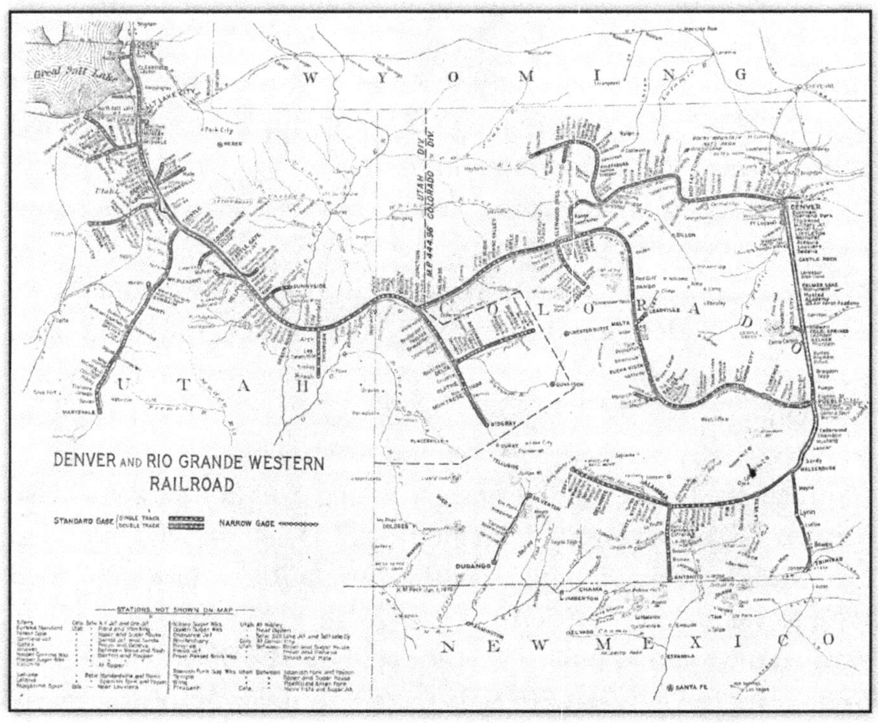

Map showing the rail line from Denver to Craig, Colorado (the railroad nearest the Wyoming line). The then-named Moffat Railroad reached Hayden in October 1913 and Craig later that year, but the line went bankrupt and never went beyond Craig, much less to Salt Lake City. Elkhead is about twelve miles north of Hayden.

For the first several weeks the Jones family camped on James Oldham's place on Dry Fork while neighbors helped them put up a "soddy"—a small log cabin with a dirt floor and a sod roof. "When it rained, the water and dirt came pouring through," Minnie Jones recalled.[181]

Herbert Jones was forty-six and his wife, Minnie Mae, was forty-four. Both looked much older than their years; their hair was grey, their expressions worn. The youngest child, Minnie, was barely one year old; their oldest child, Susan, was twenty-one and living in California. Building their homestead would require a phenomenal amount of physical labor, but unlike many of their neighbors, the Jones were not particularly fit or skilled. They had two teenage sons, Frank and Paul, who could do a full day's work and they were soon working for wages in the valley. Herbert had a double hernia, and though he knew how to mix and form concrete, he was not familiar with fencing, cutting logs or even planting crops. He did not know how to ride a horse. Minnie Mae had been through twenty-one years of giving birth every other year and was weary. She loved to play the piano and could happily play all day when she was near an instrument. Like their neighbors, the Jones got some chickens and cleared land for a garden. They papered the inside walls of the cabin to keep the wind from blowing through, and hauled water from a nearby spring. They didn't have any livestock, nor did they fence their claim. They didn't raise grain to sell or attempt irrigation for hay. Minnie Jones Camilletti recalled:

> There was a little hay and this and that round. Makes you wonder how we lived. We had a spring but it wasn't piped down or anything like that. We had to carry water. They raised huge gardens. We could raise most anything up there. The season was short but on the other hand we didn't have a frost like they do along the river. We raised the most terrific strawberries I can remember. I think we raised a little grain but no big deal. And perhaps a little feed for the chickens.[182]

All around them, families were "busting a gut" in physical labor, trying to use the short time without snow and mud to improve their claims.

Homesteaders—both men and women—grubbed acres of sagebrush, swinging a homemade tool that was a combination of an axe and a hoe; they dug reservoirs and miles of ditches by hand to cultivate a few acres; they carved skis from wood so that they and their children could move about over the snow; they hauled water, planted, put up fence, dragged logs from the forest and built cabins, barns and corrals.

Although they aspired to have cash to buy provisions in town, and a garden and livestock sufficient to feed their families, Elkheaders often lived off the land, just as the Ute had. They hunted for elk and deer and when that game could not be found, or they could not afford ammunition, they snared rabbits, killed sage grouse with a rock, even caught, skinned and boiled porcupine. In the summer they camped in the nearby forest to fish and gather berries. Finding food was a year-round, daily chore for most people. During the long winters, which typically began in October and ended in April or May, daily work included chopping wood and keeping a fire going.[183]

Industriousness was heralded above almost any other character trait. Part of this was the firm belief that anyone could succeed if they tried hard enough. As the *Steamboat Pilot* opined in June 1909, "Those who want a kid-gloved job turn around and go back home. There are fortunes in Routt county soil, anywhere from the eastern border to the western, and any man who can acquire 160 acres and is not afraid of work can develop a fine ranch."[184] No one seems to have questioned this ethic, even while individuals were heeding the needs of the community, and at times, subsuming their own advancement for the good of the whole.

Some homesteaders like Israel Boloten who arrived on foot in Elkhead in 1908 had an enormous capacity for work. They had already endured a lifetime of hardship and were prepared to survive, if not prosper, just about anywhere. Ferry Carpenter remembered meeting Boloten on the road where he and his partner, Jack White, were fixing fence. Boloten was a very short, sturdy, muscular man who wore plain, inexpensive clothes and lace-up boots. He arrived in Elkhead with $75-80 in his pocket, almost exactly what he would need to file on a homestead. Boloten asked Carpenter about land and a job. Carpenter told him that all the best land had already been taken but referred him to the Adair-Solandt Ranch, about five miles away, where he could probably find work.[185]

Boloten grew up in Russia dreaming of going to America. His mother died when he was one year old and he was raised by his grandparents and later, by an uncle. When he was eight, he was apprenticed to a shoemaker; by the time he was fourteen he was earning three dollars a month plus his room and board. He worked all over Russia, Siberia, Turkestan and Manchuria until his passport expired and he was arrested. He bribed an official and then spent six months hiding in the Caucasus Mountains. With another bribe of vodka he won a release from military service and made a plan to immigrate.

Boloten read about Teddy Roosevelt during his shoemaking apprenticeship and developed a fascination with the American West. Without his Russian passport and with no country to return to he made his way to Libau, Latvia, where he secured passage on the ship, SS *Smolensk*, bound for the United States. Boloten was just a few weeks shy of twenty-one years old. Like most of the other travelers he was listed as "Hebrew." He landed March 13, 1907, in New York City with five dollars, but managed to wire a cousin in Chicago who sent him twenty-five dollars. He joined the cousin and together they fixed shoes in Chicago while Boloten took English classes at Hull House. A year later he moved west to Wisconsin, where he milked cows on a dairy farm and then moved farther west, to South Dakota, where he worked as a stoker in a hotel and later, as a waiter. He read about Routt County in the *Denver Post* and decided, "That is the place for me."[186]

Within a few weeks of his arrival on foot in Elkhead, Boloten claimed 160 acres of dry land on the side of a hill above Calf Creek. The land was nearly treeless and had no water. Boloten immediately began working for anyone who would hire him; he gained a reputation as a laborer who did not complain. He fixed fences, plowed land, tended cattle and seemed to never let a day go by without filling it with work, paid or unpaid.

Like many men in the area, Boloten left Elkhead in the winter to work in the nearby mines in Oak Creek, or for the railroad at its switching station in Phippsburg, or as a hired hand on the larger ranches in the Yampa Valley. Even in Elkhead, where hard work was the norm, Boloten was known for his labor. He spent almost nothing on himself and used the money he earned to trade. He would later recount a story of buying cattle in Meeker for $75 a head and selling them to a fellow Elkheader, Reece Horton, for $125 each a few weeks later. With that money he went to the bank and borrowed money that he used to buy and sell hay.

Boloten was labeled "the Jew" and sometimes referred to as "our Jew friend." Boloten's story of his youth in Russia conforms to the fate of many Jewish people at the time, but Boloten rarely stated he was Jewish during his time in Elkhead, nor did he show any signs of practicing his faith. Only decades later did he speak of being Jewish and that was while explaining his lack of formal education.[187] Was he a Jewish man in an area hundreds of miles from a synagogue or Jewish community, who chose to keep his religious identity quiet? Looking back from such a distance, it is difficult to know how Boloten was treated in Elkhead. Anti-Semitism was rife during that time and in that part of the country. There was no Jewish community nearby to either document discrimination or defend people like Boloten. Some people did not like him, and as his wealth and influence grew, and as he became a sheepman, some people spoke derisively of him. The known descriptions of him did not attribute his perceived character flaws to his religion or ethnicity, but would people have said the same things if he had not been known as being Jewish?

After proving up on his homestead in 1913, Boloten changed his name. According to his lawyer, Ferry Carpenter, Boloten thought "the word Israel was very Jewish and he wanted to change it to Isadore."[188] He also dropped an "o" to make his surname Bolten. Carpenter went on to say that he didn't think he "got a lot of good out of changing it," suggesting that his Jewish identity was already established.[189]

Bolten always held himself as a member of the more educated, forward-looking group of Elkheaders. He seems to have been accepted by that group; he was so industrious and soon had money to improve his land, buy more land, and enter into trades. Charles Fulton, Ferry Carpenter, his partner, Jack White, and Reece Horton all signed the papers to substantiate Bolten's homestead claim. He was the Russian, the Jew, but was also quickly an insider.

Unlike James Oldham, who was also single, initially disliked, and had seemingly wandered into Elkhead after trying several different ventures, Bolten was friendly and willing to lend a hand to his neighbors. He sought partnerships wherever he went and a few times brought struggling families into his businesses. If he knew he would be away for the winter working in a mine, he would rent out his cabin in return for work on his homestead and tending his livestock. He also spent time living with other Elkheaders, particularly the Fredrickson family, who were known for their large garden and good cooking. He would trade labor for his board and save his cash to buy livestock or hay.

In one sense, Bolten differed from his neighbors: he was not much interested in horses and he did not partake in the status that a good horse could confer on an individual or family. Even after he had money, he chose to walk rather than spend money to purchase and care for a horse.

For most settlers, horses were an integral part of life and work. Without automobiles, nearly everyone relied on horse power. Having a horse that could pull a wagon meant you could haul supplies to and from a market, or you could earn money hauling freight. Horses were used to haul logs for a cabin down from the forest. They were used to plow new land, to pull machinery that cut and stacked hay; many people used them to help pull up brush when they were clearing land. (People tied one end of a rope around the horn of the saddle and the other around the base of the small tree.)[190] Settlers used horses to round up cattle and later, sheep, or to tend livestock on unfenced, typically public, land. Horses pulled sleds over the snow in the winter both for personal conveyance and to haul provisions. Horses were essential to life because they did a great deal of work. Horses provided power.

Breeding, training and handling horses was a specialized skill. Nearly everyone in Elkhead could ride, but only a few people tried to raise and train horses, and even fewer people had the skills to operate horse-drawn machinery. On Dry Fork, Charles and Cliff Fulton built their ranches around cattle, but their real love was horses. The brothers were said to "have a way with horses," which meant they could train unbroken colts, handle horses that others found impossible, and could match horses into teams to pull a wagon or a sled. Horses were their side business but were central to their identity as a family.

The Fultons were also known for their work ethic, particularly in regard to their efforts to bring water to their pastures. According to his son, Charles Fulton "built more ditches, reservoirs, flumes, headgates, laterals, fences, roads, bridges, and cleared more scrub oak and sage brush and drained more swamps than some reclamation jobs that have cost millions . . . The adobe hills, basalt rocks, or oak stumps were not as tough as his spirit."[191]

Dry Fork was not dry when water was abundant in the late spring, but in the summer, as soon as the fields began to wither, the small stream would turn to a trickle and then to hard dirt. The Fultons tried to capture the water in the springtime and store it so that they could use it in the late summer and early fall. Most of their efforts were in vain. The soils were porous and the ditches did not hold. Their conflicts with their neighbor James Oldham over a stallion, a fence line, and a main ditch ended up costing them dearly; after Oldham won the $1,500 judgment against Charles, the family lived under the constant threat of losing their homestead.

The Fultons were not alone in building a complex set of waterworks. All around Elkhead, as people tried to cultivate their land, they spent thousands of hours, and precious cash, attempting to capture and direct the fickle and seasonal supply of water. The newspaper regularly carried news of these water projects: dams surveyed and built, headgates (the mechanism for opening and closing off a source of water into a ditch) installed, and most arduously, miles and miles of ditches dug. With an average of less than seventeen inches of annual rainfall (including snow melt), cultivation meant diverting, storing and managing water. No crop could grow and mature without being watered.

The growing season was also incredibly short. Frosts could continue into June and were likely again in late August and September. As soon as the weather got warm, the soil got dry. And the soils in Elkhead are mostly clay. They lack humus, the vegetative material that can keep soil loose and able to retain water. When clay is wet it is sticky and forms heavy clods when turned with a shovel or plow. When those clods dry they are like cement, only breakable with a pick. There was a common belief at the time that rain would follow the plow and through some magical process the soil would become loose and workable when it was plowed. In truth, plowing made the situation worse: organic matter was vulnerable to wind and sun and in a heavy rain or during a snow melt, soil not held in place by roots could wash away downhill.

Along the bends in the creeks, on the small valley floors, homesteaders tried to grow hay. With some irrigation the native grasses would produce more hay; without irrigation the hay is much thinner. Of the close to 150,000 acres in the Elkhead district, less than 4,000 could be irrigated. Homesteaders hand cut and loosely stacked their hay in mounds. When winter covered the ground with snow these stacks could be opened and the hay pitched from a wagon or sled to cattle and horses. The numbers were never in the homesteader's favor because 160 acres, or even a desert claim of 320 acres, could not keep many head of cattle alive. Roughly speaking it takes fifteen to twenty acres of brushland in Elkhead to keep a cow grazing healthily for a year. It takes approximately two tons of hay to feed a cow through the winter. To raise two tons of hay requires one to two acres with irrigation and about two-and-a-half to three acres without irrigation. Only the largest ranches in Elkhead, those that were formed before the area was opened to homesteading, had enough acreage to handle more than a few cows. Nevertheless, people tried.

They also experimented with several other crops: strawberries, potatoes and oats were the most successful. Almon and Nina Galloway cultivated strawberries at their Dry Fork home. In September 1909, the newspaper noted that they "set out a fine strawberry patch" and that their neighbor, Jim Barnes, was giving away strawberry plants to his neighbors. Others thought the climate and soil were perfect for potatoes, which had the advantage of being easier to cultivate, transport, and in a pinch could be fed to cattle and pigs. Oats and wheat would grow on hillsides where a horse could plow and where a ditch could presumably carry water. None of the homesteaders had enough land to cultivate more than fifteen to twenty acres of grain; the acreage put into strawberries or potatoes was much less.

Wherever people cultivated crops or held livestock they needed fences. As late as 1912, large cattle outfits were still moving herds of steers through the open land of Elkhead and into the Routt Forest Reserve to the north. Elkhead was also on the way to the railhead at Rawlins, Wyoming, where cattle were shipped to both coasts on the Transcontinental Railroad. Consequently, there were often loose cattle that could destroy a grain crop or eat and trample their way through a garden in a few minutes. A loose bull could impregnate cows, and livestock that was not confined could wander off to join the renegades and never be seen again. The loss of a horse was particularly worrisome—had it been stolen or was it lost? The newspaper reported regularly on lost horses, giving a full description, a dollar value, and sympathizing with its bereaved owner. The message was intended to alert everyone that a horse was missing. If someone tried to sell the horse or trade it, they could be caught and tried.

Homesteaders typically built pens or corrals for their livestock first, and later, when they had the materials, built a perimeter fence around their claim. Digging postholes in the rough ground and stringing barbwire was arduous work. It was also difficult to know where the corners were in a land with few surveyors and infrequent markers. To put up fence around a 160-acre parcel meant a minimum of a mile of fence calculated as the crow flies, not the distance of the actual fence that would need to follow the shape of the land.

Frank Corbin, the Fultons' neighbor on the south side of Dry Fork, followed a work path very like Bolten's. He sought cash and hired himself out with whoever had means to pay for labor. Corbin was from East Providence, Rhode Island, and had grown up in a densely urban area with parents and older siblings who worked making jewelry. His father, William, was a bench hand (meaning both hands were free to work) and his sisters worked as chain makers. No one in the family seems to have had time for much education; by the time he was fifteen, Frank Corbin was working beside his father. When Corbin was twenty-one, he and his older brother, Lewis, left home and wandered west. They ended up in northwest Colorado in 1906 and soon filed for homesteads on Dry Fork. Neither of the brothers had any experience with horses or cattle but they both managed to find work. Lewis became known as a local cowboy. He was also a hard partier and one night he and two buddies drank themselves to death in Hayden. In 1910, Hayden was a "dry" town—the nearest legal alcohol was nearly a day's ride away in Steamboat Springs. Lewis Corbin and his friends began the evening with a bit of whisky but soon turned to drinking wood grain alcohol. After the men finished the grain alcohol, one of the men, who worked in a barbershop, led the group to the shelves full of hair tonic. All three died sudden, painful deaths that night, presumably from lead in the tonic.

Frank Corbin took charge of his brother's body and arranged for the memorial service in Hayden. Although Lewis died without a will, leaving his homestead claim in a legal limbo, Frank used the land as though it belonged to him and soon expanded his small herd of cattle. That winter, in December 1910, Frank Corbin married Edna Hughes, the daughter of his neighbors George and Willmenia (Minnie) Hughes, and they moved into Corbin's simple cabin together.

Frank Corbin, Edna Hughes Corbin and their daughter, Claudia, at the Adair-Solandt Ranch, 1913.

Single men far outnumbered women of any age in 1910. Although few in number, the women worked just as hard or harder than the men in Elkhead. Their work was more diverse. Women in Elkhead certainly followed conventions of the time, focusing their efforts on caring for children, cooking, cleaning and laundry. They also tended the chickens and maintained the vegetable garden. But, given the circumstances, particularly the extreme weather and the isolation, they often took up what was considered "men's work": riding horseback to tend cattle, grubbing sagebrush to clear land, irrigating, butchering, chopping firewood, fencing, and shooting predators. They sometimes also wore men's clothing to do the job.

Grubbing sagebrush to clear land was common labor in Elkhead. Here Jesse Ferguson would have used an axe-like tool to chop the sagebrush out by the roots and then piled the brush up to burn.

Mary Murphy grew up in Iowa, the daughter of Scots-English and Irish-English parents. She married George Murphy and they had four children, but none of them survived their childhood. When George was forty-six and Mary was thirty-two, they homesteaded in Elkhead on a southerly stretch of Dry Fork about a half-mile downstream from the Galloways, and about a mile downstream from the Fultons and Oldham. Mary was known as an inveterately generous and jolly person. She loved a good joke and once hung a bushel of apples on Ferry Carpenter's fledgling apple trees that he had so proudly planted near his cabin. She spent a lot of time alone on the homestead while George earned cash by hauling freight to Rawlings, Wyoming, and back. Mary kept a flock of chickens, turkeys and geese, and tended a large garden. She was competent on horseback and looked after the livestock while George was away. She cooked meals for bachelors and provided a sympathetic ear when people were in trouble. She was also known as a "crack shot"—someone who could handle a rifle or a pistol with excellent marksmanship.

Her neighbor Paroda Fulton, the former schoolteacher, gave birth to her first son, Ben, in the family cabin in 1909. In 1911, John was born, followed by Bill in 1913, Cliff in 1916, and Charles in 1918. Like the women around her, Paroda became a resourceful cook: she "could fix a gorgeous meal out of an apron full of bear cabbage, dock or dandelion and a tough old sage rooster," her son John remembered.[192] She made periodic trips into the higher mountains to pick berries in the late summer and canned fruit and made jelly for the winter.

Chokecherry bushes are common at certain elevations in Elkhead. They produce clusters of small dark fruits that, although too tart to eat directly, can be turned into fine syrup and jelly. Paroda's chokecherry jelly was famous. Above all, Paroda was known and respected for her healthy children and her calm and resourceful nature.

On August 19, 1910, just two months after the Jones family had moved into their soddy on Calf Creek, Dr. Solandt returned from Elkhead and stopped by Ferry Carpenter's law office in Hayden. He had terrible news. Little Herbie Jones, the four-year-old son of Minnie Mae and Herbert Jones, had died suddenly at their home on Calf Creek. Solandt told Carpenter that he thought the cause of death was amoebic dysentery, but the real problem was malnutrition and starvation.[193] He asked if Carpenter would be willing to officiate a burial on Calf Creek and if he could take some supplies to the family, immediately.

Carpenter made the long ride past his homestead cabin, across Dry Fork, and north to the Jones homestead on Calf Creek. Along the way, he stopped at the Murphy homestead. Mrs. Murphy told him to catch and saddle her pinto horse while she got rice to feed the family and a black silk underskirt to line the coffin.[194] They rode together the remaining miles up Calf Creek. As they approached the Jones's simple cabin, they could hear men's voices. Al Galloway, a neighboring homesteader on Dry Fork, was sawing wood and hammering together a coffin. Carpenter and other neighbors helped dig the grave near the creek, just below where the sod-roofed cabin stood, near a grove of aspen. Reece Horton, another neighbor, arrived on horseback, leading a milk cow and carrying its young calf across his saddle. While Carpenter was working outside, Mary Murphy made sure the other children had something to eat. She found a pot of old boiled potatoes on the stove; she heaved them into the brush, washed the pot thoroughly, and cooked a large pot of her rice. Afterward, she prepared the body for burial. She lined the coffin by tearing her silk underskirt into long pieces.

A few hours later, with nearly every homesteader seated on logs outside the cabin, Carpenter led the group in singing "Nearer My God to Thee" and then read John 14:1, "Let not your heart be troubled: ye believe in God, believe also in me. In my Father's house are many mansions; if it were not so, I would have told you. I go to prepare a place for you." When he got to the line "Come let us rise and go hence," he was surprised to see the pallbearers jump up and carry the coffin down to the grave near the creek. Carpenter completed the service; the first child known to die in Elkhead was buried.

A few days later the newspaper published a short notice:

> AUGUST 19, 1910
>
> It was a great shock to the people of this section to hear of the death of Herbert Jones's small boy, Sunday. Dr. Solandt was in attendance and brot the sad news down the creek. The Joneses are recent settlers up here, but have already won the respect of their neighbors and the sympathy of the community goes out to them at this time.[195]

There were surely other struggles and tragedies in Elkhead but Herbie Jones's death was a turning point. Before the Joneses staked their claim and brought all their children out to live in the one-room cabin, the area was mostly a place of speculation and adventure for single men. Herbie's death reminded everyone to stay focused on the essentials: to keep food on the table, to stay warm in winter, and that the only doctor was many miles and hours of travel away.

The death of a child also served as a kind of antidote to the boosterism and hyperbole that was part of the spirit of the time. Everyone wanted to find the crop that would bring in steady cash or have enough cattle to sell and earn the title of ranch as opposed to homestead. The passing of the young boy pushed people to realize that children might die for the risks they were taking, for the ambition and dreams they were pursuing. It was a shock to Carpenter, a young bachelor, full of ideas and enthusiasm, to dig a grave with his neighbors and say a prayer for a small child.

The funeral on the hillside above Calf Creek in August 1910 was also the first time Elkheaders had gathered to accomplish something collectively. Although the event did not mark the end of intense individualism and self-reliance, it did mark a beginning: it was a time when the assembled mourners acted for the common good and openly and publicly cared for one another.

Ferry Carpenter's homestead cabin, circa 1908. Carpenter is on the right; to the left is probably Fred Schaefermeyer, who cut and stacked the logs.

CHAPTER EIGHT

From Mine to Ours

(1910–1911)

September 2, 1910

The dry weather continues and we had two cold nights, Wednesday and Thursday, which frosted down the potatoes and nipped the young alfalfa.

Mrs. Bryon Shelton and Sam have been spending the latter part of the week at Charlie Fulton's.

Al Galloway has been cutting oats while Frank and Paul Jones shocked them.

Jack White is getting down logs for a new house.

Herman Foster has been helping Fred Schaefermeyer on his reservoir.

Lou Segur and bride drove out to their claim on Wolf Mountain Sunday.

There were 97 people at Ferry Carpenter's dance and 65 horses tied to the hitch racks.

Owing to the dry weather the grain in this section was so well ripened that the frost did not affect it.

September 16, 1910

The bids for carrying the mail to the Elkhead post office were not rejected completely as reported but were returned, owing to a technicality in the lowest bidder's bond, and new bids must be in by Sept. 26th.

The three school teachers who filed on adjoining claims near the Fletner cabin have let contracts for the construction of cabins and expect to move here as soon as possible and commute.

The Lighthizer boys finished staking the second cutting of alfalfa on the McKinley place on Saturday.

Miss Bessie Jones has been visiting Miss R. Carpenter and Miss Hetty Terry at the Murphy's the last week.

A.D. Galloway and H.M. Jones drove to town Wednesday.

Jack White has the poles hauled and strung out to stay his fence with.

Charlie Schaefermeyer was up to the Schaefermeyer Bros ranch Sunday.

A.P. Wood drove the president and vice-president of Hugus & Co. up to the Adair-Solandt place on Friday.

The Cary roundup outfit was working this part of the county last week and took a bunch out down Deep Creek.

Mrs. Sam Lighthizer visited at the Geo. Murphy place on Saturday.

Coyotes have been making raids on the poultry yards in this region lately. Jack White's Thanksgiving turkey was carried off the Schaefermeyer's place and chickens were turning up missing pretty regularly until the Murphy dog brought the thief to bay and Mrs. Murphy shot it.

Herbert Jones has moved his family into their new residence on Calf Creek.

Art Horton was a Hayden visitor on Saturday.

The Oldham-Fulton case over a dead calf has been dismissed by the prosecuting attorney for lack of sufficient evidence.

Sam Adair will probably bring a thresher in to this part of the county to thresh the grain.

Fred Schaefermeyer reports a record-breaking oat crop this season.

Ferry Carpenter broke his plow in 3 places trying to plow up oak brush roots last Saturday.

"East Elkhead," *Routt County Republican.*

Ferry Carpenter turned twenty-four in 1910, just a few days before Herbie Jones died. With his college degree, homestead and talents on the dance floor, he was one of the county's most eligible bachelors. According to Carpenter, the problem in the country was a dearth of "she stuff," particularly in Elkhead. He lamented how quickly telephone operators and teachers were snatched up and married. In truth, there were several young single women in the area, but either there was not mutual interest, or he was not ready to marry. He enjoyed his life as a bachelor. Carpenter created a story that he was looking for a wife to make his real intentions more locally acceptable, and humorous. After the death of Herbie Jones, Carpenter threw his energies into establishing a school district in Elkhead. He was not immediately successful. In fact, when the district was finally established, many months had passed and Carpenter was back in school, more than a thousand miles away. Establishing a school district, a governing unit, was a community event; the first big collective decision taken by Elkhead settlers.

The census taken in the spring of 1910 found 40 households and 90 individuals living in the roughly 220 square miles that people were beginning to call Elkhead. The population was growing, and more and more children needed schooling.

When Carpenter told the story of the school district he always began with Herbert and Minnie Mae Jones and their eleven children, and added that he and his business partner, Jack White, hatched a plan to open a school so that they could recruit female teachers and prospective wives. Carpenter said that on the very day Jones filed on his homestead on Calf Creek, he took the newly enlarged list of school-age children and petitioned for a school district. What actually happened was much more complicated and interesting. In 1910, Elkhead was still a cluster of homesteads—not a place with an identity of its own or where people had much experience with cooperation, much less civic projects. Yet, there were stirrings of community: friendships, partnerships, joint ventures, and a few public works that served the whole. There were still many single men in the area, but the population was gradually shifting toward married couples, and more and more of them had children.[196]

Jack White was Carpenter's old friend and classmate from Evanston, Illinois. Carpenter convinced him to come to Colorado to homestead near him and become a partner in the cattle business. White homesteaded on Morgan Creek, on the far eastern edge of Elkhead, but near enough to Carpenter that they could care for their livestock and homesteads together. Jack was a good-humored young man who was not particularly driven or competitive. He was loyal and hardworking. After forming the partnership in 1908, Carpenter asked his father if he could borrow money to buy land and cattle. His father loaned the money but with the stipulation that after Carpenter graduated from Princeton University he would go to law school. He wanted his son to have a career with earnings outside of the volatile cattle business. Carpenter purchased a school section, an entire square mile to the north of his homestead, from the State of Colorado; he passed along $2,500 to White to buy cattle.[197] For the next several years, while Carpenter completed his bachelor's degree and his law degree at Harvard, White maintained their homesteads and tended the cattle.

Ferry Carpenter and Jack White, circa 1910.

Arthur and Anna Fredrickson who homesteaded on a shelf above Elkhead Creek. Circa 1919.

Even though Carpenter was hardly a full-time resident during this period, he took an active interest in local affairs. He wrote letters to the newspaper and fellow homesteaders and returned faithfully every summer to improve his homestead and agitate for the development of Elkhead.

In the early days of homesteading the dominant ethic was "you are on your own." Many people turned to homesteading intent on leaving the world of wage labor, bosses and the hierarchy of a typical work environment. They longed to be independent. A few who had been sharecroppers looked forward to at last having their own land and being able to work and earn a living without paying rent. Reflecting this sentiment, the stories that people told about each other and those they printed in the newspaper in Elkhead's early days, centered on individual achievement: Fred Schaefermeyer could notch and saddle logs for a whole cabin in a few days; the Fulton brothers could train a team of workhorses; Anna and Arthur Fredrickson raised three healthy children on nothing but what their garden, chickens and a milk cow could produce.[198] Being strong and self-reliant was a norm, or at least a common aspiration.

The most independent people in Elkhead, those who had only themselves to depend on, who handled their money and property alone, who were responsible solely for their own well-being, were the single men. In many ways, the single men, those who never "got hitched," set the social norms for everyone. During the period of early settlement, these men were the successful homesteaders. A group of at least thirty men, including John Jykadorke, James Oldham, Fritz Nash, Steve Shipka and Ed Knowles, moved through Elkhead, homesteading, buying land, and when they were eligible, using their Union soldier time as credit toward the five years they needed to "prove up." Their names appear on some census records; occasionally the newspaper mentioned their passing in and out of the area. Most, however, left little record behind. They took jobs in the mines in the winter, or traveled to warmer and lower elevations and worked as ranch hands. They returned in the spring and spent the summer and early fall tending their homesteads and picking up part-time work. As itinerant, seasonal homesteaders they were not particularly concerned with establishing a home, much less building a community. They really could accomplish everything they needed to do alone. They were only very rarely caught asking for help.

After the initial round of land acquisition, another group of settlers, consisting mostly of young couples, began to put down roots in Elkhead. A few had children. Several of the older children married across families, creating new ties. New customs and habits emerged as families formed and became permanent, year-round residents.

During the first several years of homesteading, almost all of an individual's or a family's labor had been spent building individual ranches and homesteads. But gradually, as people got to know each other, an ethic of neighborliness developed. People began to form friendships and to rely on and care for one another. Julia Smith Pizor called it "real neighborliness." She described some of the customs that connected people who had recently been strangers and now found themselves living on the same hillside, or along the same creek. "If anyone had too much of something they'd give it to somebody else. The clothes the kids had outgrown we'd pass them on to someone else. Everything was pretty much worn but it was real neighborliness."[199]

During that period, there were also certain tasks, like threshing, that were best done together in what people came to call "exchanged work." "We always worked together," Julia Smith Pizor said. "Everybody got along; you had to get along. We'd exchange work. One would help one, then he'd go back and help the other. Especially in threshing time: you went and helped your neighbor."[200]

Julia Smith Pizor, second from left, berrying with friends and family in California Park circa 1910.

Slowly, the need for cooperative projects like roads, bridges, mail delivery, telephones, and eventually, schools, began to emerge. Neighbors cut trails, widened paths, and scraped grass and brush to build roads that could accommodate a wagon. Horses are fairly nimble and can climb steep slopes, wade through or even swim across rivers, and they don't mind rocks, brush, thick grass, and other conditions that would stymie movement of a wagon. But horses can pull far more weight than they can carry. A typical horse can carry a third of its weight or 250-300 pounds on its back but can pull double that in a wagon. The sawmills on Bears Ears and Pilot Knob also needed roads to haul lumber to market in Hayden. Paradoxically, the best time to haul was in the winter when a horse could pull a sled. If the path or road is wide and level, and if the snow is packed or, even better, coated with hard, smooth ice, a horse can pull 1,000 pounds. The sawmills and small coal mines moved the lumber and coal down to the valley in the winter to take advantage of the slickness of packed snow and ice.

In Elkhead, transportation by any means was a challenge. Even today, the ground there is soft, and any moisture, be it from rain, melting snow, or a creek overflowing, could turn a path into a mire of mud. People call the expansive clay soil "adobe" because when it gets wet it becomes slippery and sticky. The wet clay forms clods that stick to the bottom of shoes, hooves or wheels. Each step or turn adds a new layer of clay until the whole chunk flips off and a new clod begins to form. Even dogs and cats have trouble with the mud; it gets between the pads of their feet and splays their toes until they have to stop and pick the mud out with their teeth. When the clods dry they are harder than the soil, more like rocks than dirt.

For the homesteaders, mud season was inevitable and dreaded. There was no way to create a path or build a road that would always be dry and never muddy, although paths and roads could be sited and maintained so that the times were shortened. To do this, Elkheaders would need to build roads along hillsides so that the natural drainage would take the water away or add "cut outs"—small ditches that serve as drains. In a place with so little annual moisture, it is incredible how much time, energy and ingenuity was needed to drain water away. Being stuck, as in stuck in the mud, was one common form of helplessness. "Mud season" was a common term for spring.

Creeks, like Elkhead and Dry Fork, were impassable in the spring and early summer and could be difficult fords at other times of the year. The first mention of a road building effort in the local paper was in 1908; the first mention of a bridge was in 1910, when Elkheaders finally spanned Dry Fork. The "Elkhead Items" section of the *Routt County Republican* reported the news: "The bridge over Dry Fork of Elkhead is being put in. This will be a great convenience to the people of that section who have forded the stream for years."[201] If homesteaders were not doing all the work themselves on road and bridge building, they were expected to help the county crew.

Ferry Carpenter and Charles Fulton borrowed the horse-drawn scraper from the county, and with a team of horses (probably Fulton's) built and maintained roads in Elkhead.

Homesteaders went to Hayden for supplies, medicine, and occasionally for entertainment. They also went to town to get their mail. More than any other service or convenience, Elkheaders pined for mail delivery. Having a post office, or at least a regular carrier, not only put their place on the map, it meant regular contact with the outside world. Without the mail, people felt cut off from their family and friends, and unable to complete business transactions. How would they know if someone had died if no one could reach them by letter? How could they make arrangements for a visit if they could not send a letter?

Elkhead petitioned for a post office in early 1909 and the paper announced on September 3 that the petition had "been heard in Washington" and the "prayer granted." Two homesteaders, Cornelius White and John Kitchens, served as first postmasters. The following year, Senator Guggenheim sent word that both a post office and a star mail route would be established. Elkhead sent bids to Washington, but these were declined on a technicality.

Elkheaders set up a temporary post office at the Adair-Solandt Ranch and named John Adair the postmaster.

There was a telephone at the Adair-Solandt Ranch as early as 1908: that year, James Oldham advertised his timothy seed in the newspaper and gave the Adair mutual line as a number to reach him. The mutual or party line was connected to the main line near Hayden by a strand of wire stapled to the tops of fence posts. The line was so unreliable, however, that whenever there was a real emergency someone rode a horse to Hayden. If there was urgent news to send it was usually communicated by telegram from the Hayden railway station. After 1910, Elkheaders put in time during the warmer months to work on the phone line, making repairs and sometimes extending the line to a homestead cabin. Carpenter had a phone in his cabin that branched off a line going up Morgan Creek. As late as the 1970s, Elkhead was part of a mutual telephone company, maintained by residents who lived along the party line.

A few weeks after the Jones family moved to Elkhead (and before Herbie died), Carpenter started circulating a petition to form a school district among the neighbors. Carpenter was back in Colorado for the summer after his first year at law school. He spent the requisite time on his homestead but he was fascinated by the courtroom dramas going on at Hahn's Peak. That summer, he took a bedroll to the courthouse to follow the proceedings of a murder trial. While in Steamboat he met with Emma Hull Peck, a former county superintendent of schools, who explained how to establish a school district in Colorado. Peck told Carpenter that families could petition the state for recognition as a district if there were at least ten children of school age in the proposed new district and if there remained at least twenty school children in the district they would be departing from. Elkhead was considered part of the Hayden and Deep Creek districts, though neither had an interest in opening a school so far from town. The petition

Carpenter circulated proposed to cut off 222 square miles to form the new District 11.

Emma Peck was the first woman to hold elected office in Routt County. She married Henry Peck when she was nineteen and together they built a small ranch near Steamboat. While she was homeschooling their three boys on their ranch, her husband, who was interested in politics, ran for the post of county school superintendent. He held that office from 1894 until 1896 when he decided to run for county assessor. Emma Peck put her name in to take his place. She was elected by a wide margin and was re-elected for three more terms between 1912 and 1920. Well-liked and greatly respected, she was described as "an unusual combination of indomitable courage, irrepressible energy, self-sacrifice, bubbling enthusiasm and good humor."[202] Women could not vote in statewide elections until 1893 but they could vote for school elections as early as 1876.[203] Nevertheless, women like Peck were finding positions where they could use their education and civic drive. Peck traveled all over the new county, helping to establish districts and encouraging communities to build schools. By 1898, Routt County had forty-three new schools and Steamboat Springs had a high school. Emma Peck held the position until her husband became ill and the family moved to Missouri. While Peck was in Missouri, a succession of women—Laura Monson, Florence Lighthizer and Mamie Weyand—held the post.

George W. Smith, editor of the *Routt County Republican*, regularly wrote about local schools and he nearly always championed Carpenter's plans. Alongside celebrating the tonnage of oats shipped or the industriousness of homesteaders, he promoted schools as a way to attract families to settle in the region. In early August 1910, he wrote,

> Ferry Carpenter took Sunday dinner with Mr. and Mrs. J. Kitchens. Ferry is circulating a petition to form a new school

> district. Two families who have taken up homesteads in the proposed district have 28 children—11 in one family and 17 in the other. Fact. At this rate Routt County will soon lead the state in school census. Come on school marms. Some nice looking ranchmen up here. Now is your chance.[204]

That fall, Smith entered the race for county school superintendent and won, ensuring that the nascent district would have a strong advocate at the county level. But the petition that Carpenter started was not immediately successful. Single men with a small cabin and a few cattle did not want to pay taxes to support a school. Among the few families with children, some did not intend to send their children to school. They needed the children to work on the homestead. Most crucially, few homesteaders had cash to support a district. Districts levied their own taxes and paid for their own teachers and supplies; they had to build their own buildings without any help from the county or the state. Carpenter, the enthusiast and persuader, ran out of time.

Before he left at the end of that summer, Carpenter held his big birthday party and dance at his homestead cabin. As usual, he invited everyone in Elkhead, Hayden and the Yampa Valley—family, friends, acquaintances and people he thought he would like to know. His older sister, Ruth, came from Evanston. Ruth was known as the dynamo of the family, the only person who could (and did) boss Carpenter around. She had sandy, red hair and bright blue eyes like her brother. She was small, but wiry and physically strong. She liked outdoor work and when she visited she helped Carpenter and White, branding their calves, fixing fences and herding the cattle on horseback. Many people found Ruth abrasive and abrupt. She seemed to have jumped the women's suffrage movement and emerged a young woman who assumed she was equal to any man. She excelled in school and passed through her four years at Wellesley without an academic scratch and emerged with a tight cadre of female friends. Like Carpenter, she had enough money from her father to live independently. And like her brother, she was fervent about addressing civic problems and correcting social ills. Together they were a formidable pair, bantering and sparring, while at the same time encouraging each other to lead and serve.

Around a hundred other guests came to the party. Carpenter tried again to persuade residents to sign the petition, but when he left for school a few days later, catching the Denver-bound train in Steamboat, the petition was still short of signatures.

After he left, Carpenter's effort appeared to languish, but in the late fall and winter, a few influential homesteaders, George and Mary Murphy, Paroda Fulton, Ed Smith (the owner of the sawmill), whose daughter Julia was boarding in Hayden for high school, and William Kleckner, whose young son, Galen, was spending the winters in Hayden to attend primary school, joined the campaign to form a district. George Smith took office as the county superintendent in January 1911 and in February he announced his receipt of the Elkhead petition; it named 44 children of school age. The next week Smith called a meeting of all those interested in having a school to "come and help decide this matter." On March 10, he complained that "people seem to have decided opinions on both sides, and the superintendent is 'up against it' in a sense."[205]

At some point, probably while he was away at school, Carpenter used his knowledge of land and mineral ownership in the area to figure out how the district could support itself without putting a financial burden on homesteaders. He suggested drawing the district lines so that they included valuable anthracite coal seams around Pilot Knob, on the eastern side of Elkhead. Because this area was so mountainous and remote, few people considered it part of Elkhead; there were only one or two bachelor homesteaders living there.

The idea of taxing the commercial coal owners, particularly the investors who were holding on to valuable mineral rights, waiting for the right moment to sell for a profit or to open the mines, had not occurred to nearby school districts. There had been speculation about the value of underground coal deposits but no one in the area had thought of including them in a school district to increase the valuation. At the time there were no operating mines in the Elkhead area and there was confusion about who owned the minerals. In most cases, minerals were unsevered from the surface, meaning that if a homesteader claimed 160 acres, his or her patent included all the minerals below the surface. However, with speculation of coal lands growing, by 1910, the U.S. government stepped in and tried to reclaim mineral rights under some Elkhead homesteaders. Jack Jykadorke homesteaded along a small creek in California Park. Jykadorke, like his neighbors Ed Knowles and Pete Eckman, appears to have always been a bachelor. When he came to town, the newspaper quipped that he had come to taste a bit of civilization before disappearing again. While providing up on his homestead, Jykadorke worked on temporary jobs in coal mines, in the sawmills, or, in the summer, putting up hay on the larger ranches in the valley.[206]

In October 1909, Jykadorke encountered a Department of Interior official on his property in California Park who told him that in order to receive the patent to the surface he would need to relinquish his claim to the coal underneath. Apparently Jykadorke had never completed the paperwork for his claim and although he had been there for six years, his land and mineral ownership were in dispute. There were several similar adjustments, or last minute requisitions, of minerals around Elkhead. In 1910, George Murphy successfully held on to his mineral rights below his homestead on Dry Fork. The newspaper commented, "All the Dry Fork region extend congratulations to Geo. Murphy on the successful outcome of his contest with the government over his coal rights. The outcome means a lot to those in this neighborhood who have been in doubt as to whether they were to receive fair play at the hands of the Interior department or not."[207] But on Cottonwood Creek, closer to California Park where Bob Harmon started a "punch mine"—a hole dug into the side of a hill or mountain to remove coal usually with a pick and shovel—the national government took back both the land and the minerals.

Before lands were opened for homesteading, the state of Colorado and the federal government were legally entitled to choose lands they wished to keep; if there were valuable minerals to be found, they had to option to reserve mineral ownership. The state of Colorado automatically got one square mile of surface and minerals in every township—typically, Section 36—but early surveys were incomplete, lines were often redrawn, and minerals were difficult to locate.[208]

Anthracite coal was discovered in deep seams along the eastern edge of Elkhead beginning in the early 1900s. Large mine owners in Denver, and investors from other parts of the country, bought homesteads and grabbed land and mineral rights. Henry B. Babson, an inventor and investor who became wealthy through his involvement with the Victor Talking Record Player, knew Carpenter and his family in Chicago. He invested in land and minerals on Pilot Knob, an area rich in anthracite coal.

When Hayden and Wolf Creek residents realized that the new Elkhead district would be taking away valuable assets from their school districts, they tried to convince Smith to block it from forming. Smith, however, did not have much choice. The very minimal requirements in Colorado law had been met. In mid-March he called for a vote among Elkhead residents.

> The people of Elkhead will vote on the formation of a school district April 15. They will first try to decide the location of the schoolhouse or houses, and then vote on the formation

of the district. If formed, this district will have a valuation of $175,000. This will be taken from districts two and three. District three has drawn taxes from three townships of coal land lying north of Morgan Bottom district for years, and the new district includes this. The proposed new district has 44 school children.[209]

The home of George and Mary Murphy on Dry Fork circa 1910.

Mary Murphy hosted the April 15 gathering. She and her husband had a small but comfortable log cabin on Dry Fork a few miles from Carpenter's homestead. Mary Murphy likely roasted some poultry—she was known for her flocks of chickens and turkeys—and unearthed stored carrots and potatoes she had raised in her garden. Smith opined in the paper that "those who were in time to partake of the bountiful dinner provided by Mrs. Murphy speak in the highest terms of her culinary ability."[210] The Murphy homestead, though not centrally located, was famous for its hospitality; moreover, as the Murphys did not themselves have children, they were supporters who lacked a strong opinion as to where the schoolhouse should be located. In a 222-square-mile district, the question of location was not easily resolved. The school's placement would inevitably advantage some families over others. And as the school would be Elkhead's first public structure, the community might be inclined to develop a physical center around the building. No one had plans to develop a town and sell lots, but everyone knew that the school would increase nearby property values and encourage speculation.

Apprehension about the first school probably influenced the order of Smith's agenda; he wanted to make sure that the community could come to an agreement about the location before they voted on forming a district. Elkheaders had joined together at Herbie Jones's funeral, attended a few dances, and there were growing ties between families through friendship, marriage and shared work, but the community had never tried to come to an agreement before, much less decide to tax themselves and spend money on a school.

Twenty-five people came to the first meeting and voted for Almon Galloway, another married but childless homesteader, to chair the meeting. L.C. (Shorty) Huguenin, father of two school-aged children, was named secretary. The group then named a committee of five to recommend a location for the schoolhouse. While the committee deliberated, the other twenty attendees took an "intermission" and waited.

The committee of five swiftly and neatly avoided controversy by recommending two schoolhouses, one on Calf Creek near the Adair-Solandt Ranch and another west of Jim Barnes's place on upper Dry Fork. Their recommendation was immediately agreed to without dissent. The group voted sixteen to three to form the district. School officers elected were: William Kleckner, president, Paroda Fulton, secretary, and Arthur Fredrickson, treasurer. As legal residents of District 11, the voters decided to have regular school board meetings at the Adair-Solandt Ranch and to elect their board of directors at their next meeting.

On that chilly April day in 1910, Elkhead became a discrete entity, its own political unit. It was no longer merely a place somewhere north of Hayden. Just eight months after the death of Herbie Jones, the first step was taken toward building what Murphy, Carpenter and others knew the community needed: schools, and a public place to come together.

CHAPTER NINE

Wading Around in the Knee-High Vegetation

(1911–1913)

July 7, 1911

Elkhead Celebrates

Sixty-four people gathered in the grove below Frink's place to celebrate the fourth. A big picnic lunch was spread under the trees and the many varieties of eatables were passed around. Only the bachelors, homesteaders, and cowpunchers were allowed to eat thru two tables. After lunch a number of games were pulled off. Frank Jones won the lemon race (potatoes were too scarce). Everett Adair took the free for all foot race. Rose Barnes was voted favorite in the ladies' relay; then followed a tug of war and jumping contest in both of which Frank Corbin was star performer. Shorty Huguenin was judge. Geo. Hughes and Bill Montieth's fiddle music proved too much for those with dancing blood in them to resist, so several quadrilles were called off with four couples to a set and quite a lot of grass was tramped down. Thunder clouds and home chores caused the crowd to break up, altho a few went to the Hughes' ranch and danced until morning.

September 27, 1912

Elkhead School Closes

Friday evening the log schoolhouse on the Adair-Solandt ranch was crowded to its full capacity. It was the last day of a successful five month's school by Miss Heermans. The entertainment began with a play by the pupils entitled "Idle Irene." The little folks entered into the spirit of the play with great zest. Sam Lighthizer, soon after the play was calling off the quadrille, while Bobbie Bowers, Art Horton, Eph and Bill Rider took turns at the fiddle. After the famous baby boys of this community were stowed away, the box suppers were auctioned off and the bachelor homesteaders had the feast of their lives. It was a gray dawn before the merry party broke up.

"East Elkhead," *Routt County Republican.*

Leila Ferguson was eight years old in 1911 when her family boarded a train in Kansas, seeking a new life in Colorado. The train stopped in Steamboat Springs and she and her mother and younger brother, Richard, waited there while their father explored Routt and the newly formed Moffat County, looking for land. The Fergusons were among the very first young families to move to Elkhead and they arrived just as the fledgling community began to build its first one-room log school. The Ferguson family would live in Elkhead for the next thirty-five years, outlasting nearly all their neighbors. Leila and Richard would graduate from Elkhead schools and become adults in the community.

The Ferguson family arrived from the small town of Medicine Lodge in south central Kansas. Leila's father, Alexander, worked as a farmer while her mother, Jesse, tended the children. Jesse's son from an earlier marriage, James Hood, was a teenager. He helped support the family as a laborer. Alexander Ferguson grew up in Iowa, the son of a carpenter; his father had migrated to Iowa from

Pennsylvania. Jesse Winters, Leila's mother, was the daughter of a German immigrant who farmed in central Illinois.

In the early spring of 1911, the Fergusons sold what furnishings they had in Kansas and boarded the train for Colorado. They shipped a sewing machine, a plow, and a few white Holland turkeys and Black Lang Shang chickens, good breeds that Alex and Jesse Ferguson hoped to establish in their new home. After lodging his family in Steamboat Springs, Ferguson spent nearly two months searching for land to homestead. He finally decided on 160 acres in Elkhead. When Leila described his vision and the journey many years later, she captured both his determination and his high hopes.

> My father bought a team and wagon and went around over the country looking for a homestead. We came from Kansas where trees were very scarce. He didn't realize what a chore it would be to clear land, so he was looking for land with timber on it. Elkhead has lots of quaking aspen, not so much valuable timber, but timber. The grass was lush and beautiful. Father thought he wanted to raise stock and when he waded around in that knee-high vegetation it appealed to him, so that was where he decided to locate a homestead. He came on up to Steamboat Springs where we were living in a little house waiting for him and he said he had found us a new home.[211]

Jesse Ferguson quickly assembled a few mismatched chairs and bought a dresser from a second-hand store in Steamboat. Leila said, "I was only eight years old and I cried. We hadn't had such looking chairs in Kansas and I thought it was terrible to have such chairs."[212] Mr. Ferguson bought a big tent, took the tent in the wagon out to the homestead and set it up with some of the furniture and the chickens and turkeys.

> It was a two-day trip from Steamboat to the homestead at the pace we traveled. We camped out overnight. I never will forget the food mother cooked over the campfire; she fried some bacon and some canned hominy, fried it and seasoned it. To me it was the best tasting stuff I nearly ever ate. We got to our homestead and all we had was a tent; no corrals, no barns, no anything.[213]

The Ferguson homestead was located in Section 18, on the south-face of a long slope that ends in Dry Fork. The unnamed hill was covered with aspen, oak brush and sagebrush with small patches of grass in the open areas. There was very little level ground for fields, much less a garden, and the only source of water, a small spring, was far below the house site. The nearest neighbors were James Oldham and the Fultons, who lived along Dry Fork. Herbert Jones and his large family had filed on a homestead about two miles to the northwest the year before. Charles Pizor, a bachelor, had homesteaded a half mile to the east and Ferry Carpenter and Jack White were several miles away to the south.

While the Fergusons were cutting logs to build a cabin in a rush to move out of the tent before the snows began, the fledgling Elkhead school board levied and collected a tax on all land and mineral owners and contracted with a local carpenter to build the first school. Henry Babson, the wealthy Chicago investor who owned most of the mining interests, paid his new tax bill without protest. The district hired Clayborn Hayes, a homesteader, to build a log schoolhouse on Calf Creek, near the Adair-Solandt Ranch.

In mid-July, the building was finished. The school directors, George Murphy and Jack White, found that it passed inspection. Neighbors hauled the furniture—a blackboard, desks and a potbellied stove—from Steamboat and installed them in the classroom.

School began on August 28, 1911, with Miss Williams as the first teacher. Eighteen children enrolled. Jack White took the school census and reported present Myrtle, Marvin, Frank, Nettie and Pearl Rose Barnes; Leila Ferguson; Eleanor, Adelbert and Louis Haller; Galen Kleckner; Florence, Helen, Yoleta and Tommy Jones; Roy Johnson; Charles Riley; and John Workman.

The oldest was Myrtle Barnes, age seventeen, and the youngest were Marvin Barnes and Tommy Jones, both six. Miss Williams was "one of Routt's most efficient teachers" according to the newspaper.[214] The school was well attended.

School children in front of the Adair/Red Top/McKinlay Ranch school. Circa 1913-1914. Rear from left to right: Leila Ferguson, Helen Jones, Lewis Harrison. Other children not identified.

Elkhead began to compete with other small rural schools in the county over who could hire the most qualified and experienced teachers. A typical teacher at that time had a high school diploma but little if any training in pedagogy. Eligible young men and women could teach with a provisional certificate for a year until they were able to sit for the teacher's exam. The exam was administered by the local county superintendent but written and graded by the State

Teachers College in Greeley. It was long and difficult. The August 1910 test began with ten questions on arithmetic, including:

> 6. As agent, I buy the S. ½ of the S.W. ¼ of a section of land at \$12.50 per acre; I have it fenced for \$.0.35 per rod. What is my commission upon the transaction at 5%?
>
> 7. A, B and C rent a pasture for six months for \$100; A puts in twenty-five head of cattle for the whole time; B, thirty head for 4½ months; C, forty-five head for 3 1/3 months. Find the rent to be paid by each.[215]

The morning portion of the exam included essay questions on the theory and practice of education. In one example, the test-taker was asked to describe five ways she had been helped by her reading of John Dinsmore's "Teaching a District School." In the afternoon, there were essay questions on geography, Colorado school law and civil government. On the second day of the exam, the aspiring teachers sat down for essay writing on reading, with a heavy emphasis on John Ruskin (an influential English thinker), natural science and U.S. history. Most of the questions were national or international in scope, but there were a few that were specific to Colorado and the practice of agriculture in the state. Aspiring teachers were expected to know why it took longer to boil water on Pikes Peak than in New York, and what Congress had done over the last twenty-five years about irrigation. There were several questions related to the formation of national parks and forest reserves. The final afternoon was for essays on physiology and grammar.

Leila Ferguson loved school but she soon found that she was unable to walk the distance between home and school every day. She did not know how to ski, and her family did not have a horse. As soon as the snow began to accumulate, the three- or four-mile trudge was too much. The other seventeen students were able to get to school and finish the term. School closed in mid-December 1911 with a short ceremony and program. Miss Williams vanished; it is likely she was hired away by another district.

The Elkhead school board was determined to offer at least nine months of school, but when the fall term ended at the Adair School on Calf Creek, the promised Dry Fork School had not yet been built.[216] Jack White advertised in the newspaper for bids to build the second school "on or near the Frank Corbin place." Frank Corbin had a small log cabin on upper Dry Fork, upstream from Oldham and the Fultons and near the Jim Barnes homestead. When winter storms began, before construction could start, the district used the Barnes home for the school term that began at the end of January 1912. Harold Felton, an itinerant schoolteacher from Syracuse, New York, had just passed the teachers exam. Little record remains of his time at the school. After he completed his contract he moved on to other districts in the county and the Barnes home was never used again as a schoolhouse.

Leila was unable to attend school due to the distance and the heavy snows. She and her brother were stuck in their rudimentary cabin, playing board games. "We couldn't coast because the snow was so deep; we didn't have trails to coast. We had no skis. When it would be nice and Dad had a trail beaten, we'd go out and play awhile. We didn't have clothes to play in the snow very much."[217] Leila's mother, Jesse, tried to teach her math but gave up in frustration. Jack White brought her some magazines, *Cosmopolitan* and *Harper's*, and she read every word of every article and advertisement. She longed for books and dreamed of a library.

The winter was unusually long and harsh. Throughout January and February there were two and a half feet of snow on the ground. The only way to move around was on snowshoes. When Elkheaders managed to get to Hayden their visit was noted in the paper. The Elkhead mail route, established with so much effort the year before, struggled to maintain service. Romaine W. Haller, father of Eleanor,

Adelbert and Louis, a homesteader from Michigan, had the contract to carry the mail to and from Elkhead every Saturday. It was known as the Seventh-Day Adventist route. In mid-January 1912, Haller started out from his homestead on Upper Elkhead Creek with a two-horse sled, but the horses floundered in the deep snow after a few miles. He borrowed snowshoes from a neighbor and made his way the remaining ten or so miles to town. On his way back, on snowshoes and with the sack of mail on his back, he was overtaken by dark, wind and cold. He crawled under a small bridge and somehow stayed alive until daybreak. He then snowshoed another five miles to Ferry Carpenter's reservoir. George Murphy found him there; he had become snow-blind. Despite his ordeal, Haller held on to the mail route and the tiny income it provided. His injured eyes recovered.

When Haller's wife, Angelina, had severe difficulties in labor in late February 1912, Dr. Solandt was called from town. Like Haller, he began the journey with a team of horses but had to switch to snowshoes after he came over the divide into Elkhead. He was able to reach the cabin in time and delivered a baby girl, Dorothy, later that night.

The winter stretched on, putting a strain on everyone's efforts to stay warm and fed. Leila's family ran short of food. When her father, Alex Ferguson, was finally able to go to town he was denied credit at the grocery store. Hugus and Co. owned a chain of stores in Colorado and Wyoming and they held interest in cattle, and later, in sheep. They also owned an interest in the local bank. Leila's father felt the grocery store was trying to run them off the land because "nesters," or homesteaders, were fencing off the otherwise open range.

The Fergusons survived mainly through the generosity of their neighbor Myrtle Davis. James and Myrtle Davis came to Elkhead from West Virginia after spending a few years in eastern Colorado where James worked as general farmer. The couple, with their three young boys, Walter, Edward, and Archie arrived in Routt County and stayed briefly on a ranch in the Yampa Valley before they found land to homestead far up Cottonwood Creek, a tiny tributary of Dry Fork, on the side of Pilot Knob. Myrtle Davis had married when she was fifteen or sixteen and had never learned to read or write. Leila Ferguson, at age nine, became her amanuensis, writing letters home to her family in West Virginia and reading their replies. Myrtle spent most of her time alone with her children on the homestead as James left the family for weeks at a time to work on ranches in the valley and in the coal mines. Myrtle was apparently a crack shot. Although there was no season on deer and shooting them was considered illegal, she would regularly hunt and butcher the animals for her neighbors. During the winter months she would walk the nearly four miles as the crow flies to the Ferguson homestead and tell Leila and Leila's brother, Richard, that there was "a pretty waiting for them down at the spring." Leila and Richard "would just tear out of the house. She'd have a lot of nice venison for us, the very best cuts of venison, all wrapped up in a flour sack. She never gave it to us, it was always just down at the spring."[218]

The Ferguson's closest neighbors were Steve and Gratis Cook. The Cooks came to Elkhead in early 1910, from Arkansas. They were a large family that included Steve's mother, Nancy, his half-brother and his wife as well as their three young children. Steve's son, Henry, eighteen, from an earlier marriage in Missouri, and Steve and Gratis's two youngest children, Ray (nine) and Samuel (three), who had both been born in Arkansas, filled out the household.[219] Like many men struggling to support a large family, Mr. Cook left home for weeks at a time to work at the sawmill, cutting timber. Gratis Cook depended on her neighbors for help. The Fergusons were the nearest neighbors, but Alex Ferguson took an intense dislike to the Cooks. "My father turned up his nose very much at the Arkansawyers," Leila Ferguson said, "this family especially.

He'd get so vexed at Mother for going to visit. Mother would tell him 'I've got to talk to somebody; I can't just sit out here and never see anyone . . . even if it's a Cook.' Well, he said 'I could live here all my life without talking to the Cooks.'"[220]

Jesse Ferguson, despite her husband's misgivings, visited often. She taught Gratia Cook how to bake bread. "The woman learned; she made beautiful looking bread. Whenever her loaves came out of the oven, they were great big nice-looking loaves, she would put them in the middle of her bed to cool." Jesse Ferguson also gave her seeds and showed her how to plant and tend a garden.[221]

The Cooks did not have a team or wagon and depended on others to buy staples in Hayden. Leila Ferguson recounted:

> One time she sent money to town with my Father; she had a little money to buy groceries . . . She chewed tobacco. She didn't smoke, she chewed . . . My father never chewed or smoked. She wanted two dollars' worth of chewing tobacco. She wanted a five-pound pail of lard, flour and a little stuff like that but anyway he thought a too large percent of her money was to go for tobacco which should be spent for groceries. So, he politely forgot to buy the tobacco. He brought back the groceries and she looked and asked why not. "Well, you know I just forgot to get it." She was the angriest woman you ever saw. She went around telling the neighbors. She said she'd never send Mr. Ferguson to town again for any groceries. She had to do without groceries for weeks till she could find somebody going to town.[222]

The partnership between Ferry Carpenter and Jack White continued to thrive, with White managing the cattle and land while Carpenter completed his law degree. White, who was known as the more easy-going of the two, and who apparently had no interest in going to college, met a woman homesteader at a dance in Steamboat. Like Carpenter and White, she came from Chicago. Anne Ehrat was the daughter of Swiss immigrants who came to the United States in the early 1890s. Her father worked as an accountant and later became a wealthy cheese merchant with a fine home in Rogers Park, a suburb of Chicago. At the age of twenty-one Ehrat headed for Colorado alone, intending to homestead. Her arrival in Steamboat was noted in the local paper in October 1910. She stayed for a few weeks at the Cabin Hotel and then staked a claim on Cow Creek, north and west of Steamboat. Her combination of glamour and grit drew a lot of attention. She was "unconventional." In January she played 60 rounds of "500" with three male friends in a hotel parlor. Her friend from Evanston, Beverly Lukens, joined her in Routt County sometime after; together they were referred to as the "charming homesteaders of Cow Creek."[223]

Ehrat typically took the train back to Chicago around Christmas and would spend the winter months in her family's home. She returned to her homestead in late spring. She proved up and gained full ownership of her land in the fall of 1912. Around that time, Jack White met her at a dance in Steamboat. Ehrat came dressed in her riding outfit, defying the dress code by wearing pants. The couple were soon engaged but they kept their romance a secret, at least from White's Elkhead neighbors and Carpenter. Ehrat took a disliking to Carpenter, perhaps because she felt that Carpenter was taking advantage of White and tended to treat him like a younger, less competent brother. In August 1913, when the couple announced their plan for a wedding in Chicago with just a few weeks' notice, Carpenter was surprised but quickly arranged to take the train to Chicago to be his friend's best man. The Carpenter-White partnership, however, soon began to dissolve. Ann White insisted that Jack White sell his Elkhead lands. She sold her homestead on Cow Creek and together they bought a ranch along the Yampa, east of Hayden. White and Carpenter, friends since boyhood, saw each other less frequently. White gradually withdrew from the Elkhead community.

Spring came late to northwest Colorado in 1912. The two-and-a-half feet of snow on the ground in January was slow to melt. Families ran out of food. Some, like the Fergusons, found help from their neighbors; others were not so fortunate. In April, Lilly Maynard died in her homestead cabin, leaving her husband Ernest and their baby, Charles. Lilly was only twenty-one; she was still nursing her one-year-old baby. She and her husband had arrived in Elkhead from Indiana and Arkansas two years earlier. Leila, who was nine at the time, said that it was "nothing but malnutrition that killed her."[224] A short note in the paper attributed her death to jaundice and noted that the funeral would occur at the Maynard home. For the first time, the anonymous writer offered condolences in a message from the community as a whole: "The community extends sympathy to the bereaved husband in this hour of sorrow."[225]

A few weeks later, in early May, Clayborn Hayes, the builder of the first schoolhouse, was struck by lightning and killed. He had been working on his land and apparently took cover under a tree during a storm. The charge hit the tree and split, killing him instantly. Hayes was from Cameron, Missouri. His parents brought him and his brothers and sisters to Colorado to hunt for gold in the 1880s. He married Margaret (Maggie) Williams, who had emigrated from Ireland in 1870, and who had five children from an earlier marriage. They moved to another gold mining area in Garfield County, Colorado, and had a son, William. In 1904, the family, including two of Maggie's children from her first marriage, homesteaded in Elkhead. Clayborn's body was found by a man measuring stream flow on the upper Elkhead river hours after the storm passed. Again, the paper sent condolences from the entire community.[226]

A third tragic death, another relatively young adult, struck the fledgling community that year. Josiah Riley was unusually ill-prepared and unsuited to homesteading. He arrived in 1910 with his wife and eight-year-old son, from New Jersey, where he had been working as a mechanic in a garage in Millville. Although he was only thirty, he suffered from pneumonia and rheumatism and came to Colorado hoping to improve his health. He homesteaded near Charles and Paroda Fulton on upper Dry Fork. His son, Charles, enrolled in the new school. When Riley emerged from the long winter, he was too sick to work. His neighbor, Romaine Haller, brought him, his wife Adelaide, and son to Hayden to stay with a family in town, but with no hospital and little medical care available he died a week later.

Although these deaths shook the community, several births and a marriage also gave people hope. Everyone wanted to look forward and to revel in accomplishment. As the newspaper put it, you could choose between being a "booster" or a "knocker."[227] If adults were dying, it was because they had brought their health problems with them or their death was an accident that could not have been prevented. At the time, the paper made no mention of malnutrition or suffering. Living so far from medical care was a given, just one of the common hardships that everyone endured, like heavy snowfall or high winds that knocked down the grain crop. When Clayborn Hayes was found dead under the tree, hours passed before a working phone was found and the coroner dispatched. People did not expect to be rescued. In many ways, they had come to Elkhead to prove that they could make it on their own, that they were tough enough. Some, like Josiah Riley, came to regain their health in a new climate, on their own ground. No one was inclined to complain; no one was about to discourage new people from trying to make a life in Elkhead. There was also a sense of accomplishment and relief among the survivors of the winter of 1912. If they could make it through that much snow, anything was possible.

The widows, Ernest Maynard, Maggie Hayes and Adelaide Riley, did not immediately leave Elkhead. They kept their children in school and worked to prove up on their land alone. Maggie Hayes's daughter from her first marriage, Kitty Williams, filed on her own homestead, one of the first women in Elkhead to exercise that right. Ed Smith's daughter, Julia, graduated from high school in Hayden the same year and returned to Elkhead to claim her own land adjacent to her parents'. While perhaps these women were not as bold as Ann Ehrat, they were independent in a way unknown to their mothers and aunts. The rules and conventions governing what women were capable of were changing in the West, and particularly in places like northwest Colorado. A combination of necessity and determination meant that these women's circumstances would change years before those of their peers.

At the end of May, Albert and Edith Smith welcomed a son, Harold Smith, at their homestead on lower Dry Fork. The Smiths had come from Des Moines, Iowa, two years earlier with their two young sons, Joseph, age three, and Albert, age one. They loaded their seven cows, two horses, two dogs, some farm machinery and a few pieces of furniture, including a reed organ, into a boxcar and traveled on the Moffat railroad to the end of the line in Steamboat. Like the Fergusons, the Albert Smiths hired a wagon and continued on to Elkhead. Both of Albert's parents were German, but he had been born in Iowa. Edith's parents came from Virginia and New York, but she also grew up in Iowa. The family's first home was on the Harrison homestead on Calf Creek. There they lived in an eight-by-twelve-foot "soddy," which usually meant a cabin with three log walls dug into a hill so that the dirt roof became a continuation of the hillside. Ferry Carpenter was apparently concerned about the family's well-being and later that summer arranged for them to move into one of several outbuildings for laborers on the Adair-Solandt Ranch. From there, the family moved to the Frink homestead on Dry Fork, where Harold was born.[228]

In July 1912, Erasmus and Hannah Smith's son, Ira, married Bessie Jones, the second-oldest daughter in the Herbert Jones family, on Calf Creek. They had been neighbors since the Jones moved into Elkhead in 1909. Like several couples who would eventually marry, Ira and Bessie immediately filed on a homestead near Bessie's parents on Calf Creek.

Another sign of hope and renewal was a new surge of families arriving to homestead, or to take over relinquishments. In the spring of 1912, the Bisels arrived and soon became cherished friends of the Fergusons in the Bull Gulch/Little Arkansas neighborhood. Ben Bisel had been a coal miner in Marion County, Illinois, but when he was unable to work due to rheumatism, he and his wife, Nellie, and their three young daughters, Helen (ten), Hazel (nine) and Opal (six), moved to Elkhead. The family found Elkhead through their connection with the Maynards; Ben's brother Dan was married to Maude Maynard. Ben Bisel had grown strawberries in Illinois and declared northwest Colorado an ideal place for the fruit. He bought 167 acres for $1.25 per acre, a form of homesteading known as a relinquishment. With the help of neighbors, the family built a two-room log cabin. In Opal Bisel's words the family "set up housekeeping with 'Routt' county furniture."[229] Chairs and tables were made from crates. The three girls slept on a large storage box and their parents slept on a bed made from woven wire with folding legs that could be raised and attached to the wall when not in use. Ben Bisel built his wife a rocking chair using aspen branches. The family had a trap door in the floor below the kitchen table where they stored root vegetables in the dirt under the house; they hung their meat in a sack from a tree or buried it in a large crock in a cool corner of their garden.

Although the Bisels were remembered for their efforts to grow and market strawberries, they also gathered and sold chicken feed. The children accidently found a sandy outcrop with a seam of petrified oyster shells. Ben Bisel "pounded or ground up the shells, put it in bags mama made on her sewing machine, labeled them and took it to Hayden and sold his chicken grit."[230]

L to R: Jesse, Leila and Richard Ferguson; Opal, Helen and Nellie Bisel. (Helen Bisel sitting to the left of her mother, Nellie.) Opal Bisel identified the "four Cook boys" as being in the photo (top right). Mrs. James Stephen Cook was known as Gratis in Elkhead but is listed in U.S. Census as Jennie. In order of oldest to youngest her four sons were: Henry, Samuel, Roy and Leonard.

The Freemans arrived later that summer and homesteaded on Wolf Mountain above Morgan Creek, near Jack White's ranch. The Freemans, like the Fergusons, were from Medicine Bow, Kansas.[231] James Freeman was a plumber and a tinner who arrived in Routt County alone at age twenty-six, seeking a homestead. A few months later, in late 1912 or early 1913, he sent for his wife, Ethel, her mother, and the couple's three children: Louise (four), James (three) and Carl (one). They built a simple log cabin on their land

and James quickly sought work wherever he could find it—haying, cutting logs at the sawmill, or tending livestock for his neighbors. Over the next five years, the Freemans had four more children including twins, Louis and Lester, born in Elkhead.

Frank and Fannie Hayes, also from Medicine Lodge, Kansas, arrived on Thanksgiving Day, 1913. The large family initially moved into Isadore Bolten's cabin and claimed land to the north along the upper reaches of Calf Creek. Frank and Fannie Hayes's family (of no relation to the Clayborn Hayes family) included seven children: Percy, Guy, Ina, Ray, Roy, Ruby and Morgan. Percy was sixteen and Morgan was only a year old. A few years later, Robert was born on the homestead. Frank was a skilled carpenter and found work making cabinets, windows and doors for his neighbors and for the school district while he farmed his hillside claim. Fannie had taught school for a few years in Kansas and was soon recognized for her intellectual interests and book reading.

Ferry Carpenter completed his last semester at Harvard Law School in the spring of 1912 and passed his bar exam that summer. He was full of plans both for his new law practice and for the Elkhead community. The railway, which had reached Steamboat in 1909, was finally approaching Hayden. Optimists like Carpenter projected a boom approaching, if it was not already underway.

The children on the Calf Creek side of the district had not had school since January, so the district school board hired a teacher and school restarted in May 1912 for a five-month term. Elkhead was in the difficult position of trying to provide schooling to children who lived many miles apart without sufficient funds to operate two schools. Rotating between the two ends of the district was the only solution. During the summer of 1912, work began in earnest on the Dry Fork School.

When the second one-room schoolhouse was finally completed on upper Dry Fork in September 1912 there was another all-night celebration. Fred Schaefermeyer, an Elkhead bachelor with a talent for notching logs for cabins and barns, and Jim Barnes, a homesteader with a large family on Dry Fork, supplied the music with their mouth organs (harmonicas). As usual, the dance lasted until after dawn.

School on Calf Creek ended a few days later. Miriam Heermans, the wealthy daughter of a mechanical engineer from Evanston, Illinois, celebrated the term as her predecessors had, with a community presentation and dance. The children put on a play called "Idle Irene," sang, and recited poems to a room full to capacity. The school board had realized that they could raise some money at these events and auctioned off box suppers. "The bachelor homesteaders had the feast of their lives," the Elkhead correspondent noted in the paper.[232] Four fiddle players, Art Horton, Bobbie Bowers, and Eph and Bill Rider, played for the all-night dance while Sam Lighthizer called. "It was a grey dawn before the merry party broke up."[233]

The Elkhead community finally had two schools and a regular schedule. The new district was bringing in enough money to build simple log or frame schoolhouses, provide furnishings and hire teachers. Families with children who were moving in would be assured that their offspring had access to education, and no one would need to move into Hayden to put their children in school.

The balance of residents had shifted in just a few years from mostly bachelors, to married couples, many with young children. In 1908, there were at least twelve bachelor homesteaders and only five families with school-aged children. Eight more households, including the Adairs, Galloways and Hortons, either had grown children or were childless. Four years later, in 1912, there were twenty-one families living in Elkhead with school-aged children. An additional ten households included a young married couple. A few were living and working on other's ranches, but almost all were homesteading and working to prove up on their land. Homesteaders had claimed nearly all of the acres of sage and grassland and had pushed into less accessible and wooded lands. The nascent community had a mail route, a rudimentary telephone line and a few rough-hewn roads that came to be called "two tracks."

Ferguson family in front of their homestead cabin in Little Arkansas, Elkhead, on Easter Sunday, circa 1915. L to R: James Hood (face hidden), Tommy Jones (a neighbor), Susie Jones Hood, Richard (Dick), Jesse, Alex and Leila Ferguson.

The summer of 1912, with the influx of families and good prices for grain and cattle, Elkhead had something of a building boom. George Hughes added rooms to his house. Cliff Fulton put up a frame house on Dry Fork; Alex Ferguson, Leila's father, went up into the forest to haul logs for a large cabin. The Ferguson family had spent the summer in a tent and the children played in the hills, gathering wildflowers and exploring. "We never thought to be afraid of anything; our folks never taught us to be scared of things," Leila said. "We just wandered all over the hills and played."[234] The family put in a large garden and expanded their flock of chickens. When a bird nested in a fold of the tent, Leila's father insisted that the tent stay open until the eggs hatched and the birds flew away. The family felt an enormous surge of joy and opportunity: for the first time they owned their land, the improvements they made were theirs, and they had good, caring neighbors. All that was needed to prosper was hard work.

CHAPTER TEN

The Breach: A Murder in Elkhead

(1914)

January 16, 1914

Jim Oldham advertised the sale of Charles Fulton's place and the sale was dated for last Saturday. As Oldham had to put up $200 to pay Fulton for his homestead exemption and did not have the money to put up. The belief is expressed that Oldham is at the end of his string so far as the collecting of an old judgment he has against Fulton.

February 20, 1914

A.D. Galloway has been putting up ice on his ranch the past week.

The Wayandt Wagners and Gelman families spent Sunday at the Galloway ranch.

Dr. Solandt and Leslie Kinsey visited the McKinley ranch one day last week.

Mrs. A.A. Frederickson visited the Galloway ranch one day last week.

We hear that E.D. Smith had a narrow escape from being buried under the snow at the mill the other day. He had dug thru the snow to a pile of lumber when the snow caved in but Ed got out of the way enough so the snow just caught his feet. He might have been suffocated or crushed had he been two feet further in.

February 27, 1914

Thomas Haxton and family expect to be down from Steamboat this week and will take up their residence on their claim in this neighborhood.

A.A. Fredrickson has bought some hay of Adair-Solandt and is hauling it from the Hayden valley.

Reece Horton and wife spent Sunday visiting the Galloway ranch.

Sam Lighthizer and family expect to move to the ranch next week.

Reece Horton bought a cow of A.A. Frederickson a few days ago.

July 19, 1914

George Murphy was down from his Elkhead ranch Saturday.

Ferry Carpenter and Jack White recently found one of the Adair-Solandt cattle on the range in dying condition from larkspur poisoning. They applied the new forest service remedy and the steer came through all right and is now fattening up for the fall market.

Ed Fulton is in Steamboat attending the Oldham trail. After this is over Ed will go to Ohio but expects to return soon.

A.D. Galloway expects his father in from Michigan on today's train.

R.E. Norvell, Sam Adair, Sam Lighthizer, Dr. Solandt and G.W. Smith summoned as witnesses on the Oldham case, were excused Wednesday evening and all but Norvell returned home that night. Tush Holderness going after them in his auto.

"East Elkhead," *Routt County Republican.*

Land was what people longed for, saved for, dreamed of and sometimes died for in this particular (and late) moment of homesteading. To own your own ground was to have a "stake," to possess a chance for a better future, a means to lift yourself and your offspring out of poverty, or at least to improve your condition. Land, that piece of the earth that could be tilled, or grazed, was where you could grow your fruits, grains and vegetables, and raise your own meat. Land held the promise of self-sufficiency. There were a few people who homesteaded as an investment, never intending to support themselves or feed themselves off the land, but most people in Elkhead thought of their land as their home, their livelihood and their source of well-being. Land became a part of one's identity, an expression of independence, a capacity to work and a sturdy personality. An artist might take pencil to paper, or paint to canvas, to make a drawing or painting their unique creation; these individuals took what they had, the land with its trees, brush, rocks, creeks, springs, and created by hand their own place, unique in the world. Nobody went to the store and bought a homestead; no one contracted out the essential work of building a home. And for most people, there was no turning back, no bank account to draw on if things didn't work out, no home to return to when the homestead failed. Their land was their start in life.

Naturally, the reality of what occurred there was far more complicated: self-sufficiency was an ideal, and eventually an illusion. The boundaries between pieces of land were ambiguous and individuals were not alone; they lived more and more in a community, whether they chose to conform to what they called society, or not.

When men like Oldham, the Fulton brothers, Adair and Carpenter arrived in Elkhead, it was possible to imagine a way to be independent and self-sufficient. Ironically, part of that plan entailed not confining themselves to the land they owned, but also allowing their livestock to roam onto adjacent, unclaimed property. Where water was scarce, they would freely make use of "extra" water flowing by. When most of the land was unsettled, those who were there first could use and profit from unassigned "common" or public land and water with impunity. As more people claimed land and built fences around their holdings, free use disappeared. Those who had been able to raise large herds of horses or cattle had to figure out how to manage with much less.

James Oldham, the solitary homesteader from Illinois who came to Elkhead by way of a failed attempt at silver mining, did not shift his vision or compromise his ideals. He was not a particularly flexible or adaptable person. He built a ranch on Dry Fork and he was there first, but after two or three years he had close neighbors, and in a few years more, he was surrounded by other men and women with similar grand ideas and high hopes. Without any land, livestock, or equipment actually being taken away, Oldham had lost, and he felt his losses deeply. The pitifully small amount of water that ran down Dry Fork in the wet season was no longer solely his. He had to share it with the Fultons, and farther up the creek, with the Barnes, and later, with Frank Corbin and the Robinsons. Downstream even more homesteaders were trying to figure out how to capture a bit of the water flowing down the creek so that they could irrigate their meadows. The Galloways, the Murphys, the Lighthizers, the Georges and the Erasmus Smiths all depended on Dry Fork water. The public domain that had surrounded his homestead in 1900 was now claimed and fenced. He could not let his horses and cattle roam and graze freely. Someone else owned the land, and needed that water and grass.

Another problem that Oldham faced in Elkhead was that he never found a partner. After the failed courtship of his neighbor from Missouri, Rose, he did not go to dances or appear interested in finding a spouse or a close friend. All around him, single men were marrying, and married couples, some with children, were moving in. Two adults working the land had a huge advantage over a single man. And women, at that time, the designated social creatures, were more likely to build connections between families, more likely to work for the good of the whole and ensure the survival, if not the well-being of their family and their neighbors.

As the land around Oldham became built up—fences, ditches and reservoirs, log cabins and barns and corrals—Oldham became more isolated. He turned against his neighbors. After he sued Charles Fulton over a "scrub" stallion and a dead calf in the ditch, he sued John Adair for assault. After Fulton lost his first insanity charge against Oldham, Oldham sued him for malicious prosecution. He showed more and more signs of being afraid of his neighbors. He told a few of the men he trusted, Ed Knowles and William Kleckner, that the Fultons were hiding in mounds of hay on a wagon as they went to feed their cattle. He was sure he could see the ends of rifles sticking out from inside the hay. Then he thought that his mail was being intercepted. He refused to allow the Elkhead mail carrier to bring his mail and stopped the casual practice of picking up Carpenter's mail, or having Carpenter pick up his mail. He got his own post office box in Deep Creek on the other side of Pilot Knob.

Oldham began to see patterns and plans in the actions of disinterested, uninvolved men. Dr. Solandt was an investor in the Adair-Solandt Ranch and rarely involved in the actual workings of the business. When Dr. Solandt started across Oldham's property on snowshoes one night, trying to reach a patient, Oldham intercepted him and told him he was not allowed on the property. Later, Oldham went to the drugstore in Hayden to get a prescription filled and was alarmed to see Dr. Solandt behind the counter; he later refused to buy the medicine. He confronted Solandt on the street in Hayden and accused him of being with the "gang."[235] Nothing Oldham did assuaged his fears or lifted his gloom. Neighbors described him as despondent. The newspaper editor, George Smith, said he was solemn and sorrowful.[236]

Oldham was particularly irritated by the Fulton brothers. On one side of his property he had Charles, who with his highly competent wife, Paroda, was thriving. Their family was growing with one new baby boy every couple of years. They were well-liked and trusted. Paroda was on the school board and she opened their home to everyone. On the other side of the property was Cliff Fulton, Charles's younger brother. He was an industrious, good-looking young man and had been considered a fine prospect for young ladies in the area. Anticipating his marriage to Mary McDowell, he had built a frame house. Much farther downstream on Dry Fork, Ed Fulton, a third brother, owned land near the Lighthizers though he did not live on his property full time.

In late 1913 or early 1914 George Murphy, also a neighbor on Dry Fork, told Charles Fulton that Oldham wanted Charles dead. Murphy also told Fulton that Oldham was carrying a gun and advised Fulton to carry one for protection. He loaned Fulton his pistol. Fulton probably had a rifle but evidently did not own a pistol. As the threats escalated, various people in the community sought help. A trader in town, Dave Sellers, knew Oldham and attempted to broker a deal where Oldham would drop his charges against Fulton, and Fulton would agree not to bother Oldham. Carpenter wrote to Oldham's brother Frank, who was living in Ouray, Colorado, and sought his help. He also sought the advice of an eminent psychologist in Denver, Dr. Edward Lazell, who advised relocating Oldham to another community. It was an audacious plan but the psychologist, citing research on paranoid disorders, convinced Carpenter that the only solution was for Oldham to start over in a new place with new neighbors. Several individuals together filed two more insanity charges against Oldham. Finally, in August 1913, Carpenter, representing the prosecution, negotiated a settlement after the first day of the third trial. Carpenter raised $1,000 from four individuals, a sum worth about $23,000 in today's currency, and offered it to Oldham if he would leave the county. The $1,000 was to help Oldham begin a new life somewhere else. Oldham agreed and signed a contract that was printed in the local papers. "It is hereby agreed by James W. Oldham, that he will, within twenty days, settle up his affairs in Routt county and depart therefrom."[237]

What would happen to Oldham's ranch, or to the $1,500 judgment against Charles Fulton for malicious prosecution, was unclear. In the winter of 1913, Oldham took the $1,000 in cash and left for Craig, the county seat of the neighboring county to the west. For a few weeks no one heard a word. Then, sometime in early 1914, Oldham reappeared on his Elkhead ranch. In February 1914, Oldham quietly transferred his property to his brother, Frank. At the same time, he offered his ranch for sale for $9,500, a sum that his neighbors considered extremely high. Oldham made it known that he wanted the community to raise the money to buy him out, and though no one told him "no," no one made an offer, either.

In May 1914, a school district election was called to elect new officers. Jack White had sold his land in Elkhead and could no longer serve on the school board. Paroda Fulton was expected to be elected in his place. The community gathered on a Monday afternoon for a routine meeting on the Galloway homestead on Dry Fork.

The Galloways had recently left their home and were in Adrian, Michigan, caring for Almon Galloway's dying father. Galloway left his small ranch in the care of Ferry Carpenter, who planned to graze his Herefords on the meadows along the creek. The Galloway place was centrally located and the cabin was available for the school election.

Monday, May 4, 1914, was a chilly, rainy day. The creeks were high, and several people had to ride around upstream to get to the Galloway place. The cabin was nestled close to a hillside, overlooking a hay meadow bordered by Dry Fork. There was a log cabin, a small barn, a chicken house and a small corral. The cabin was a simple one-room log building with a window on each wall and a door facing the creek, the barn and corrals. With the Galloways in Michigan, there was little furniture in the house; people stood or crouched along the walls. Ferry Carpenter came over from his homestead; Sam Lighthizer, George Murphy and Ed Smith came on horseback from below the Galloways' on Dry Fork. William Kleckner and his wife of eighteen years, Ida, came a long way from their ranch on upper Elkhead Creek. The Fredricksons and Hallers were also there from Elkhead Creek. Frank Corbin joined the group from his homestead near the Fultons on Dry Fork, as did Frank Hayes, Isadore Bolten, Jim Barnes and Alex Ferguson, Leila's father. As usual, the Fultons were all there—Charles, Paroda, as well as Charles's brother and neighbor on Dry Fork, Cliff. Oldham rode up and after tying his horse to a corral post, took a place sitting on the cabin floor with his back to the wall. He was wearing a vest under his jacket and had on his usual loose-fitting pants. He looked worn and grey, joyless and older than his forty-four years, but not much different than what his neighbors and acquaintances were accustomed to.[238]

The meeting was called to order by the president of the school board, William Kleckner.[239] E.D. Smith was nominated to succeed Kleckner as president and Paroda Fulton and Ferry Carpenter were nominated to fill White's position as secretary. Paroda Fulton narrowly beat Carpenter. George Murphy continued on as treasurer. The district was in good financial health and was now able to support two simultaneous six-month terms at the two one-room schools. The district renewed Mary McDowell's contract and hired a new second teacher, Mary Officer. Both were to start the next day.

McDowell was from a large farming family in the Missouri Ozarks. Her father died, leaving her mother with nine children to raise on a small farm in Burdine Township, Missouri. She left home to teach for a few years in Oklahoma and then decided to join a sister in Colorado. Her plan was to get her teaching degree at the Teachers Normal School in Greeley, but instead she took a job teaching in the one-room school on Dry Fork in the fall of 1913.

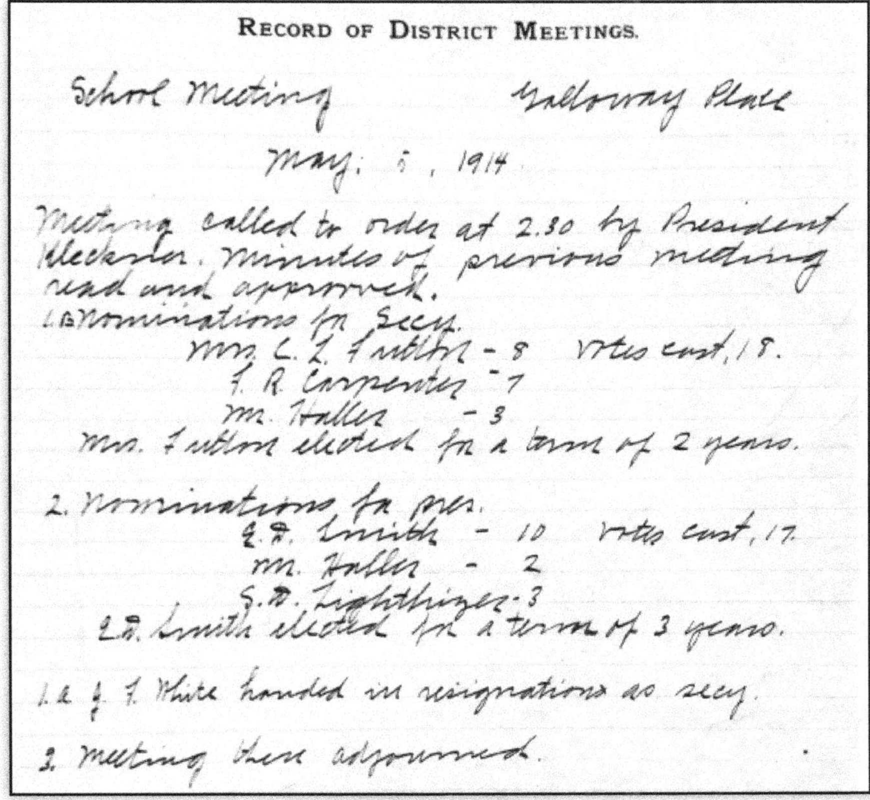
RECORD OF DISTRICT MEETINGS.

School Meeting Galloway Place

May 5, 1914

Meeting called to order at 2.30 by President Kleckner. Minutes of previous meeting read and approved.

1. Nominations for Secy.

Mrs. C. L. Sutton - 8 votes cast, 18.

F. R. Carpenter - 7

M. Haller - 3

Mrs. Sutton elected for a term of 2 years.

2. Nominations for pres.

E. D. Smith - 10 votes cast, 17.

M. Haller - 2

S. D. Lighthizer - 3

E. D. Smith elected for a term of 3 years.

1.a J. F. White handed in resignations as secy.

3. Meeting then adjourned.

Elkhead District 11, school board election minutes from May 5, 1914.

Her mother and two younger brothers soon sold the family farm in Missouri and relocated to a modest holding north of Steamboat in the small community of Sydney.

Mary McDowell was quickly recognized as a talented and dedicated teacher. She plowed ground around the schoolhouse for a school garden and began a practice of preparing lunch for the children. She turned the students' attention toward studying their own environment and chose tasks that would lead the children to contribute to the community. She later bought the Bisels' abandoned homestead and over the next several years a number of children boarded with her during the winter so that they could attend school regularly. Her students were her primary focus and she knew exactly where each of them stood on their studies. When Ed Smith despaired of his youngest daughter, Ione, ever learning math, McDowell arranged for the girl to come and stay with her for several weeks; she tutored her until she was up to grade level.[240]

Mary McDowell chopping wood in front of her homestead, circa 1919.

Early school on Dry Fork, circa 1913-1914. Mary McDowell, teacher, in white blouse in back row. Leila Ferguson in back row with bow in her hair. Frank Barnes on far right with hand on dog.

At the district meeting at the Galloway place, the voting and other school business finished quickly. After the ballots were counted, people lingered in the cabin to talk. The rain let up and though some people stayed inside, others began going out to the corral to get their horses and prepare for the trip home. Smith and Lighthizer ambled toward the corral talking about a proposed new road that would save time when they hauled lumber down from Pilot Knob. On his way out, Oldham spoke briefly with Carpenter and Lighthizer and asked if there were any offers for his property. They told him they didn't know of any and Oldham continued toward his horse, pausing for a brief conversation with Kleckner. Seconds later, as the Fulton brothers, Corbin, Lighthizer, Bolten and Kleckner were untying their horses, gunfire rang out. Lighthizer said he had just gotten his slicker from where he had hung it up in the barn and was starting to get on his horse: "I got a foot in the stirrup and started to raise up when I heard the shooting begin."[241] He laughed at first, thinking someone was playing a joke. Bolten thought someone must be shooting for target practice. Then they all saw Cliff Fulton run a few steps, stumble and fall face down. Charles Fulton was also running away from the corral and down toward the creek. Ida Kleckner and other women yelled, "Jim, Oh Jim" and screamed. Bolten ran for the barn. Ida Kleckner fainted, and William Kleckner ran to her side.[242]

Frank Corbin and Sam Lighthizer were the first to fully understand what was happening. Oldham had fired into the group, wounding both Cliff and Charles Fulton. As Oldham paused to reload the automatic pistol with a new magazine, both Corbin and Lighthizer left their horses and ran at him. Lighthizer tried to get his slicker off and was shaking his left arm loose as he ran. Oldham fumbled with the gun and then reached into his vest and maneuvered a second, smaller, gun which he fired at Lighthizer, hitting him in his upraised hand. At that moment, Corbin lunged at Oldham and knocked him to the muddy ground. Corbin grabbed the big Luger pistol and gave it to George Murphy, who had run up behind him. Others around him yelled, "Get the other gun!" There was a struggle as Corbin and Bolten tried to subdue Oldham and get his finger off the trigger and the gun out of his vest. After they got hold of the second gun, the men hog-tied Oldham's hands and feet and carried him into the cabin. Corbin searched Oldham's pockets and removed a jackknife, a pair of pinchers, the unused second magazine, and a handful of cartridges for the smaller gun.

Frank Corbin then went back outside and immediately saw Charles Fulton coming toward the cabin with his hand on a gun in his pocket. When the shooting stopped, Fulton had gone to his brother Cliff who told him, "Well, I am killed."[243] He stayed with his brother for a few minutes while Barnes got him something to drink, and then walked swiftly toward the cabin where Oldham was tied up. Corbin met him on his way and said, "You are liable to get into trouble. Give me your gun."[244] Fulton handed him the gun that he had momentarily forgotten he had.

Soon afterward the group dispersed. Someone rode to town to get the sheriff. Someone else went to the Adair-Solandt Ranch to call for help if the phone was working. Carpenter somehow reached Annie Elmer, now a nurse living in Steamboat, and told her to come immediately. Paroda Fulton and others gently loaded Cliff Fulton into a wagon and made their way to the Fulton ranch. Alex Ferguson held Cliff in his arms. Charles Fulton, wounded in the leg, and Sam Lighthizer, with a wound on his hand, rode with the wagon to the Fulton ranch to wait for help.

Those who stayed in the cabin guarded Oldham for several hours before deputy sheriff Emory Clark arrived. Carpenter later said he worried that the crowd would lynch Oldham. Everyone knew Cliff would not live. Oldham was bruised in the scuffle but not seriously harmed. Clark took him on horseback to Hayden. Sheriff A.H. Chivington met them and commissioned a railroad motor car to take Oldham to the county jail in Steamboat to await trial.

Dr. Solandt was in Craig, a day's ride away, but Dr. Enoch was in Hayden. Enoch reached the Fulton ranch around six in the evening and found Cliff Fulton "cold all over, a purplish color over [his] face, hands, and feet and practically pulseless."[245] Enoch counted three bullet wounds; one had entered his back and gone all the way through his body. Cliff Fulton died at around seven in the evening.

Despite the West's reputation for violence, Routt County had experienced very few murders. The last time someone had been killed near Hayden was in 1908, when Simp Tipton shot his neighbor Eph Donnelson. Like Oldham and the Fultons, the two neighbors shared water from the same source and were in conflict for several years about their headgates, ditches and fences. Tipton shot Donnelson at close range when the two met on horseback on the county road. According to witnesses, Tipton first asked Donnelson about his intentions with his water. When Donnelson began to explain, Tipton said, "Shut up or I will shoot you!" to which Donnelson replied, "Well, then blaze away."[246] The Tipton murder served as a cautionary tale, probably known to every adult and child in that part of the county. The message was simple: land—and especially water—were matters of life and death, and could drive men to seemingly insane acts.

The response to Oldham's murder brought many forces into play. The community was relieved that no one else was seriously injured, especially considering there were children present. They were glad to know that Sam Lighthizer and Charles Fulton's injuries were minor and that they would fully recover. There was also an unspoken and unacknowledged relief that Charles Fulton had not used his gun to kill or injure Oldham, nor had the community lynched Oldham, as Carpenter had feared they might. A sense of decency was upheld: Elkheaders could go on as sane, respectable people and lament the lunacy of only one in their midst.

After the murder, the community's immediate goal was to ensure that Oldham went to prison for life. Some also felt a persistent urge to dismiss the incident; the Oldham murder was not a story people wanted to tell outsiders. Moreover, to tell the story was to relive the terrible mystery of why a person would kill another; it meant opening up the possibility that the community had failed somehow. The only explanation for what transpired was that Oldham was insane, but if he was insane, how could he operate such a fine ranch and plan such a horrible crime? No one wanted to allow the event to taint Elkhead's identity or thwart its future. Oldham had fired into the very center of community life, at a school district meeting where he knew almost everyone would be gathered. He had chosen the most public place and an almost ceremonial event to express his fear and anger toward his neighbors. He had wounded two hardworking men, Sam Lighthizer and Charles Fulton, both with families to support, and killed a young man in his prime, a man of "more than ordinary intelligence and industry" who was "sober, accommodating, clean and trustworthy."[247]

James Oldham, Colorado State Archives, circa 1916.

Oldham's act was a breach, violent and destructive. The only remembered words Oldham spoke immediately after the murder were to Frank Corbin. When Corbin tackled him and knocked him to the ground, Oldham said, "they kept me a prisoner here for six years"—as if the murder freed him.[248] Perhaps he thought that if he eliminated his immediate neighbors he might be able to return to who he had been: master of his own territory, alone on his land, free in his solitude. Or, perhaps he sought to be free of the charge of insanity that had chased him for at least six years. No matter his intentions, Oldham would never be a free man again; he would never belong to a community of free people.

The funeral for Cliff Fulton was held in Hayden at the Congregational Church on the Wednesday following the Monday shooting. Businesses closed and the high school was dismissed for the afternoon. Over the following days and weeks, details of Oldham's trials appeared in the news, but Elkheaders turned away from the tragedy. They focused even more intently on the future of their blossoming community.

There was ranch work to do; there were children to teach.

CHAPTER ELEVEN

The Rock Schoolhouse

(1915–1916)

December 31, 1915

Nearly 200 people gathered at the new Elkhead school house to celebrate Christmas day. The marriage ceremony of Thomas McManus and Gertrude Sprague took place at 2 o'clock, the Rev. Chapman from Hayden officiating. The ring ceremony was used, and the Christmas tree and festive trimmings of the room made a very pretty setting for the service. Mrs. William Kleckner had provided a bountiful wedding dinner which was served in the Domestic Science room in the basement. The afternoon program was as follows:

Opening prayer and talk by Rev. Chapman
Song by everyone.
Song by the Elkhead boys and girls.
Recitation by Jeannette Haller.
Duet by Lela Gibbs and Eleanor Haller.
Recitation by Jessie Morsbach
Recitation by Allie Kleckner
Recitation by Leila Ferguson

After the program, the Christmas tree was lit up with candles and Santa Claus put in an appearance and distributed sacks of candy and nuts to all the children. Fritz Woshram sang Stille Nacht in German, which was enjoyed by all. Dr. Solandt, who was scheduled to talk, telephoned up that he could not get away, and to tell everyone a Merry Xmas from him, this message was received with applause, and a like Greeting returned to him over the phone. After sunset, the Xmas tree was removed and its place taken by the musicians, and a big never-to-be-forgotten Christmas dance was soon in full swing and lasted till broad daylight.

"East Elkhead," *Routt County Republican.*

The resourceful school teacher, Mary McDowell, was returning for the summer term in early May 1914. She was to be joined by the newly hired, Mary Officer, who would teach in the other one-room log school on Calf Creek. The district would finally have both schools open at the same time. Mary Officer came by train from Steamboat. She paid eighty-nine cents for the fare, an amount she had borrowed from her father against her first month's salary. She had just turned eighteen and had not yet graduated from high school. McDowell and Officer met in Hayden and stayed there overnight waiting for George Murphy to accompany them out to Elkhead. That night, they learned that Cliff Fulton had been shot and killed by James Oldham. The two teachers got a message to "wait until things had quieted down a bit." Mary Officer said she had "terrible pictures in her mind." She dreaded going out to the school and wondered what she was getting herself into. "What kind of people were there? These thoughts were in my mind all night long."[249]

The next morning, George Murphy arrived with his wagon and took the teachers as far as his homestead, in the southern part of the district along lower Dry Fork. Officer spent the night with the Murphy family. Their hospitality and good sense reassured her, and she began to stop her "quivering." Mary McDowell went on to the Fulton ranch, where she would board for the term. Her fiancée had been killed but she held to her commitment to teach. The following morning, George Murphy's wife, Mary, saddled up two horses and Officer tied the suitcase containing her very few belongings behind the saddle. "Mrs. Murphy led the way on her horse and we followed the cow trail. We stopped for a while to rest the horses; I don't think Mrs. Murphy needed it but I surely did."[250] Mary Officer found the schoolhouse "a tiny log building with many flies and mice." Eight students, four Jones and four Haller children, arrived for school the next day. Mary Officer, feeling somewhat overwhelmed, began by explaining who she was and where she was from. While she was talking, she opened the desk drawer to check for supplies and "out came a whole bunch of mice, who were as frightened as I. I sat down suddenly on the chair at the desk, which was rather wiggly, and the chair and I both fell to the floor." The students laughed while Officer tried to get up in a dignified manner. "Children, we've had our fun and laughter, now let's settle down," she said, collecting herself and attempting to regain control. Tommy Jones, the youngest son of Herbert and Minnie Mae Jones, raised his hand. "Miss Offither," he said with a lisp, "I'm going to kick you in the thins: I ran the other teacher out." Officer finally had her mettle up and replied, "If you kick me in the shins, you won't ever be able to kick again!"[251]

Mary Officer with her students outside the Calf Creek School, 1914.

Leila Ferguson, now twelve years old, began eighth grade at the Dry Fork School with Mary McDowell. There were eight students in eighth grade in 1914: Leila, Ezra Smith, Helen Jones,

Lewis Harrison, Frank Barnes, Galen Kleckner, Eleanor Haller and Ina Hayes. The new school board, elected on the afternoon of the Oldham shooting, began to mull over whether to continue holding school at two locations during the fall and winter, or whether to go back to rotating terms. There were several problems, not the least of which was recruiting qualified and experienced teachers. The other problem was what to do with eight students who were quickly approaching the end of elementary school, then the eighth grade. If they were going to continue their education their only option was to go to high school in Hayden, where the Elkhead district would be required to pay tuition.[252] Going to school in Hayden also meant that their families would likely move to Hayden, at least in the winter. Depending on Hayden to educate their children was not an appealing option, especially when Elkhead expected to grow. Would the community continue to expand without a high school?

Homesteading continued at a steady pace in Elkhead, though suitable land was becoming scarce. Some of the new residents could afford to buy property; others came with almost no money and tried to homestead leftover lands on steep hillsides with no water. Among those who arrived in 1915 were the Mitchells, the Morsbachs, the Rices and the Graves.

The Mitchell family arrived in 1915 from Mayes County, Oklahoma, where they had been cotton sharecroppers. George and Dolly Mitchell brought their son-in-law and their six children, Cherrie, Gladys, Claude, Donath, Joseph and Alma, who ranged in age from six to sixteen. Cherrie, the oldest, was pregnant with her first child. The Mitchells filed their "homestead rites," as they called them, and moved into a simple two-room log cabin on Bull Hill, on the lower edge of what became known as Little Arkansas. All nine of the Mitchells survived their first winter trapping rabbits and melting snow for water. The family sold animal hides to buy supplies. The women and girls spent much of the winter converting flour sacks into baby clothes. Cherrie's baby was born in the cabin the following spring.

Mitchell children: Gladys, Claude, Donath, Joseph and Alma. Gladys later wrote how fortunate they were to go to school. They had been working in the fields in Oklahoma.

The Morsbachs, like the Fergusons, Freemans and the Frank Hayes family, were from Medicine Lodge, Kansas, a small town close to the Oklahoma border. Henry Morsbach married Ethyl in Kansas when he was twenty-two and she was twenty. They had three children, Rudolph, Jesse and Oliver, before they had been married four years. The young family moved to Hayden in late 1914 and bought an option on an eighty-acre homestead west of Hayden. For some reason this property did not work out for the family and in the spring of 1915 Morsbach claimed land on upper Calf Creek, challenging the homestead of a man named James Bennett. Bennett had apparently left Colorado without completing the homesteading process and did not have a patent or title to his land. Morsbach was willing to live on the edge of the forest, farther up Calf Creek than anyone had attempted to farm. A fourth son, Frank, was born in 1918. Morsbach and his boys were known for their hard work and innovative methods. Morsbach was an experienced grain farmer and a skilled carpenter. He built several silos, tall round towers, entirely from small lengths of wood. On his modest acreage he raised sunflowers and grass hay; he chopped and mixed them together to create a silage, which he fed to his livestock during the winter.

Earl and Vella Rice left southwestern Missouri to start over in Alberta, Canada. Soon after, they moved to Routt County and sometime in late 1914 or early 1915 they filed on a homestead on lower Dry Fork, very close to George and Mary Murphy. Like the Fredricksons, the Rices focused on raising food they could eat or sell in town and avoided the cattle business. They won many awards at the county fair for their carrots, cabbage, onions, pearl potatoes, table beets, wheat, blue stem and alsike clover.[253] In 1920, they fulfilled a promise made to a dying friend in Missouri to adopt her twelve-year-old daughter, Oklahoma Golden Womack. Okla, as she was called, weighed only seventy pounds. She had been living with her grandmother who had already raised fourteen children. Okla adapted quickly to life in Elkhead, attended the Rock Schoolhouse, and became an accomplished viola player.

The fourth family, the Graveses, arrived around the same time with a large group of children and very few resources. Chris and Bellezora (Belle) Graves were from Arkansas and Kentucky, where they had scrambled together a life as day laborers and sharecroppers on various farms. They had five of their own children, Myrtle, Lance, Boyd, Golden and Lloyd, and two from Belle Graves's earlier marriage, Ollie and Walter Nelson. No records exist of them owning land in Elkhead; they seem to have found an abandoned soddy or one-room log cabin and squatted there, uncontested. In many ways, the Graves home was the most isolated and difficult to reach because it was far from the nearest road and miles away from other homesteads along Calf Creek or Dry Fork. The Graveses were also probably the most desperate family to settle in Elkhead, with so many young children, so few skills, and not even enough money to file on a homestead or purchase a relinquishment. Although they moved to Colorado from Livingston County, Kentucky, Belle Graves and the children had been born in Arkansas. For this reason, apparently, Elkheaders began referring to the Graves family as Arkansawyers and the area they settled as Little Arkansas.[254]

Chris and Bellezora Graves's frame cabin in Little Arkansas.

Over half of the land contained in the Elkhead school district was never opened for homesteading. Of the 140,800 acres in the district, the federal government kept more than 90,000 acres that contained either valuable forest land or potentially useful minerals, such as coal, that the federal government did not want to lose.

Beginning around 1910 more and more homesteads were patented with their coal interests excluded. The mineral rights were kept by the government and the homesteader had title to the surface only. For a landowner, this was a difficult position to be in; if the owner, or lessor, of the coal rights decided to mine the coal, they could enter the property and open their mine, regardless of how the surface was being used.

Speculation on mineral leases and ownership spiked after the railway reached Hayden in 1913. Though many people thought of the train as opening the land for settlement and providing transportation to and from Denver, its primary purpose was to haul resources out of the region. Between 1909 and 1915, newspapers in northwest Colorado were full of rumors that the vast coal lands of northwest Colorado would soon be developed and that rail lines would be extended to Salt Lake City. Investors, primarily from Denver and Chicago, bought or leased hundreds of acres of coal lands north of Hayden. The small "punch mines" on Pilot Knob and up Cottonwood Creek on the eastern edge of the Elkhead district fueled speculation in high-quality anthracite coal. Sam Perry, owner of many mines in Colorado, including the Oak Hill and Moffat Coal Mining Companies in Oak Creek, invested in significant swaths of land on Pilot Knob and into California Park. He was joined by Henry Babson, a wealthy investor from Chicago, and many others.[255] In 1914, the Hayden newspaper confidently reported that a spur line would be built from Hayden to Pilot Knob to haul out "several hundred acres of anthracite coal, the largest undeveloped field in the U.S."[256] Rumors circulated that Belgian investors had already bought the right-of-way to the anthracite coal fields. Hayden (with a population of close to 500 in 1913) would soon become a metropolis.[257] Meanwhile, there were no real changes: no one expanded the existing mines or opened new ones, and no rail lines appeared. Speculators simply held the mineral rights, waiting until the market was right before developing the coal.

By this time, Ferry Carpenter had opened his law office in Hayden and often road his bicycle between his log cabin on the southern edge of Elkhead to his office on the main street of town. Hayden aspired to be a small city. Now that the railroad had reached the town, and with all the speculation to the north, everyone expected Hayden to grow. Carpenter was naturally privy to a lot of information about the valuation of the coal lands, as well as property and mineral right sales. He was the town lawyer as well as a friend of the town's newspaper editor, George W. Smith. Smith and Carpenter also saw each other at Sunday services at the Congregational Church. There is no evidence that Carpenter invested or benefited from developing coal lands, but he certainly served as a conduit of information for investors. His parents in Evanston knew Henry Babson and it was through Carpenter that Babson came to invest in Elkhead coal. Carpenter was a promoter and he was shrewd about money. He had a fascination for taxes and moving wealth from investors and corporations into public works. He knew that if he could raise the valuation of the Elkhead district he would not only sell school bonds but also insure that wealthy land and mineral owners paid most of the tax, and relatively poor homesteaders and small ranchers would pay very little.

Carpenter also had a knack for making an investment sound like a philanthropic package: wealthy landowners could help lift the schools out of the mire, enabling struggling homesteaders' valiant children to get an education and escape poverty. As did many idealists of the time, Carpenter could bundle the plan in a Christian message of uplifting the downtrodden neighbor. Wealthy people were not just paying their taxes, they could be part of building something grand; they could aid in the progress of mankind.

Homesteaders, eking out a living on small parcels of land with very little cash ever passing through their hands, were naturally conservative about money, taxes and debt. Almost all of them had come from situations of hardship and they were all accustomed to getting by on very little. The economy that they trusted was based on bartering and reciprocity; when they had to "go out" to work in the Yampa Valley or in the mines around Oak Creek, they were back to being wage laborers with far less independence.

Ferry Carpenter claimed that Mary Murphy, George Murphy's self-sufficient and industrious spouse, was the first to mention the idea of a community center. After Herbie Jones's death and again after the Oldham murder, she chided Carpenter and her neighbors; in her home state of Iowa, a settlement like Elkhead would build a school that would serve as a hub of community. The school would be a public place where everyone was welcome, where there was space for everyone to gather.

The Murphys often hosted community picnics and dances but their cabin was small and was not centrally located. Carpenter held his come-one come-all birthday party in August every year and tried to have a dance floor large enough to accommodate everyone, but he, too, had limited space and lived far from what might be considered a physical center of Elkhead. As talk of a community center grew, the idea merged with plans for a central, consolidated school that would include a high school. As Elkheaders warmed to the idea, Carpenter complained that everyone wanted the center either on their property or right next door. Surely the location of the center would make the surrounding land more valuable, especially if the community actually grew large and important enough to have a town.

Sometime in 1914, Carpenter latched onto the idea of mapping the Elkhead community. He offered to pay a local surveyor, Parker Carsons, out of his own pocket. He gave Carsons this charge: locate every residence on a map of the district, count how many children live at each residence, and then draw concentric rings connecting the ranches and homesteads until he found the exact physical center of Elkhead. Carsons dutifully traveled to every frame house, log cabin, soddy, dugout or tent.

At each of the thirty-six homes he found he noted the number of school-aged children. The result was a legal-sized blueprint map. Three rings encircled nearly every habitation and a large dot marked the exact center.

The physical center of the community, as defined by the survey, was in a remarkable place; it was high above Dry Fork and Elkhead Creek on a south-facing slope. It was a perch, a place people sometimes called a "crow's nest," a small shelf below a rocky outcrop with a view over nearly every home in the community. It had several problems: no water or road access, and it was owned by the State of Colorado. Isadore Bolten's homestead was the nearest residence, about a half mile away. The future school and community center location would be an uphill climb for nearly everyone.

In Carpenter's many renditions of the story, his next step after commissioning the map was to convince the voters, and taxpayers in the district, that they could—and should—borrow and build. He convened several meetings but found that the homesteaders did not want to vote—in fact, they refused to vote. It was as if they had the sense that simple majority rule was not going to create the unity needed to actually build a community center and school. Carpenter wrote for pamphlets from Michigan extolling the virtues of a central, consolidated school. He thought some of the Midwesterners might be convinced by published wisdom from home. He went to Denver to wrangle a land swap so that the district could build on the centrally located land. He downplayed the value of the two little one-room schools and the inexperienced teachers the district was able to recruit. He rhapsodized about how a community center would lead to the expansion and development of Elkhead. And he brought home incredible news from the county assessor: the valuation of the district had surged to $705,000, making Elkhead the fourth most valuable school district in the county, behind only Steamboat, Oak Creek and Hayden.[258]

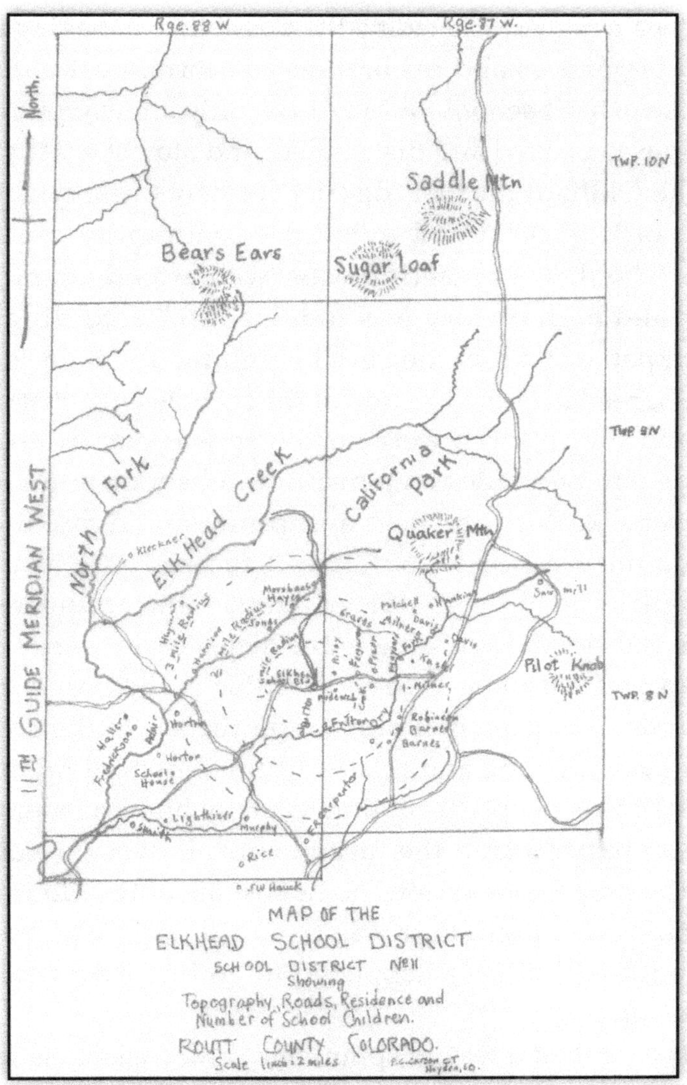

Elkhead District 11 in 1915 (originally a blueprint). Concentric circles (visible on the left side of the map as "3 mile radius, 2 mile radius and 1 mile radius") defined the center of the community as the proposed site of the "Elkhead School Building." Families with school-age children, listed north to south and west to east: Kleckner (2), Hugenin (2), Morsbach (3), Hayes (5), Mitchell (5), Jones (6), Graves (3), Davis (3), Harrison (1), Riley (1), Ferguson (2), Cook (1), Maynard (1), Haller (3), Fredrickson (1), Fulton (1), Robinson (2), Smith (4), Lighthizer (1).

Elkheaders were excited by the possibility of having a place to hold big dances and celebrations, a central post office and, of course, a high school. In May 1915, only a few months after the map was printed and distributed, and almost exactly a year after the Oldham murder, district residents finally gathered to vote on a $5,000 bond to build a community center and school. The district meeting was "well attended and much hot air and high oratory was indulged in," according to the Hayden paper.[259] From the very beginning, the homesteaders had disagreed over the location of the schools—the district was large and the children were far too spread out. In Elkhead's hilly terrain, two miles on a map could be four miles on foot or horseback. With the neat and professional looking map showing the exact center of Elkhead, marked with a large dot like a bull's-eye in the middle of a target, the arguments over location subsided. According to the map, nearly every home in Elkhead was within a three-mile radius of the proposed new school site. The principal opposition turned to the cost. The idea of such a young and relatively small district taking on a large debt was deeply troubling to many homesteaders. Leila Ferguson remembered the "arguments all over the country" about the proposal and how "to hear some of the old ranchers talk you'd have thought it was five million; it was the most terrible thing that ever happened to go into debt that much for a schoolhouse."[260]

Carpenter had a way of spinning out the vision. He said the new school would be a beacon. "We had a lot of open land," he said, "and we expected a population two or three times as great."[261] Paroda Fulton, equally convincing and with far more experience as a teacher and parent, saw the central school as practical and necessary if the community was to thrive. Together, the single bachelor from Evanston and the ranching mother of three from Mt. Ayre, Iowa, pushed the proposition through.

"I never will forget when my father came home from the school meeting where they voted it in, and voted the location, what a happy man he was," said Leila Ferguson.[262]

Rock Schoolhouse. With so much volunteer labor the schoolhouse went up very quickly. In October 1915 the district was out of money and needed to wait through the next tax season until it had enough money to hire teachers.

Work on the new school began immediately after the vote. From the start it was a community project built with a huge amount of volunteer labor. Carpenter and the Elkheaders who supported the idea wanted a distinguished structure; they felt that with $5,000 Elkhead could have a school of lasting function and beauty. Frederick Seeley, a sixty-five-year-old Danish retired general contractor from Denver, was hired to oversee the design and construction. Because the building site was so close to a long columnar basalt dike, the plan was to save money on materials by building the walls out of local stone.

The Frew brothers were known locally for their stone work and were soon hired to begin dynamiting the dike and cutting and setting stone. Thomas and Frank Frew had grown up in Fremont, Colorado, the sons of a German coal miner. They both followed their father into the mines, but Frank moved to Steamboat and began a different career as a stone and brick mason. He brought his brother to Elkhead to help him with the huge job. Like Seeley, they set up a tent nearby and got to work in early June.

The design of the building was based on what were called classical proportions, the Golden Mean, or proportions of 1 to 1.61803. Translated into a schoolhouse, the dimensions for the building were roughly thirty by fifty feet. The design called for one large room that could be divided into two classrooms using a folding solid wood partition. Wisely, Seeley added a full basement with plenty of windows and a concrete floor. This meant that the massive stone walls, two feet thick in the basement and one-and-a-half feet thick upstairs, were securely anchored. The basement added plenty of space for the furnace, kitchen and cafeteria.

There was no road, not even a path, up to the school, and when asked to build a road to the site the county refused. Charles Fulton and Carpenter borrowed the county road grader when it was not being used. With Fulton driving his four horses and Carpenter manning the wheel they carved several miles of road into the hillside and connected the school site to the main road leading to the Adair-Solandt Ranch. Nearly everyone got involved in some way. When the elderly Mr. Seeley got sick and complained that he could not cook and was not accustomed to living in a tent, Paroda Fulton invited him to stay with her family on their ranch. He walked the mile or two uphill to work every day. The neighbors began gathering stones and hauling them down to the site with horses and sledges. Those who had a wagon contracted with the district to haul lumber and supplies from Hayden.

When the walls were about six or seven feet up, Seeley and the Frew brothers got into a dispute about how the window openings should be taped. The Frew brothers quit in protest and refused to work with Seeley. Carpenter was in his law office in Hayden when he got the news and rushed out to Elkhead to arbitrate. "I explained to the two boys that Mr. Seeley was in charge; I'd stand them a lawsuit before I'd pay them until they got busy and finished."[263]

That summer, while the massive rock school was being built, Mary McDowell taught in the frame cabin on Dry Fork and moved the first eighth grade class through the curriculum. She plowed up the ground around the schoolhouse and had each child tend a plot of vegetables. As they harvested their garden she taught the children how to cook lunch and can food on the small woodstove in the schoolhouse. Leila Ferguson was one of the eighth graders. "I marvel at what that woman did," she said. "She taught more things than three or four teachers do today. She was really quite a wonder."[264]

Mary Officer had survived her term on Calf Creek but left the district in November 1914 and never returned. In her place, Mrs. Leroy Baker taught the younger children on Calf Creek in the summer of 1915. Both schools were slated to close when the Rock Schoolhouse was completed. The plan was to move one of the schools to the far southern corner of the district on lower Dry Fork so that young children living there would not have to ride, ski or walk the three or more miles to school.

The Bisel family, who had arrived a few years before with high expectations of raising and selling strawberries in Elkhead, hastily decided to return to Illinois. They had been neighbors and close friends with the Ferguson family and connected by marriage with the Maynards. Jesse Ferguson and Nellie Bisel had spent a few months in Hayden together one winter looking for paying work and avoiding the worst of the snow and what Leila referred to as the "starvations." In early 1915 the Bisels' second daughter, Hazel, who was eleven years old, developed a heart condition and Dr. Solandt, the physician in Hayden, advised the Bisels to take her to a lower elevation immediately. The family left Hayden that day on the train for Illinois. They abandoned their homestead and all their belongings. "We left the dishes on the table," Hazel's younger sister, Opal, said.[265] Hazel died nine days later in Illinois and a few months after her death, her mother Nellie also died. The father decided there was nothing to go back for; the family never returned to Colorado.

In late August, there was another unexpected death. James and Lois Robinson had homesteaded near where Mill and Cottonwood Creeks join to form Dry Fork, about two miles east of the Rock Schoolhouse. The Robinson family had come to Elkhead in 1908 from Elmdale, Kansas. Their first son, James, was born in Kansas, but the younger two children, Robert (Bobby or Robin) and Janie, were born in Elkhead. In September 1915, Lois Lock Robinson died in the homestead cabin giving birth prematurely to their fourth child; she was buried in the Hayden cemetery a few days later. Her husband, James, decided to keep the two boys at home but to send Janie, who was three years old, out to live with another family. The Galloways on Dry Fork took her in and other neighbors pitched in to help Robinson with his homestead and the older children.

Many of the men in Elkhead found some paid work at the schoolhouse in the summer of 1915. Several earned a few dollars hauling materials from Hayden and Lloyd Smith, Albert Smith's oldest son, earned almost $200 scraping the site and excavating the basement. Others like Ed Fulton (Charles and Cliff's brother who had moved to Elkhead after Cliff died), Alex Ferguson and Frank Hayes earned a few hundred dollars doing carpentry and cabinet work. James Freeman, who had been a plumber in Kansas before moving to Elkhead, was paid seventy-one dollars for installing the new furnace. All the lumber was hauled in from the Pilot Knob sawmill some ten or more miles away.

The Frew brothers stayed on the job after Carpenter's intervention and completed the walls in late August. For the 727 stone pitches they built they received $872.40. The general contractor,

Seeley, went back to Denver with $627 for his summer's work. Local men, both paid and volunteer, then built the roof and put in the first floor. They hung large framed glass windows on the east and west walls. They installed sturdy wooden double-front doors and mounted blackboards on the north walls, away from the glare of the natural light. When the folding wood partitions were open, the full thirty-by-fifty-foot room became a dance floor. Closing the partitions created two classrooms—one side for the elementary school children, the other side for upper elementary and high school.

The school building was complete in just five months. The district was out of money, but stunned and proud. Carpenter, newly elected as treasurer, published a list of every expense in the newspaper showing how the district had spent the $5,000 and come out with just 57 cents in the bank.

The Rock Schoolhouse soon after it was completed. Bobby Robinson and his brother, James, playing outside. Third boy unidentified.

The first program in the new building was held on the evening of Friday, November 5, 1915, to honor the eight eighth graders who were ready to graduate. Horses and buggies arrived from near and far and the event was covered not only by the Hayden paper, the *Routt County Republican,* but by the *Steamboat Pilot,* which called the rock building the "model country school edifice of the county."[266] After the usual round of recitations and songs, Carpenter gave a graduation address, a new form that the children found tedious. Afterwards, Carpenter asked his mother, who was visiting from Evanston, how she liked the speech; Leila Ferguson overheard her cut him off to say, "I didn't like it, Ferry. It was too long!"[267] The eighth graders got their graduation certificates and the official ceremony ended.

Then the real fun began. Homesteaders with musical talents, like Art Horton, Jim Barnes and Sam Lighthizer, brought out their instruments and began to play while young and old formed squares for the first dance in the new schoolhouse. Around midnight, after the youngest children had fallen asleep, a midnight supper was prepared in the basement kitchen and announced by a dinner waltz. People ate and rested but were soon out on the floor again for more lively dancing until daybreak.

All-night dancing at the schoolhouses in Elkhead began in the smallest one-room schools and continued at the Rock Schoolhouse; decades later, when the buildings were no longer used as schools, the dances continued. "All jump up and never come down. Swing your partner round and round," was a common opening call to get everyone moving in the eight-person square. The schedule varied little: there was typically a presentation in the late afternoon or early evening, the space was cleared, and dancing began after dark. In the summer months, people worked in the fields until dusk, returned home to do chores and have dinner, and then gathered at the schoolhouse in the evening. As darkness approached, the music began, a caller was found, and the floor would gradually fill as the stars came out and darkness deepened. By 10 p.m. or so, with the lights on in the schoolhouse, the dancing would be in full swing; it would continue unbroken for several hours. Everybody danced; the only exceptions might be the very youngest children and the very oldest adults who were too infirm. Dancers and the caller pulled those who might be reluctant to join in off their seats along the wall for a circle dance. Once they were on their feet and moving, someone could pull them along as a partner in a square.

These dances were open to anyone who wanted to come, no matter who they were or how they happened to be in Elkhead. Whether someone sat along the wall all night or joined the fast-moving swirl of bodies and music, the dances were a time of bonding, connection, touch and collective celebration. In one night, an individual's hand could have been tightly held in the hand of hundreds of other people—children, women and men, neighbors and perhaps a few strangers, family members and friends. The caller often rang out, "Balance and swing," a metaphor and a directive to hold your partner, lean back, and then move forward into a light embrace before you begin to spin.

As the community got tighter, and the more they built and danced together, the stronger and more aspiring they became.

Through the winter, the school was opened for parties, including a grand Christmas celebration, wedding and dance on Christmas Day, 1915. Everyone was invited and expected to attend. Families like the Mitchells came in a homemade sled pulled by two burros. Gladys Mitchell Shuttlesworth remembered:

> The Christmas tree was a marvel of delight, gleaming with lights and shining baubles the likes of which I had never seen. The tree stood from floor to ceiling—a beautiful sight to remember. Being a bit shy and rather backward I almost missed out on a present when my thoughtful father yelled

out, "My daughter hasn't a gift as yet!" and Mr. Santa said, "Step right up here young lady for a bag of goodies."[268]

Gertrude Sprague, known as Gertie, worked for Bill and Ida Kitchens Kleckner on the Bears Ears Ranch. When she became engaged to a local cowboy, Tom McManus, her employer, Ida Kleckner, decided to give her a real wedding party. Those plans were folded into the Christmas party at the Rock Schoolhouse. It was a grand affair with well over a hundred people attending. After the wedding ceremony, a duet by Lela Gibbs and Eleanor

Ida Kitchens Kleckner with her daughter, Allie, in her arms. Bears Ears Ranch, circa 1910.

Haller, recitations by Jesse Morsbach, Allie Kleckner and Leila Ferguson, and the Christmas dinner, an all-night dance party followed. The bride, Gertie McManus, apparently fell asleep on a pile of blankets in the basement. A huge snowstorm moved in during the night and no one was able to leave to go home, including the Hayden pastor, Reverend Chapman, who had come to officiate the marriage. A minor scandal ensued: Ida Kleckner served Reverend Chapman wine during the long blizzard night, and he had imbibed. Needless to say, it was a party that no one would forget. [269]

The new schoolhouse was open as a community center but not yet as a school. In the spring homesteaders organized a Sunday school (Christian but nondenominational) and the newspaper noted that there were forty to fifty in attendance most Sundays. In the spring, seventy adult voters in the Elkhead district petitioned to become a voting precinct with the new school as the polling place.[270] But still, the school had not opened as a school. It was not until July 1916 that two new teachers from "back east" were finally hired to teach at the Rock Schoolhouse.[271] Elkheaders, and particularly the 1915 eighth-grade graduates, were ready.

CHAPTER TWELVE

We're a Merry Group of Pupils

(1916–1917)

March 23, 1917

ELKHEAD SCHOOL SONG
Tune of Tipperary
composed by Eleanor Haller and Helen Jones

Way up on dear old Rimrock Ridge
Where the snow is white and deep
Where the air is clear and fresh and
cold, to school we always trudge
With such a bunch of Boys and Girls,
we could not be asleep,
And I'm sure you cannot help but
think, we're very hard to beat.

Chorus
It's a long way to Elkhead School House
It's a long way to go,
It's a long way to Elkhead School House,
To the finest school I know.

Then it's good bye, oh, little school house
Away down by the rill.
It's a long, long way to Elkhead School House,
Clear up on top of the hill.

We're a merry group of pupils,
As you presently will see,
We can sing and laugh and study and of fun we have just tons;
If you should happen in some day, we'd be busy as a bee,
For in study, work and everything, we are way up in "G."

April 20, 1917

Closing exercises of the first nine months term of school, beginning August 4, 1916, were held at the Elkhead consolidated school house Thursday evening, April 12. In spite of the fact that it was impossible to get a horse over the roads on account of the melting snow, about 30 parents and residents walked upon the crust early in the morning and were on hand for the exercises.

The lower grades gave a series of Mother Goose character monologues and the upper grades room gave a very cleverly-acted farce. The eighth-grade diplomas were presented to Adelbert Haller and to Lewis Harrison. The attendance and the work at the school thru out the long and exceptionally severe winter have shown that a winter school is feasible for the rural districts of any county. The credit for the success of the term lies with the pupils who have faced all kinds of weather to get there, in part with the parents who have assisted and co-operated in that matter, and in part with the unusual perseverance and pluck of the two young lady teachers, Misses Underwood and Woodruff who have not only not missed a day's attendance and kept a snow trail open the 2 1/2 miles from where they boarded at Harrison's but who worked with such interest and vitality as to make the scholars want to come. In recognition of their bravery and loyalty in these matters they were presented by the school board of District No.11 with a gold medal apiece with a cut of the school on one side and an inscription on the reverse side.

A dance followed the exercises, after a short war meeting at which the residents of Elkhead pledged their support to the prosecution of the war.

Misses Underwood and Woodruff drove to Hayden Friday and went out on Saturday's train to their homes in Auburn, N.Y. and with them go the best wishes and gratitude of the community they have so well served.

"East Elkhead," *Routt County Republican.*

In May 1916, when the heavy snow in Elkhead finally began to melt, the Elkhead school board met in the new building to decide, among other things, when to open the Rock Schoolhouse for classes. The delay in opening was partly due to the lack of roads but mostly due to the lack of money. Carpenter prepared a financial report that showed $74.11 in the bank. The general fund that paid for teachers and materials was overdrawn by $158, an amount Carpenter covered by transferring money from the special building fund, a piece of creative financing that no one protested. "There is due [to the district] about $1,500 in taxes," he wrote. "Of this we can figure on about $1000 from taxes and $200 from the State of Colorado."[272] He also credited the district with $157.50 for the sale of an old building, presumably the log schoolhouse on Dry Fork. If they waited until the end of the summer, he predicted they would have $1,200 in the bank, enough to get classes started in the Rock Schoolhouse.

There was also the problem of timing. Although the solid stone building went up at breakneck speed, it was not finished until November 1915, already well into winter, and not a good time to begin a nine-month term. With a group of students ready for ninth grade, the community wanted to hire a competent high school teacher. Attempting a nine-month term, the first for the district, would be far preferable for the first high school class, and would put the new school on par with Hayden and Steamboat, the other large districts in the county. Very few young people went on to high school at that time, because most young people were considered unfit for or not in need of further education. The educational dividing line was eighth grade. The Elkhead teachers had prepared the students adequately for high school and in a sense were competing against the standards set in Hayden and Steamboat.

A nine-month term was a challenge for homesteading families. It wasn't just that the district was nearly out of money after building the new school; Elkheaders were accustomed to short four-month terms that allowed families to move in and out of the district for work and made it possible for children to be in the fields during the summer crop raising and haying season. Child labor had been in competition with schooling for centuries and the situation in Elkhead was no exception. Families depended on the free labor of their children, particularly in cash-poor economies like subsistence farming. Gathering and storing hay in the summer was labor intensive. If the hay fields were irrigated by water in ditches, the

Fulton boy hauling water from a well on upper Dry Fork, circa 1915.

labor was needed beginning in late spring. In Elkhead, with its short growing season due to the higher elevation and heavy snows, essential activities like keeping a garden, canning vegetables and jams, and gathering and chopping firewood were also consuming summer and early fall tasks.

At the May 1916 district meeting, residents re-elected Paroda Fulton as secretary of the school board "with acclaim." Ed Smith continued on as president and Ferry Carpenter maintained his position as treasurer. After deliberation, the board decided to have an inexpensive summer term in the far southwestern corner of the district for the youngest children. The district had not been able to move an unused school building, or build a new one, so they borrowed Julia Smith's homestead cabin on lower Dry Fork and held the school there.

The district hired Iva or Ivy Rench to teach. Rench came to Elkhead from Delaware, Indiana, with her brother, Emil, and his wife, Lydia. She was thirty-four and unmarried. Her father had been a farmer in Ohio and Indiana but had died young. Rench lived alone with her widowed mother and taught school in Indiana before she joined her brother to look for a homestead in Colorado. In 1916 the Renches didn't own land yet, so that summer she boarded with Arthur and Anna Fredrickson, homesteaders of Swedish descent living on a mesa above Elkhead Creek.

The school board declared August 1, 1916, as the first day of classes at the new school. No teachers for the Rock Schoolhouse had been hired, but presumably by August enough taxes would be collected to pay teachers in the new school a competitive wage. Rench, a teacher in a one-room school with a provisional certificate, was paid sixty dollars per month. The district budgeted seventy-five dollars a month for each teacher in the Rock Schoolhouse and promised to hire two college graduates with first-class certificates.

At the same May meeting, the school board, stepping outside of its role as overseers of education, also decided to look into the state of the roads from Elkhead, Dry Fork and Calf Creeks. The county was not interested in building or maintaining roads in Elkhead; could volunteers build adequate roads to connect the school to the various settlements along the major creeks? The board also decided to explore the need for a community cemetery. In January, an eighteen-year-old young man, Lester Maynard, had died of locked bowels, and in April, Ruby, the seven-year-old daughter of Frank and Fannie Hayes, had died of pneumonia. Both were buried on their homesteads and the community felt it was time to designate some land for an Elkhead cemetery.[273]

Lastly, the school board decided to petition for a voting precinct with the voting headquarters at the new Rock Schoolhouse. They reasoned that only ten of the seventy-one eligible voters had been able to get into Hayden at the last election to vote. Now that the community was functioning as a political unit, it made sense that the residents could vote in all elections at the community center.

Paroda Fulton and Ferry Carpenter were the designated recruiters to find teachers for the fine new building. Carpenter's older sister, Ruth, was visiting that summer and she had recently taught a term in Pyramid, a small rural district south of Hayden. She was a Wellesley College graduate with an extensive group of friends. Everyone she met felt she was a force to be reckoned with and the only person who could out-perform her brother Ferry in determination and initiative. Carpenter turned to his sister for help finding teachers who could raise the level of education in Elkhead.

In his many stories about life in Elkhead, Carpenter always said that he recruited teachers as prospective brides for himself, his partner Jack White, and his many bachelor friends. He said he required a recent photograph of all applicants and pinned the photos all around the top log of his cabin. His unmarried friends were invited to look over the gallery and vote on the teachers they felt the district should hire. That may be true, and it certainly made a good story, but it was also true that Paroda Fulton was reviewing all the applications; it was the district that had the final say in who to hire. Perhaps Carpenter told his version of the story to provide humorous cover for his and the community's enormous ambition: Elkhead wanted to have the top school in the county, if not the state. So much was at stake. Everyone had invested a great deal of time and energy in building the new schoolhouse, and their hopes for the school were high. How better to defuse the tension than to joke about finally finding a suitable wife? Making fun of himself, the lonely bachelor hanging photos of applicants on his wall, was part of Carpenter's leadership style. He did not want to appear grand or imperious. He definitely did not want to appear to be controlling the district or setting the standards alone. He wanted to lead but still very much be a part of the community, to be inside, and yet to have influence.

Dorothy Woodruff on Ferry Carpenter's homestead porch, circa 1916.

The district put an ad in a Colorado teacher's magazine and Ruth got the word out among her friends in women's colleges in the East. Though we do not know how many teachers applied, in mid-summer the district chose two young women, Dorothy Woodruff and Rosamond Underwood, both from Auburn, New York, to take the job.

Carpenter wrote a letter to the two prospective teachers in mid-July letting them know how many students to expect and what supplies they needed to bring with them. "If you have a .22," he quipped, "you had better bring it out here as there are lots of young sage chicken to be found in that country and August is the open season on them."[274] He also arranged for the two women to stay with the Harrison family on Calf Creek, paying twenty dollars per month each, for room and board. Woodruff and Underwood, Ros and Dotty to their friends, had grown up together in Auburn and had attended Smith College together. They were both from wealthy families: Woodruff was the daughter of a button manufacturer and Underwood was the daughter of a prominent judge. Neither had ever had a job before. After graduating from college they participated in the suffragette movement, took a trip to France, and returned to Auburn to be bored with the eligible young men they were expected to marry. Their lives of privilege and social standing could hardly have been more remote from the lives of the typical homesteader in Elkhead. Neither had a teaching certificate but they were hired with the understanding that they would take the Colorado State teachers' exam at the earliest opportunity and that their college degrees from Smith were at least worth a first-class certificate.

Rosamond Underwood on the same porch, circa 1916.

When the two new teachers arrived by train in Hayden they were met by Carpenter and one of his closest friends, Robert (Bob) Perry, son of Sam Perry, owner of many Colorado coal mines and coal reserves in places like Pilot Knob in the Elkhead district. When the Moffat Line went into receivership in 1911, Perry was one of the two investors who took over the railroad. Bob Perry was a graduate of Columbia University and, like Carpenter, was known for his ready wit and storytelling. He was working for his father as the manager of the Oak Creek mine and living alone in a large cottage on a hillside near the mine. His sisters, Charlotte and Marjorie, lived in Steamboat and were friends of Ferry's sister, Ruth.[275]

Carpenter and Perry took the two new teachers by wagon to the Harrison homestead on Calf Creek. The family gave them their upstairs bedroom with a double bed to share. Carpenter said his friend was "smitten" by Underwood that day. Carpenter later learned that Woodruff had gotten engaged on the way to Colorado to a man in Grand Rapids. If he or any of the other single men in Elkhead had any illusions about finding a wife among the new school teachers, those aspirations soon dimmed.

Uriah Franklin (known as U.F.) and Mary Harrison came to the Hayden area in 1900 from Callaway County in central Missouri. Franklin grew up on a substantial farm with his Virginia-born father and nine siblings. He married Mary, and after the couple's first seven children arrived, they moved to Routt County. For over fifteen years they tried ranching in the Yampa Valley between Hayden and Craig. Franklin bought and sold horses and dabbled unsuccessfully in the telephone business. The family lived on and off in Elkhead and in the summer would take some cattle there to graze, but it wasn't until 1915 that the Harrisons moved to their homestead. That same year, the family built a log-and-frame house and a log barn. They intended to settle on Calf Creek permanently. Their older children, Emma, Edward, Mark, Marj and Thomas, had by then left home.[276] Their youngest daughter, Ruth (twenty-two), and their sons, Frank (often referred to as "Boy") (eighteen) and Lewis (twelve), lived with them. The Harrisons had a few cattle, some chickens and raised a big garden. Their new house had an upstairs room under a steep roof. They cooked and heated their home using a woodstove supplemented with coal. For the struggling family, the chance to board the teachers was a privilege and a financial rescue. Frank had been supporting the homestead by working in the mines in Oak Creek. He was able to come home that winter to help his parents on the small ranch simply because Underwood and Woodruff's contributions of forty dollars per month put the family on firmer financial ground.[277] Lewis, the youngest child in the family, agreed to be the teachers' guide and wrangler. He saddled their horses and led the teachers up to the school in the morning and returned with them in the evening. Mary Harrison cooked for them and did their laundry.

Harrison family at their homestead cabin on Calf Creek. L to R: Lewis, Uriah F., Mary, Frank and Ruth.

School began as promised on Tuesday, August 1, 1916. About twenty-five children arrived on the first day. Woodruff taught the lower grades; she started with ten boys and one girl. Underwood taught the high school; she began the year with six girls and two boys, including Lewis Harrison.

By October, when haying and other farm work were on the wane, enrollment grew to fifteen in the elementary school: George and Dolly Mitchell from Oklahoma sent Alma, Richard and Claude; Alex and Jesse Ferguson from Kansas sent Leila and Richard. Chris and Belle Graves from Arkansas sent Lance and Boyd; widowed James Robinson sent his two sons, James and Robert (whom the teachers called Robin); Charles and Paroda Fulton sent their oldest son, Ben; Herbert and Minnie May Jones sent Tommy and Minnie; and Henry and Ethyl Morsbach sent their three boys, Jesse, Rudolph and Oliver. Minnie Jones was the only girl in the class until Alma Mitchell enrolled. Woodruff struggled with fractious small boys like Tommy Jones and the three Morsbach brothers, who had become adept at disrupting class. She also had Ray and Roy Hayes, sons of Frank and Fannie Hayes. Ray was thirteen and nearly as big as a grown man. He was only in third grade and

School children at the Rock Schoolhouse, 1916-1917. Rosamond Underwood on far left. Dorothy Woodruff, turned to look over her right shoulder, in right center.

suffered from attacks of rage, particularly when he was teased by the younger boys.

Underwood's high school class was much smaller, though it also grew in the fall. The core group included Leila Ferguson, Helen Jones, Florence Jones, Ina Hayes, Eleanor Haller, Lewis Harrison and Ezra Smith.[278] Several of these students were among the eighth graders who had graduated in the fall of 1915. They had been waiting almost a year for the high school to open. In addition, the Jones family sent Yoleta, the Mitchell family sent Gladys, and the Graves family sent their oldest daughter, Myrtle, to join the class.

These three photos of the inside of the schoolhouse are probably the only interior pictures ever taken. The first is of the high school where Rosamond Underwood taught. The second two (next page) are of the primary grades where Dorothy Woodruff taught. 1916-1917.

What actually went on day to day in the school is impossible to reconstruct. What the students recalled years later was a feeling of awe and appreciation. Robin Robinson, whose mother had died the summer before, was six years old and starting first grade.

The Robinson cabin was two miles from the schoolhouse on the map but due to the rough terrain, probably a three-mile walk or ski. "Most of the best land was taken up when my dad filed on

his homestead,"[279] Robinson said when explaining why the family located in such a remote part of the district. After his mother's death, Robinson's sister lived with neighbors, but he and his older brother stayed with their father on the homestead. "I'll never forget the first morning when Lewis Harrison and the two new teachers rode up to the school," he said. "I thought Miss Underwood was the prettiest girl I'd ever seen . . . I don't think there ever was a community that was affected more by two people than we were by those two girls."[280] He said that the teachers inspired him and his fellow students to "work their hearts out." Robinson also remembered the long walk or ski to school and managing through the winter having only boiled wheat to eat at home.[281]

Leila Ferguson, whose parents homesteaded near the new school on the same south-facing hill above upper Dry Fork, had finished eighth grade and was ready to begin high school with Rosamond Underwood. When she looked back on her time at the Rock Schoolhouse after her own career in teaching, she described the new teachers as women with "fine educations, fine principles and were fine characters. They truly had the interests of the children at heart. What they didn't know about teaching methods they made up in zeal."[282]

Gladys Mitchell and her siblings walked to school from their homestead far up Calf Creek, a distance of at least two miles. "What a welcome inspiring sight met our eyes," she later wrote, "as we climbed to the crest of a steep grade, rounded a break in the long chain of rimrocks that ran for miles through this countryside, and beheld the huge stone structure firmly anchored to higher ground, solemnly overlooking the lower foothills. Truly a challenge to all who entered its doors. Beautiful Elk Head school."[283]

The morning typically began with the whole school singing together while Underwood played the piano. Woodruff was in charge of the opening exercises and then the group divided into two rooms, separated by the large wooden folding doors.

The subjects that the teachers taught were not set by the state or any authority above the district level. Nor were they under much supervision by the school board. Nevertheless, the teachers absorbed and passed on high expectations from the community, especially in the high school curriculum. Underwood taught grade school arithmetic to her younger pupils and algebra to the ninth graders. She also taught spelling, grammar and composition, ancient and American history, geography, civil government and physiology. She and Woodruff were relieved when they learned from Carpenter that they were not expected to teach domestic science, but they added cooking and other domestic arts to their lessons as the year went on.

Subjects were taught by recitation. In both the lower and upper grades, the teacher would call a group up to the front. Students sat on a bench to read aloud, worked problems on the blackboard, or stood in a small circle to answer questions about their reading posed by the teacher. In the upper grades, in which all the children could read and write, the group at their desks could continue with their schoolwork while other pupils were engaged with the teacher. In the lower grades, it was often a struggle to keep the children who were waiting at their desks from disrupting the lesson in front. The strength of the method was that it prepared students for presentations and performances. They learned to stand in front of others and recite, or answer questions, sing or perform in a drama.

The teachers were very aware of Elkheaders' high standards and their own lack of preparation, but the students simply regarded them as beautiful and sophisticated Easterners. The teachers described their efforts as stumbling and improvising; the students were dazzled and fascinated. Somehow, the combination worked. There was no lack of focus: the school was the center of everyone's attention and the center of almost all community activity. The mail was delivered there, church services were held there on

Sunday, dances and performances were part of every holiday celebration. Like a homestead, the school could not fail: too much was at stake, and there were no other options. Parents scraped together the little money they had to buy books and supplies, they

School group portrait, 1916-1917. L to R back row: Elzie Scott, ?, Roy Hayes, Ray Hayes. L to R middle back: all unknown except for third boy, Ed Davis, and sole girl, Fredonia DeCora. L to R middle, second and third steps: Alma Mitchell, Minnie Jones, Flora Huguenin, Richard Ferguson, Ben Fulton, Archie Davis. L to R: front row: Homer Scott, Janie Robinson, Bobby Robinson, James Robinson (likely), John Fulton.

gave up the labor that particularly the older children would otherwise have contributed to the household, and they carried concerns about the heavy debt on the district and the difficult prospect of paying off the bond. In such a small place, where nearly everyone attended every school board meeting, the children were well aware of the sacrifices being made. All eyes of the community were upon them.

After morning classroom work, everyone ate lunch together. The teachers packed a lunch in a bag on their saddles; the students carried lunch when they walked or skied. Like Mary McDowell and other teachers in the district who preceded them, Underwood and Woodruff were struck by how little food the children had for lunch. It was not uncommon for a child to bring a cold pancake smeared with lard. The teachers did not have time or skills to get a vegetable garden started so they began supplementing lunch, first with hot cocoa and cookies and later, with soups. Woodruff and Underwood were also concerned about the children's scanty clothing, or lack of clothes that fit. In a letter to her parents, Woodruff wrote, "We had two very cold days, and the condition of the children's clothes nearly broke my heart."

Morsbach, Jones and possibly Hayes boys skiing up from Calf Creek to attend school.

> Some of them haven't any shoes or stockings, and they wear coats to match their overalls for warmth. Tommy had a torn

> shirt next to his skin, a ragged coat, and a duster around his neck. I wish you could have seen Robin, bare legged, overalls, a coat of his big brothers, in shreds, which came to his knees, and his hands dangled inside the sleeves. They are all cheerful and take it as a matter of course. Rudolph said he always ate radishes to keep him warm.[284]

The teachers appealed to their friends and family members in Auburn to send secondhand clothes. Throughout the year, they received barrels of clothing, books and supplies as though they were missionaries living in a foreign country.

Physical education, physiology and health were considered vital to a country child's education. There was no gym in the two-room schoolhouse, although the basement could be used for some physical activity on very cold days. The weather was often sunny, and the teachers accompanied the students outside to play games, throw balls and ski. Carpenter created a Boy Rangers group and often led the boys in calisthenics or took them on snowshoe hikes. Later in the year the children practiced folk dancing using a Victrola for music.

Elkheaders took frequent opportunities to display the learning of their children; performance was part of nearly every celebration, activity and event. When a visitor came to the school, children were asked to stand and recite.

The first "Exercises," as they were called, were in October, close to Columbus Day. The entire community was invited, as it was to every event at the schoolhouse, and most of the parents and many single residents came. The children sang the songs they had been practicing in the mornings, put on two short plays, and ran through their recitations. Although not followed by an all-night dance, the event was the first of many in which students showed the community what they were learning at the Rock School.

Elkhead, through people like Paroda Fulton, Ferry Carpenter and Mary McDowell, was influenced by the Country Life Movement, a social reform that identified the school as the heart of a rural community and put no bounds on how a school could nurture a child.[285] Advocates suggested, for example, that schools should attend to the health of children. The Elkhead district arranged for the local doctor to spend a day at the school evaluating the health of each student. Dr. Solandt would have been the obvious choice as he had cared for nearly every family in Elkhead, but in late September 1916, on his way back from taking an Elkhead patient, Jane Sprague, to the hospital in Steamboat, Solandt was killed in an automobile wreck. The driver lost control on the narrow road and Solandt was crushed underneath his Model A. The doctor who served the Mt. Harris coal mine, Delbert Livingston (D.L.) Whittaker, came and examined each pupil, particularly their sight and hearing, but also their teeth and general health. He found several who needed glasses, including one of the Cook boys and two high school students, Ina Hayes and Gladys Mitchell. The district immediately procured glasses. They also sent Lewis Harrison, who needed nine teeth pulled, to the dentist.[286]

A few days before Halloween, the community held a masquerade party with an all-night dance. On the day of Halloween the teachers organized a party for the children. Woodruff noted with wonder that none of the children had ever been to a children's party before. The students made popcorn and the teachers used molasses to form popcorn balls. The guests brought cookies and cake and along with crackers and cocoa and after bobbing for apples everyone had a feast. Woodruff described the guests as "fond mothers and babies, neighbors and cow punchers!"[287]

The teachers taught a traditional week, Monday through Friday, but they were often at work on Saturday and Sunday as well. The summer term teacher, Iva Rench, started a Sunday school at the Rock Schoolhouse and she asked Underwood and Woodruff to take over at the new building so that she could start another Sunday school in her one-room school on lower Dry Fork. Rench, her brother and his wife, stood out in Elkhead at least partly because their religious beliefs prevented them from partying and dancing. The newspaper described Rench as an "unusually well-informed Bible student" but others were not so charitable. [288] They described her as "too dictatorial" and "a typical old maid school teacher."[289] Fortunately for Underwood and Woodruff, Rench's Sunday school plan never came to fruition because the school board and parents soon realized that it was enough to ask children to walk or ski five days of the week to attend school. Church services and weekly Sunday school would have to wait until the following summer.

About one Saturday a month the teachers rode on horseback to visit families. Home visits were a standard part of a rural teacher's job, and for many teachers who were living on a meager monthly salary, a home visit meant a hearty meal donated by the family. For Underwood and Woodruff, the home visits were a chance to ride and explore the beautiful country around them, and they became a way to see and experience their students' living conditions. In late August the teachers visited the Jones family. Underwood's letter provides a sympathetic description of their situation.

> We stayed for supper with the Joneses—(there are six at home plus the parents Jones—and there have been eleven in all.)
>
> They used to have better days in Michigan but came out here absolutely stranded five years ago. They have a log cabin, beautifully situated in a grove of "quakers," with a wonderful view and a marvelous garden—flowers and all. That's the extent of their wealth though. The walls of the cabin are lined with newspapers—there were three or four homemade chairs of wood, and a tiny stove, a wooden table and an antiquated phonograph, (a present from an uncle) in the two rooms downstairs. The place was neat as wax—but

> pitifully empty. Mrs. Jones had been spending the day at the schoolhouse with her husband, who was doing some mason work there—and she played for 7 hours on the piano. She used to love music—had been practicing all her old pieces and had been blissfully happy at touching a piano again. They gave us their best for supper—poor things—they make flour and water do in place of the cream sauce Mrs. H. always cooks her vegetables in. I have three of the girls in my room—and they're so nice and well-behaved, and Dotty has two more.[290]

The same Saturday they visited the Morsbach and Hayes families along Calf Creek. Dorothy Woodruff wrote her sister, Anna, about the visit with Frank and Fannie Hayes. Fannie Hayes was pregnant with her eighth child.

> We also stopped by the Hayes' where my "queer" Ray lives, and we also have two others from there. Mrs. Hayes is a gaunt silent woman with the sadness of ages in her face. She told us all the details of losing a little girl last Spring, while Ray and Roy hung on the door, and were too shy to come in. Ray was a strange picture in overalls which had one leg torn off above his knee, while the other dangled around his ankle. He has become my strong ally, and doesn't give me any real trouble, except for occasional wild bursts of tears.[291]

In September, the pair visited the Huguenins, who were homesteading below Aigner Mountain, north of the Harrison home where the teachers were staying. Louis C. Huguenin, usually referred to as L.C. or "Shorty," had grown up in a Swiss immigrant family in eastern Colorado. Like many of his neighbors, he was from a very large family of twelve children and had left home to find free land. When a friend was injured after he fell off a barn roof at the Cary Ranch, Shorty moved to Hayden to take

Minnie Mae Jones playing the piano in the Rock Schoolhouse, circa 1916.

his job. Huguenin's wife, Stella Lazarus, was also from an early homesteading family. Her parents left Michigan in the 1890s and homesteaded in the Yampa Valley. Her father was Ed Smith's early partner in the sawmill business on Pilot Knob. Shorty Huguenin met Stella Lazarus in Hayden after she decided not to move with her parents to Oregon. Shorty was an entrepreneurial man who worked on and off as a housepainter, paper hanger and barber in Hayden. Stella was known for her cooking and had worked in a restaurant in Hayden. The couple had two daughters, Flora and Marie, and worked and lived in Hayden until 1916, when they moved to their small log cabin at the base of Aigner Mountain in Elkhead. Stella "detested it out there," her daughter Marie said. "She was a person that liked to be around the public and have people around her."[292] She found Elkhead isolated and difficult. "We lived, of course, on wild meat and my mother used to pick wild raspberries and thimble berries and even strawberries."[293] Later that year, the Huguenins began building another cabin near the Rock Schoolhouse so that their daughters could get to school during the snowy months. Shorty opened a store near the school and ran the post office. The Huguenins expected that the teachers would move from the Harrison home to their cabin to be closer to the school once the snow got deeper. But for whatever reason, although the cabin log walls went up, forming what the locals called a "hog pen," the structure remained without a roof and the teachers never moved in.

The Huguenins took Woodruff and Underwood to upper Elkhead Creek, where they all went fishing and had a picnic. The teachers found the Huguenins relatively prosperous and the children well fed and clothed in contrast to the group on Calf Creek.[294]

In late October, the teachers visited the Chris and Belle Graves family, much farther up Calf Creek. Woodruff had three Graves children in her class: Myrtle, Lance and Boyd. In one of her letters to her parents, she described the poverty they encountered at the Graves homestead. She could not believe that a family could survive on so little food and in such a tiny and insufficient house. Woodruff found Belle Graves gaunt and with only two teeth that looked like tusks. The log cabin was a filthy and cramped single room. Rosamond described the cabin as a "miserable hovel."[295] Seven people shared a stove, three beds and two stools. When Woodruff asked Belle Graves if she liked Elkhead, the reply was "Naw—'ppears like me and Chris don't care about nothin' anymore!"[296]

Boyd Graves later claimed he had gone to school only two days in his life and those were when he went in place of his brother. The family left Elkhead the following fall. The newspaper barely noted their leaving except to remark that Miss Rench, the schoolteacher, had purchased the Graves ranch and that the family had moved to town. Soon after, the Graveses went to Texas for a few years and then moved back to the Arkansas Ozarks. Lance Graves died in a 1919 influenza epidemic and Belle Graves died soon after, while giving birth to her ninth child.

In November, the teachers rode to the Fulton homestead on upper Dry Fork, now so well developed with barns and corrals that it qualified as a ranch. After Cliff Fulton was murdered by James Oldham in 1914, the community learned that Oldham had transferred all his property to his brother Frank who lived in the southern Colorado town of Ouray. After Oldham was convicted, Isadore Bolten stepped in to buy Oldham's ranch.[297] This maintained the odd arrangement in which the Fulton lands along Dry Fork were separated by the Oldham (now Bolten) property. The Fulton ranch occupied the widest and most productive sections of upper Dry Fork. The flat, irrigable lands along the creek were hundreds of feet wide in places, forming lush meadows of native grasses. Upper Dry Fork is particularly sinuous in this section, practically doubling back on itself as it winds west and then south. Tall cottonwood trees lined the banks; although not especially useful for building or for firewood, the trees created an inviting park-like environment of shade and tall grass in the summer.

Charles and Paroda Fulton homestead on upper Dry Fork.

The Fultons, who were known for their horses, had also invested in cattle and later sheep and, like their neighbors, tried to cultivate oats and other grains. Charles Fulton was an energetic engineer and was always looking to find a way to direct water from Dry Fork Creek. He built several dams and miles of ditches in his efforts to make the bottomlands along that section of Dry Fork productive. Relative to their neighbors in Little Arkansas or on Calf Creek, the Fultons were among the most prosperous families. Ed Fulton, Charles's and Cliff's older brother, moved permanently into Elkhead after Cliff died, and he and Charles together managed many hundreds of acres.[298]

Underwood and Woodruff found Paroda Fulton, now with four young boys, competently managing the household. She was still on the school board and the teachers spent most of their visit planning the elaborate Christmas Day celebration, a tradition that had begun when the schoolhouse was still empty the year before. They watched Paroda cook dinner with a baby on her hip and spent the night in the Fulton home. "They live in the usual log house," Woodruff wrote, "—two very tiny rooms downstairs . . . and one room with a curtain across upstairs." [299] The teachers slept on one end of the upstairs room with a baby in a crib beside their bed.

The first snow came in October. By mid-December there were several feet on the ground. A few days before the Christmas party, a big blizzard set in and snow accumulated quickly. Nevertheless, 117 people arrived on Christmas afternoon for the festivities, which included a floor-to-ceiling fir tree, decorations fashioned by the school children and contributed by various families and guests, a visit by Santa Claus, several meals, singing, performances by the students, lively fiddle and piano music and an all-night dance.

In January, several families moved closer to the school so that their children could continue attending. The Mitchells, the sharecropper family from Oklahoma, moved into the unused one-room log schoolhouse on Calf Creek and the large Jones family closed up their cabin on upper Calf Creek and moved into Isadore Bolten's cabin about a half mile west of the school. Adelbert and Eleanor Haller, who had been walking from the far side of the Adair-Solandt Ranch, moved in with Charles and Paroda Fulton on Dry Fork.

By February, visitors to Hayden were reporting five feet of snow in Elkhead. The snow was often soft, without a hard crust, and children were finding it nearly impossible to ski. Some, like the Mitchells, managed to walk to school, breaking a trail for each other. The teachers learned how to ride their horses through the snow and how to quickly dismount and lead their horses when they slipped off the snow-packed trail.

On Valentine's Day the district hosted an all-night community-wide party and dance as well as a play performed by the students and readings of their prose and poetry.

Only one student, young Charles Riley, left school in the middle of the term; his exit, however, was not due to the cold and snow, but because his mother, alone on the homestead after her husband's death, moved to Hayden that winter and later, back to her home in New Jersey.

Frank Hayes, who lived with his wife Fannie and their seven children on Calf Creek, offered carpentry classes to the boys. Together they built partitions in the basement so that the girls could have a "cozy" room apart from the kitchen, furnace, gym and lunchroom. Isadore Bolten, the Russian bachelor, offered cobbling classes and showed the children how to fix their broken shoes. He had recently invested in a herd of sheep and gave the students a guest lecture on ranching. Ferry Carpenter was a popular and frequent guest. Underwood felt inadequate in her knowledge of government and politics, but Carpenter, as a lawyer with political aspirations, was fluent on the subject. He enjoyed teaching and gave several lectures. He also taught the children how to make cornbread and led a "sugaring off" when the sap started to run in March. The Camp Fire Girls, organized by Woodruff and Underwood, made candy and cakes to sell at the community gatherings.

The school celebrated the last day of school, Thursday, April 12, with the usual closing program and community dance. The roads were impassable and the snow so deep that no one could ski. Nevertheless, thirty parents and community members walked up to the school early in the morning, while there was still a crust on the snow. The school board honored the teachers for their perfect attendance and the example they had set in the opening year. The children gave their performances and Adelbert Haller and Lewis Harrison received diplomas for having completed the eighth grade.

The next day, Frank Harrison hauled Woodruff and Underwood's immense trunks to Hayden on a homemade sleigh and the teachers left on the train for Auburn. The Elkhead community waited for the snow to melt and the ground to dry and then set to work preparing fields, planting, irrigating, gathering wood—all the tasks that needed to be squeezed into the summer months so that they could survive the next long winter.

CHAPTER THIRTEEN

War Years, Boom Years

(1917–1918)

October 5, 1917

Everybody is very busy these days gathering their crops. Spud digging is the order of the day.

The Campfire girls expect to raise a neat sum from the dance tomorrow night. The proceeds go to the Red Cross.

G.W. Mitchell has moved into the old school house where he will live thru the winter.

Adelbert Haller was hauling lumber for their school cabin the past week. We expect there will be a number of neat houses near the school before many years. This is the third one started.

The Campfire Girls cleared $34 at the dance given for the benefit of the Red Cross.

The Elkhead newspaper, Rimrock Echoes, will be read the second day of November. If you wish to hear items from a real newspaper you should be present.

School attendance is small lately due to threshing and spud picking.

The L.C. Huguenins now live in the teacherage and the girls will get to attend school regularly now.

Miss Mary McDowell is now teaching at the stone school house this making three teachers in the building. She teaches just in the morning.

"East Elkhead," *Routt County Republican.*

A few years after the Rock School was built, the Elkhead District commissioned Herbert Jones to build a sidewalk in a semicircle around the front of the school. It was probably the only work he ever did in Elkhead that recalled his previous life in Michigan, where he had been in the business of concrete sidewalks. The sidewalk is not all that long, perhaps sixty or seventy feet, but it retains its classiness and peculiarity, forming a protective arm around the building and keeping the sage and oak brush at bay. The sidewalk creates something of a promenade: stroll to the western end and Bears Ears Peaks, the two rocky promontories draped with spruce and pine trees except at the top, come into view. Out of sight, but just around the corner, was Isadore Bolten's homestead, a short walk from the school. Below Bolten, to the west, the broad meadows of the Adair-Solandt Ranch unfurl along Elkhead and Calf Creeks. If one turns on the still-smooth concrete and walks east, Dry Fork comes into view, perhaps a mile downhill, meandering between what was Ferry Carpenter's homestead and what became known as Reece and Orpha's Horton Hill. Around the corner to the east, skirting the rimrocks, or the volcanic hogback that supplied the stone for the schoolhouse, was Little Arkansas, the most densely populated neighborhood in Elkhead. A series of shelves on the long hill that drops into Dry Fork were once carefully cultivated. Far in the distance is Cedar Mountain, a symmetrical, tidy mesa that stands alone to the west in Moffat County. To the south, on the other side of the oak brush covered divide, is the Yampa Valley; and visible beyond are the Flat Top Mountains, a nearly straight line of a grey-blue, usually streaked with white snow.

Panoramic view of the schoolhouse, teacherage, the Huguenin house and three log cabins on the far right where families stayed in the wintertime so that their children could attend school, circa 1918–1920.

During the time of the Great War, from roughly 1917 to 1920, all of this land, the whole sweep, as far as a person could walk in a day and in every direction, was under cultivation or used for grazing. The tops of knobs, little swales, tiny valleys around intermittent creeks, wide spots created by the meandering creeks, the mesas and narrow shelves, were cut into by the plow, seeded, and coaxed into production. Lines of fence, barbed wire strung between oak brush posts, crisscrossed the land—a hard-won grid over lumpy, uneven ground. At higher elevations in Routt National Forest, loggers and settlers were cutting down the spruce, fir, pine and aspen and using an axe or saw to create cabin logs or lumber. A few punch mines, short burrows to extract coal from the rich seams, dotted the higher slopes of Pilot Knob to the east.

Whether to settle in or move on was always a question in Elkhead, but during the war years, as Elkheaders prospered and the community grew in numbers and strength, the balance shifted toward staying. From 1911 to 1920, homesteading reached its zenith across the United States. The government transferred 42.5 million acres from the public domain to homesteaders in the 1911–1915 period and 39.6 million more acres by 1920. Over the course of the 1910-1920 decade, 439,710 individuals and families received a patent or title to land they had successfully homesteaded. In Elkhead, homesteading pushed the population of the district to 190 individuals by the March 1920 census. Elkhead was growing and the school was the hub and heart of the community.

Heavy snows in the winter of 1916-1917 meant a lot of mud the following spring and delayed planting, irrigating and harvesting in the fall of 1917. The Elkhead District 11 school board decided mid-summer 1917 to postpone opening the school for its second nine-month term "on account of the late season and that so many of the pupils being needed in the hay fields."[300]

The United States declared war against Germany in April 1917 and passed the Selective Service Act a month later, in May 1917.[301] Ferry Carpenter, who had been to the Plattsburg-sponsored military training camp in Utah in the fall of 1916, was appointed to lead registration for the draft in Elkhead.[302] In the first round, all young men between the ages of twenty-one and thirty-one were required to present themselves on Tuesday, June 5, at their local precinct headquarters.

Carpenter set up a table at the Rock Schoolhouse and spent the day filling out forms for his friends and neighbors. Frank Corbin, the young homesteader who had tackled Oldham during his shooting spree, was among the men who came to be registered. Corbin was married with two young children. Carpenter used a fountain pen with a thick nib to answer all the questions as fully as possible on the small card. For Frank Corbin, where the question asked: Have you a father, mother, wife, child under twelve, a sister or brother under twelve, solely dependent on you for support? (specify which), he wrote "Yes. Wife, child of 2 yrs., child of 3 yrs." On the next line he answered the question: "Do you claim exemption from draft (specify grounds)." Carpenter wrote, "for support of Dependents."

The new selective service law strived to close one of the more noxious clauses in the Civil War draft that allowed wealthy individuals and parents to pay someone else to serve in their or their son's place. After President Woodrow Wilson signed legislation in May 1917, the practice of buying a substitute officially ended. Under the new law there was a process for seeking a deferment and a place on the registration form to list dependents or medical problems that would exclude a young man from service. Carpenter carefully wrote out each of the young men's vital information. On that first day of the new draft, he registered sixteen men from Elkhead, including himself. Later in Hayden nine more young men from Hayden registered, among them the sons of Frank and Fannie Hayes, U.F. and Mary Harrison, Ed and Hannah Smith, Egbert and Mary Maynard, and Herbert and Minnie Mae Jones.[303]

Carpenter was divided in his thoughts about the war. He admired Woodrow Wilson, who had been his teacher and mentor at Princeton, but he was fundamentally isolationist. In an article in the local newspaper he expressed pride in serving his country but dismay that war was necessary. He wrote from Camp Funston, Kansas, to the students in the Rock School in late 1917, "if we have lots of good pupils in schools like yours, then schools like mine won't be necessary."[304]

Like most rural communities in the West, Elkhead was initially disengaged from the war. There was little news in the local paper and conflict in Europe was remote and abstract compared to daily struggles on a brushy hillside.

That fall, just as a large crop of grains and potatoes was about ready for harvest, Elkhead families learned that the national service had called up many of their best workers, their young adult sons. The young men were to present themselves at military camp.

Carpenter, #134 in the first draw, set out for Camp Funston in Kansas to train troops. Percy and Guy Hayes enlisted and Guy was sent to France. Paul Jones entered the Navy as a fireman; after training, he was sent to Cuba. Reginald (known as Bert) and his brother, Aubrey Maynard, were sent to France, as were Clarence Horton and his cousin, Otto. Several single men from Elkhead also joined the ranks. Louis Charos, a young Greek immigrant who had been working as a miner in Mt. Harris and had a homestead claim in Elkhead, was sent to Siberia. Victor Rodregues, a young man from Mexico City who had been working on the Adair Ranch, joined the Army. Bolten, who had turned thirty-two in March 1917, missed the draft by a few months.[305]

The Great War changed Elkhead in multiple ways. Even though the young men did not all leave at once, there was an immediate sense that labor was short and that all hands were needed to hay, thresh or "pick spuds." At the same time, prices for crops and livestock began to rise. Farmers all over the United States purchased more land, put more land into production, and added to their herds. Not only was this strategy profitable, it was considered patriotic, part of the war effort.

Leila and Richard Ferguson's parents, Alexander and Jesse, borrowed money and added to their acreage by buying the Cook and the Pizor homesteads, which adjoined theirs in Little Arkansas. The Cooks, originally from Arkansas, moved into Hayden. Charles Pizor moved with his new wife, Julia Smith, to her homestead on lower Dry Fork. The Fergusons expanded. Like their neighbors, they grubbed the sage and oak brush and cultivated whatever ground a horse-drawn plow could manage. They planted grains, primarily wheat and oats, on the hillsides, and potatoes on the well-drained strips of land on hilltops and mesas. They used the rest of the land for grazing cattle or sheep. Ferguson borrowed over $10,000 at 10% interest using the family homestead, livestock and farm equipment as collateral.

Before this war-inspired expansion, Elkheaders took out mortgages only for horses. Those loans were between individuals; payment, with the agreed-upon interest, was often not due until the horse was sold again. Occasionally, these arrangements were broken: when a mortgaged horse was lost or stolen, or worse, when an owner sold the horse and simply failed to pay his dues it was a crime, not quite as grave as horse stealing, but close enough that the dispute usually aired in the newspaper. Even after the banks became the principal lenders, walking away from a mortgage was a public disgrace.

Louis Charos was a Greek immigrant who came to Routt County to work in the coal mines while he homesteaded in Elkhead. He enlisted in the Marines and left for the war in the fall of 1917. The Hayden paper ran an article outlining the state of his affairs on his homestead in Elkhead: "Louis Charos, who took up a claim north of town bot four horses and other stuff on credit and left the country the first of the week. He sold some of the horses which had a mortgage on them by the banks and never said anything about paying other bills before leaving. Louis is a foreigner and said he was going to join the army but whether he is a patriotic ignorant Greek or a rascal remains to be seen."[306]

Airing an infraction in the newspaper was obviously a way of shaming the parties, if not obtaining justice. It was also a way to let the wider community know that a borrower was not to be trusted. The article about Charos carried an unusual tone, though it appears to reflect an effort to fling insults rather than a pattern of discrimination against foreigners. Isadore Bolten, known as a "Russian Jewish" homesteader in Elkhead, was rarely subjected to such slander; on the contrary, while some residents viewed him with skepticism for his business practices, many others, including the newspaper editor, often heralded his achievements and his business savvy. Bolten followed the rules and thrived during the war. He was too old to be drafted, but he threw himself into various patriotic efforts; his name was on every list of Liberty Bond buyers. He also spent the years during the war investing. He stepped up his strategy of borrowing to buy, selling for a profit, and returning to borrow more. In a few years, Bolten transformed himself from a ranch hand and wage earner to a large land owner, investor and trader.

The local newspaper reported Bolten buying cattle or sheep, shipping sheep for a high price, or offering land and livestock for sale, almost every week in 1918 and 1919. He bought a parcel of land in Hayden and sold lots quickly, for a profit. He traveled to Moffat County and as far away as Salt Lake City to buy sheep, which he sold to Elkheaders and others in Routt County. At the same time, he pastured sheep in Elkhead and, one year, threshed 700 bushels of oats. Although he was unmarried and had no children, Bolten was active in the school—he gave talks on Russia, taught shoe cobbling, and spoke on the importance of thrift stamps.[307] In May 1918, he assumed the role of treasurer of District 11, taking the post from Carpenter, who was training troops in Brownsville, Texas. In February 1919, Bolten joined other prominent Routt County citizens by adopting a French war orphan. Then, in the summer of 1919, he changed course, buying 200 ewes in Rawlins and selling everything he owned except his property in Elkhead. He leased 240 acres, presumably the former Oldham ranch, to Jesse Armstrong for "cash rent," and also rented his 160-acre homestead to Jim Hood and the Scott family The newspaper reported in October 1919 that Bolten had left for Salt Lake City in his auto and expected to be away for at least three months.[308] That winter, Bolten's partner, Dave Sellers, wrote an open letter to a Steamboat paper gloating about his and Bolten's recent acquisition of a ranch in Nampa, Idaho, and how they were fattening 2,000 sheep on alfalfa pasture at 2,000 feet above sea level; it was a tropical climate compared to Elkhead.[309]

Isadore Bolten teaching cobbling on the front steps of the Rock Schoolhouse, circa 1919. Students L to R: unknown, Claude or Richard Mitchell, Ezra Smith and Lewis Harrison.

Most homesteaders in Elkhead had never owned property before, much less borrowed against their property. Borrowing or getting a mortgage was a new opportunity that gave people like the Fergusons a sense of power they had never known. At the same time, going into debt, paying interest to the bank, and having not just a home but a whole means of earning an income at stake piled on new pressures. "Making a go of it" took on new meaning: success had become more than getting a patent to land and keeping food on the table.

Another way to look at the new borrowing is to realize that the people who took the greatest risks were typically those who were the least likely to pay off the debt. The youngest and fittest men, and those without dependents, had gone to war. The families that took on mortgages in Elkhead were often missing a hardworking family member. The head of the household was typically an older man, probably past his prime in terms of his ability to do physical labor.

A prevailing idea in this part of the country, and probably common to many homesteaders, was that one had to grow in size to survive economically. Although few openly complained about the small 160-acre homestead parcels, people in the arid lands, like Elkhead, quickly figured out that the crops they could raise there were not heavy producers. If they had stock, they needed a lot more grazing land than 160 acres. When the banks began actively loaning money, using the homesteader's patent as collateral, nearly everyone who could, borrowed. A few people took advantage of several revisions to the Homestead Act. The Desert Claim Act allowed individuals to claim 320 acres or couples to claim 640 acres. This was not a very popular option because the land had to be irrigated within three years and there was a charge of $1.25 per acre. In 1916, Congress passed another revision called the Stock Raising Homestead Act that allowed claims of 640 acres for grazing. Few people in Elkhead took advantage of this new law because although it did not require developing irrigation, it came with the same steep charge of $1.25 per acre, half of which had to be spent on improvements to the land within three years. Hardly anyone had $800 on hand to purchase land.

During the war, prices for all commodities went up quickly, and soon they were double or triple of what they had been a few years before. The newspaper ran glowing reports of the number of bushels local farmers produced and heralded the new price per bushel or pound. Grains, like hard wheat, went from under fifty cents a bushel to over two dollars a bushel. The price of steers rose from thirty to ninety dollars.[310]

The war also caused the price of coal to rise. Whereas before there had been speculation, the new climate brought on an almost frantic scrambling for coal lands and leases. The rising value of coal meant that Elkhead school district's valuation went up. Coal companies paid hundreds of dollars in school taxes, compared to the average homesteader who paid seventy cents.[311] The district finally had enough money to hire three or four teachers. In the summer of 1917, the school board again put out word that they were looking for highly-qualified teachers, preferably graduates of eastern colleges, and they were willing to pay more than their neighbors.

Elkheaders also decided to build a teacherage in the summer of 1917 as part of their package to attract and keep excellent educators. The Congregational Church in Hayden had recently built a parsonage, which many believed gave the church a competitive edge when recruiting a pastor. The district raised private funds, apparently not wanting to try to pass another bond, and began work on a stone house a hundred yards or so from the school. They hired the Frew brothers to do the masonry work and the community pitched in to excavate, haul rocks and do the carpentry.

Stella Huguenin, who had no love of homesteading or "batching" out in the hills, offered to live in the teacherage while providing room and board for the teachers. But money and time ran out in the summer of 1917. In August, the rock walls were finished but the second story would have to wait. Nevertheless, the Huguenins moved in and made the place comfortable enough for themselves and the two incoming teachers, Ruth Bodfish and Delcina Neilson.

Ruth Bodfish was born in Chilmark, Massachusetts, on Martha's Vineyard. Her father had a grocery store in Vineyard Haven. Many of her family members were in the whaling trade. She grew up working in the store and learned Portuguese from the many immigrant patrons on the island. After finishing high school, she was sent to Northfield Seminary in Boston and then to the Boston Conservatory of Music, where she studied piano and voice. After she graduated, she considered various options for work. A man who was moving to Colorado Springs, Colorado, proposed marriage. He wanted to manage her music career, but she refused. Later, she was offered a job as a voice teacher in Denver, but her parents objected to her moving there—they felt the city was still too uncivilized.[312]

Bodfish had a close friend at Northfield, Delcina Neilson, who, in the summer of 1917, suggested they teach together in Elkhead. Delcina grew up with her two sisters, Margaret and Sophia, in western Massachusetts. After their father left the family when they were young children, their mother struggled. Eventually all four women in the family went to work in the local paper and cotton mills. In 1916, Delcina's oldest sister, Margaret, married an aspiring reverend who had recently graduated from Union Theological Seminary in New York. The young Samuel and Margaret Neilson Wright moved to Routt County in 1916, where Wright was appointed minister of the Hayden Congregational Church. Margaret wrote for her mother and sisters to join them and Sophia took a job in the Hayden school. Delcina Neilson

Delcina Neilson and Ruth Bodfish on horseback in front of the Rock Schoolhouse, 1917–1918. Snow covered the first three or four steps.

persuaded her friend Ruth Bodfish to join her in Routt County and the Elkhead district offered Bodfish, then twenty-five years old, the job of principal and high school teacher. They offered Neilson, also twenty-five, a position as elementary school teacher.

Bodfish and Neilson had not taught before but they quickly assumed the role and, like the pair before them, thrived on the work and were revered by the community. Bodfish had a talent for teaching in a small, rural school. She quickly got to know everyone in the community and started a newspaper, aptly named the *Rimrock Echoes*. Students wrote for the paper and they read it aloud every few weeks at the Rock Schoolhouse. The Hayden paper took note of the event; attendance at the readings was always high. Carpenter and other men who were away from home for the war requested copies of the *Rimrock Echoes*; the students dutifully copied each edition by hand and mailed them to the soldiers.

Because of the late snows and delayed planting and harvesting, enrollment was low when school started in September 1917. Bodfish and Neilson noted that "spud picking is the order of the day" but kept steady pressure on families to send their children to school as soon as they could relieve them of farm work. Enrollment increased from twenty-eight in September to forty-two in October. Mary McDowell, who had taught in the one-room schools, returned to teach the fourth and fifth grades in the basement.

Marie Huguenin was in third grade that year; her family had recently moved from their homestead near Aigner Mountain to the teacherage, where her mother, Stella, cooked and cleaned for the teachers. She said that during the summers, children were expected to work at home, had little time to play and "couldn't get together like we could when we went to school." Children looked forward to winter because it meant that farm work decreased, their labor was less essential, and they could go to school. Winter also meant that children could play outdoors together. "We used to ski and ski and ski," she said. "We would ski off those hills on the crust. Oh, we'd just have more fun." There were no chairlifts or rope tows to bring the skiers back up the mountain so "we'd have to work our way back over those hills," Huguenin said. "When we got home, we were usually frozen stiff from our feet up to our necks."[313]

Bodfish, Neilson and the Huguenin family at the Rock Schoolhouse. Back, L to R: Ruth Bodfish, Delcina Neilson, Shorty Huguenin, Stella Huguenin. Front, L to R: Flora Huguenin, Minnie Jones, Marie Huguenin.

In mid-winter, Bodfish and Neilson converted the nascent school library into a community lending library. They enlisted the help of the students and catalogued all the books. Elkheaders checked out books on the honor system and the library became a popular institution in a place so small and with so few books in private hands.

Marie Huguenin adored her teacher, Ruth Bodfish. Marie said that Bodfish was "the kind of person you could look up to, who would always set an example." She admired the teacher's equanimity—the way "she took things as they came" and was "never one that was griping or complaining about things."[314] Marie was aware that Bodfish had grown up in very different circumstances on Martha's Vineyard but was able to adapt to her new life and contribute to the community.

Bodfish and Neilson leaned into war work and the school became the gathering place for war-related activities. The teachers started a Victory Garden and organized a Red Cross Auxiliary headquartered at the school. The Red Cross would put out a call for sweaters or socks and Elkhead women divided up the tasks and brought their finished work to the schoolhouse to be shipped to soldiers overseas. Nearly every week, the *Elkhead News* included reports of Mrs. Murphy having completed nine sweaters or the well-turned socks submitted by students like Leila Ferguson or Ina Hayes. According to the local paper,

> The sewing department is to be very highly commended for the large amount of work which they did. They made 43 pairs of socks, 12 operating gowns, 10 pairs of pajamas, 40 comfort kits, 11 hospital shirts, 20 refugee garments. By the knitting department there we find there were 70 sweaters made and 16 pairs of socks. The work of the knitters was delayed quite a bit on account of the inability of the chapter to get yarn.[315]

The usual round of dances to mark every holiday or school event became fundraisers for the war effort. The teachers used every occasion to sell box suppers that the students prepared in the school kitchen. The dinners were auctioned off and the proceeds were donated to the Red Cross. The teachers also combined their visits to families across the district with travels on horseback to sell Liberty Bonds.

In January 1918, Bodfish agreed to care for the little girl, Janie Robinson, whose mother had died in childbirth. Bodfish noted her presence, and her day's activities, in her usual succinct style: "Beautiful. Roads packing fine. Hope to get a sleigh ride. Boy

[Frank Harrison] phoned. Going to bring out our mail. Sang a piece through in two parts in my room today. Started night gowns. Washed my head. Wrote letters. Gertrude [Janie] a little dear."[316] Robinson lived in the teacherage for several weeks and was followed by several other students who boarded with the teachers so that they could continue going to school during the winter.

School portrait, circa 1917–1918.

When young men were called up and given a date to report to camp, their parents and the school gave them a farewell dance. The largest and most elaborate of these was for Milton Wilkenson, the son of Orpha Horton and stepson of Reece Horton. Milton had left Elkhead to work as a mechanic in Los Angeles but after he enlisted he returned home for a few weeks. Over 100 people came to the schoolhouse for the dinner and dance to send him off.

Many Elkheaders compared Elkhead to Twin Mesa, another homesteading community south of Hayden. When plans were made to build the Rock Schoolhouse, people mentioned the fine two-room schoolhouse on Twin Mesa and noted that while it was a frame building, theirs would be made of stone. When Marie

Huguenin described her time in Elkhead she mused about how Elkhead was "a community in itself, just like Twin Mesa." But, she added, "Theirs wasn't the kind of school we had up there. They didn't have the class of teachers." Teachers like Woodruff, Underwood, Neilson and Bodfish, "girls that came from back East, with a definite pioneering instinct to come way out here and teach," added a new dimension to the students' lives. "They brought an awful lot to us." Marie said, noting, sixty years later, that Bodfish had "always held a spot in my heart."[317]

For American troops, the Great War was relatively short. Elkhead's young men began returning in the summer of 1919. Miraculously, no men from Elkhead were mortally injured or killed. Paul Jones suffered from serious pneumonia and spent months recovering in Boston after his ship bound for Cuba sank. Guy Hayes was badly gassed and suffered from weak lungs for the rest of his life. But all the other men were apparently unscathed. Clarence and Otto Horton returned and promptly leased the Cottonwood coal mine from the Perry family and began mining and selling coal.

Clarence Horton got married to Vada, the daughter of his neighbor Ed Smith, just before he was shipped. When Otto got back home, he married Myrtle Castor, whose family lived in Hayden. Frank Harrison came back from France and tried to buy land in Elkhead but was not successful. He married Eleanor Haller, a neighbor's daughter, and went back to work in the coal mines in Oak Creek.

Ferry Carpenter returned to Routt County regretting that he had never served in Europe but buoyant about his time spent teaching in various training camps. He revived his partnership with Jack White and together they invested in more land and cattle.

Frank Hayes, the father of eight children who had homesteaded near the Jones family on Calf Creek, died of a massive heart attack in the family cabin in February 1918. The newspaper said that one of his young sons was sleeping with him and heard him breathing deeply. The boy went to his mother's room to tell her but by the time she got to where they had been sleeping, he was dead. Bodfish wrote in her diary that Hayes's death was a "great shock," and that "most of the arrangements for the funeral at the Rock Schoolhouse "fall on Del and me."[318] She and Neilson sang a duet; school closed for the day.[319] Family members later said that Frank Hayes was sent to Colorado for his health. He had a weak heart and the mountain air was supposed to strengthen him. Two years before, Ruby, Frank and Fannie's seven-year-old daughter had died in the homestead cabin of bronchitis. Ray, their fifth child, was considered "queer" (a term used at the time to refer to mental illness) and his teachers were often concerned about his violent temper. Fortunately, Percy and Guy, the two oldest sons, returned alive from the World War and both helped their mother stay on the homestead by doing farm labor and working in the mines. Guy, who had been gassed in Europe, was not fit for heavy work in Routt County, left for Chicago after a few years and never returned.[320] Fannie Hayes held onto the homestead and kept her children enrolled in the Rock Schoolhouse. She had five children at home on Calf Creek, including the baby, Robert, who had been less than a month old when his father died.[321]

Another untimely death disturbed the community in October: that of Ida Kitchens Kleckner, wife of William Kleckner. She and her husband had lived on the North Fork of Elkhead Creek in a sawed log home since 1907. Her son, Galen, was in the Navy. It was Ida who was remembered for the fine wedding dinner she gave for her housemaid, Gertie Sprague, in December 1915, and it was she who caused a sensation by serving wine to the pastor while he was snowed in and spending the night at the schoolhouse.[322] The Kleckners called their place Bears Ears Ranch because it was so close to the base of that mountain. Ida Kleckner had been suffering from a heart ailment and sought treatment in California and Steamboat. After she died, William Kleckner sold their ranch and moved with his children to Hayden. Allie Kleckner later noted that her father seemed like a broken man after her mother's death: "Homesteading had been possible when there were two of them."[323]

Victor Rodregues returned to his job on the Adair Ranch. Milton Wilkenson, who had such a spectacular send-off at the Rock Schoolhouse, never entered the service. He died of influenza, one of the early deaths in the epidemic, while he was waiting for his call-up notice.

A strange and tragic story among the veterans was that of Louis Charos, the Greek immigrant and homesteader who left the county under a cloud of suspicion and deeply in debt. During the war he was stationed in Siberia, where he apparently rescued and married (on February 12, 1919) a young widow, Sophia Chakirido. The newspaper said he had saved her "from the clutches of roving Bolsheviki bands" that had earlier killed her husband in the restaurant they ran together.[324] When Louis's regiment returned to the United States in October 1919, Sophia accompanied him but left her child behind with her parents in Siberia. When she got to San Francisco she was detained. Charos, the newspaper noted, did not have enough money to pay for Sophia's travel to Colorado. For months she waited in California. In May 1920, she finally joined Charos in Elkhead, where he reclaimed his homestead and went back to work at the mine in Mt. Harris.[325]

Soon after arriving in Routt County Sophia asked the Red Cross for help bringing her son to the United States and, in May 1921, three-year-old Sbiro Chakirido made the trip around the world with a Red Cross nurse to rejoin his mother. A popular Chicago-based news magazine at the time, the *Saturday Blade*, ran a feature about Sbiro, datelined Hayden, Colorado. The story said the boy traveled 7,000 miles to be in his mother's arms and painted a rustic and romantic picture of the little family's life in Elkhead. "Louis Charos, ex-soldier, is tilling the soil on a 320-acre plot upon which the little family of three expect to spend their remaining days."[326]

Sophia Chakirido Charos, undated.

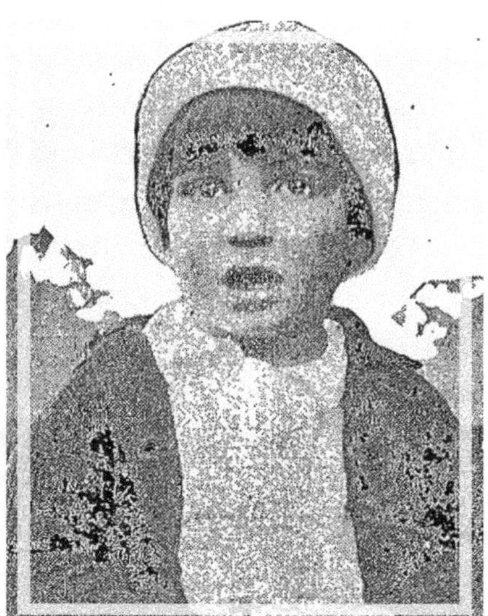

Sbiro Charos, undated.

In September 1921, just a few months after Sbiro arrived, Sophia fled to Denver and appealed to the Red Cross for help; she said she was being mistreated by Charos. She was assigned a lawyer and began filing for a divorce. Later reports stated that she sought custody of their child but did not seek alimony. Charos followed her to Denver and after visiting her lawyer demanded to know if he would have to pay alimony. Charos tracked his wife down at a downtown rooming house and later attacked and murdered her on the sidewalk in front of her rooming house. Charos fled into a "crowd of hundreds" who had witnessed the stabbing in downtown Denver.[327] A few hours later Charos turned himself in. He was tried and sentenced to life in prison. What happened to the child? Sbiro seems to have disappeared without a trace—at least, his name vanished from record. After Charos was convicted a Denver newspaper advertised for a Greek family to adopt little "Tommy" Charos, orphaned son of Sophia.[328] Louis Charos lived a long life in the state penitentiary in Canon City, the same institution that housed Elkhead's only other murderer, James Oldham.[329]

No one spoke of Charos or mentioned his crime, his wife or his child when they spoke of homesteading in Elkhead. There was no mention of Charos's return from the war or the arrivals of Sophia and Sbiro in the local papers. Sbiro was too young to be enrolled in school, nor did anyone take note of the young Charos family in Elkhead. Charos likely went to prison, still in debt to the bank and his neighbors.[330]

Even decades later Elkheaders were reluctant to mention failures, tragedies and especially criminal behavior. Oldham and Charos did not belong in a narrative of cohesion and triumph. Elkheaders were industrious and honest people; murderers did not belong. If a hole opened in the narrative it was quickly closed. Attention invariably turned to lighter and more celebratory subjects.

Delcina Neilson married Sam Shelton, a rancher in the Yampa Valley, and left teaching after one year. Sam Shelton's best friend, Earl Erwin, courted Ruth Bodfish but he left for the war in June 1918 and their romance ended.[331] Neilson was replaced by Iva Rench, who had taught a short term at the Dry Fork School followed by a year in the primary school in Hayden. Ruth Bodfish had also been courted by Ed Fulton from the first months of her arrival in Elkhead, but she seems to have delayed marriage to Fulton so that she could teach another year.

Like Mary McDowell, who had plowed up ground around the Calf Creek School, started a garden, and taught her pupils to cook, Bodfish was a natural at connecting her teaching to the local geography and the needs of the community. Several of her students, the first reporters for the *Rimrock Echoes*, later took up writing for the *Routt County Republican* and some became librarians for the school/community library. Under Bodfish's leadership, Elkhead students were recognized for the work they were doing on their parents' homesteads. Bodfish knew how important the children were to the economy of Elkhead and she frequently adapted the school schedule so that children would not be penalized for missing school because they were needed in the fields. At the end of the 1917-1918 term, both Ezra Smith and Lewis Harrison needed to leave school in mid-April to begin work. Bodfish compressed their studies and gave them their final exams over a month early.

Paroda Fulton and Ruth Bodfish (with Charles (Chuck) Fulton in her arms), in front of the Fulton home on upper Dry Fork, 1919.

Even though families needed their children, and especially high-school-aged young people, for farm work, none of the eligible high school students quit school. The following school year, 1918-1919, another three students graduated from eighth grade and were ready to enter high school. Ione Smith, Yoleta Jones and Flora Huguenin, all daughters of homesteaders, graduated from primary school in the spring of 1919. An article in the paper proudly noted that they were the third class to graduate from the eighth grade at the Elkhead School. The high school was growing in numbers, but most importantly, the idea that every child was capable of going to high school, if not college, was becoming a collective goal.

From a humble start in a one-room log structure on Calf Creek, the district had grown to have a solidly built and financed high school. Homesteaders who had resisted the idea of spending so much money on education were now intently watching the progress of the first group of high school students. Just as teachers like Bodfish accommodated the pressures and needs of that particular place, so too did parents expand their expectations for their children and adjust their demands so that their children could not only attend, but excel, in school. After three years of nine-month terms and three pairs of well-paid, well-educated, dedicated teachers, Elkhead had earned a reputation in the county—if not the state—for its high level of education. The homesteaders' identity was intricately entwined with their commitment to their school. The community hummed and thrived in and around its center, the Rock School.

CHAPTER FOURTEEN

The Triumphant Seniors

(1919–1920)

September 5, 1919

Isadore Boloten got back from Utah today in his auto.

Paul Heine, son of Mrs. Prevo, and James Kennedy of Williams Fork are two more of our soldier boys who got back from France this week.

Miss Eunice Pleasant has been elected principal of the Elkhead school. Miss Pleasant is a sister of F.M. Pleasant of Craig. Miss Ivy Rench is the assistant in the school.

W.A. Dean, who has been working for Albert Horton on Dry Fork of Little Bear, after taking a buckskin pony belonging to the little Horton girl, tried to commit suicide last week. However, the home-made cartridge was weak, and he suffered only a flesh wound from which he is fast recovering in the Craig jail. He will be tried for insanity.

September 19, 1919

Miss Reynolds, Miss West and Miss Dawley, of the Hayden school, and Miss Pleasant of the Elkhead school, spent the week-end with Mrs. Ed Fulton on Elkhead, and took the opportunity to visit the Elkhead school.

September 26, 1919

Carl Corder is selling his household furniture preparatory to leaving Routt county.

H.M. Jones has put in a small stock of goods at his store and expects to soon have a post office there also.

Tom Prevo and Mr. Freeman did some repair work last week on the teacherage. Miss Pleasant will move there in a few days. She is at present staying at the Ed Fulton ranch.

Frank Maynard, who, with his family, has been visiting his parents, has been quite sick, but is now on the road to recovery.

Altho the Elkhead school is short of supplies, the pupils have settled down to work in earnest. There is a senior class of five pupils, and about thirty are enrolled in the school.

Sam Lighthizer, Earl Rice, Mr. Omsted, Ed Fulton and Ed Smith have finished threshing their grain. Mr. Bowers did the work with his machine.

"East Elkhead," *Routt County Republican.*

Five young Elkheaders were poised to begin their senior year in high school in August 1919. Throughout the summer, school board members made inquiries and advertised for a new high school teacher, but in August they still had not hired anyone. In June, the newspaper noted that the district was "trying to get a man for principal" but there were no further announcements; apparently, no one applied for the job.

Ferry Carpenter, former school board member, was distracted. He had so many projects in motion, it was as though he was trying to make up for the years he had lost while he was away in the military. His law practice, operating out of the reopened former bowling alley in Hayden, was busy; he was buying a new line of Hereford bulls to improve his herd; he continued a campaign for a regional hospital to be built in memory of Dr. Solandt, and he was building a stone barn to house a dairy on Dry Fork which he called Kenmore. Finally, he was intent on forming a union high school in Hayden. He wrote regularly for the Hayden paper on the virtues of education and particularly on the value of a "world class" high school education.

Kenmore, a dairy started by Ferry Carpenter and various partners, located near the Galloway place on Dry Fork, circa 1920.

On a trip home to Evanston, Illinois, in 1919, Carpenter recruited two recent college graduates to be teachers, but he had them placed in the Hayden schools, not in Elkhead. He had not found anyone willing or capable of teaching high school, single-handedly, at the Rock Schoolhouse.

Iva Rench, the teacher from Indiana, who with her brother Emil and his wife, Lydia, had homesteaded in Elkhead, was rehired to teach the primary grades. Miss Rench was never popular, nor did her students find her memorable, but she was effective and reliable, so her contract was renewed.

The community attached a great deal of hope to the first five high school seniors in Elkhead. Several of them would be the first in their family to complete high school and none of their parents or siblings had finished college. They were all good students and determined to graduate despite many competing obligations at home. Each of them had a large role in their family and did the work of an adult when they were not in school. They had walked and skied to school for years, and done their assignments beside a wood-burning stove, by the light of candles or kerosene lanterns.

The five seniors on horseback. L to R: Ezra Smith, Ina Hayes, Helen Jones, Leila Ferguson, Lewis Harrison, circa 1919-1920.

Leila Ferguson, daughter of Alex and Jesse, lived close to the Rock Schoolhouse in Little Arkansas. Her family had gradually built up a homestead since their arrival and by 1919 owned several hundred acres. Her brother, Richard, was a few years behind her in school. Leila was a quiet, serious person, with a quick wit. She was tall and big boned, healthy, and strong enough to do a lot of outdoor work. At that time in her life her face often looked heavy and much older than her eighteen years. She dressed very plainly, in old overcoats covering simple dresses. She wore lace-up boots to school. There are almost no pictures of her smiling as a child or young adult.

Ina Hayes, daughter of Frank and Fannie Hayes, was Leila's best friend and her competitor for academic honors in high school. The Hayes family, like many of their neighbors, had arrived with almost no money and many young children. The youngest, Morgan, was just one year old when the family got off the train in Hayden. Ina's parents had met in Normal School where they were both studying to become teachers. Ina's two older brothers, Percy and Guy, left home to enter the war, but her mother, Fannie, despite being a widow without her older sons to help her, stayed on the homestead. Although her older brothers tried to help, Ina was the eldest at home and, as the only surviving daughter, was responsible for a lot of farm and household labor and for tending to her younger siblings. Like Leila, she was a serious, determined student. She was only fifteen when her senior year started. She had a wiry, thin build, dark brown hair and blue eyes. She was an adept skier, easily traversing the mile or so between the family homestead and the Rock School when there was snow on the ground. As a child, she had survived scarlet fever, which probably affected her stature (she was under 5 feet tall) and damaged her eyesight. She was one of the children given glasses after the first medical examination at the schoolhouse and she wore them throughout high school.

Ezra Smith lived on lower Dry Fork with his parents, Erasmus (Ed) and Hannah Smith, who owned and operated the sawmill on Bears Ears and later on Pilot Knob. Ezra worked either in the sawmills or on the family's modest ranch. He occasionally "worked out" for neighbors and friends of the family. His younger sister Ione was in ninth grade. He had an older brother, Ira, who had married Bessie Jones and homesteaded on Dry Fork, and an older sister, Julia, who had married Charlie Pizor and who had her own homestead also on Dry Fork. Being one of the younger children in a very large family may have contributed to his casual, happy demeanor. He was popular in school. When he was eleven years old, he worked as the janitor for teachers Woodruff and Underwood. Underwood described him in 1916: "'Ezra' our janitor, aged eleven, is as good as gold—and as freckled as they make 'em. He . . . has bright red hair and is really one of the funniest looking boys I've ever seen."[332]

Lewis Harrison was the youngest boy among the seniors. While he was in eighth grade his parents hosted Underwood and Woodruff and he had become their respected and revered horse wrangler and guide. Lewis was the youngest of eight children and by 1919, all of his older siblings had moved away. His sister Marj married a local ranch manager, Evan Marr, and returned home frequently. His brother Frank, who had returned from World War I, was working as a coal miner at Mt. Harris. Lewis's parents, Uriah Franklin (known as U.F.) and Mary had tried various ventures—including a telephone company, horse mortgaging, buying and selling land and livestock—before settling down with a herd of cattle on their homestead along Calf Creek. Their pastures and grain fields were prosperous compared to their neighbors. They were close to the Adair-Solandt Ranch and accessible from the main road through Elkhead. The Harrison's two-story sawed log house was a significant grade above the dugouts and single-room log cabins that sheltered his fellow students. Lewis was quick and good at math. He skipped a grade in high school and was ready for senior year when he was seventeen.

Helen Jones was much older than her classmates; she would turn twenty-one just as school started in September. For years she and her parents had listed her age as two years younger than she was, probably so that she could fit in and be eligible to stay in high school. Her parents, Herbert and Minnie Mae, were in their mid-fifties. Their homestead on Calf Creek had always been a marginal, threadbare enterprise. Helen was the sixth of eleven children; she had three older sisters and two older brothers and three younger sisters and two younger brothers. One of her brothers, Herbie Jones, had died a few months after the family arrived from Quincy, Michigan, in 1910. Every teacher, starting with the earliest in Elkhead, expressed concern about the "state" of the family. It was alarming to see the many children crammed into a one-room log home, their father, who was healthy but usually without work, and their mother, a determined person who loved music but appeared unprepared for homesteading. The family was often being rescued. Helen, however, was a steadfast student, rarely missing a day, and she gradually completed high school despite being many years behind.[333]

In late August, Ferry Carpenter was working on a Friday night in his converted bowling alley office, earning fifteen dollars per month as the town attorney. A friend stopped by to invite him to a community dance in Hayden. Carpenter said he was too busy; the weekend before had been his big birthday celebration at his

Ferry Carpenter's office, formerly a single-lane bowling alley in downtown Hayden. Carpenter had a waiting room, his office, and a small private room with a bed in the rear.

homestead with a dance performance by the Rocky Mountain Dance School from Steamboat. Nevertheless, his friend persuaded him to come to hear the Craig Orchestra, which was in town to play for the dance.

The Craig Orchestra was a creation of two musical brothers who lived in neighboring Moffat County. Floyd Pleasant was a banker in Craig; his brother John had a general store in Maybell. Both were married and had young children. They each played several instruments and with a couple of other musicians formed a popular orchestra. Their sister, Eunice Pleasant, was taking a vacation before she began teaching high school English in Tulsa, Oklahoma. Carpenter and Eunice Pleasant met at the dance. By the following Wednesday, Pleasant had completely changed her plans. Her letter to her sister-in-law in Tulsa describes the persuasive powers of Carpenter and the lure of Elkhead.

"Here is the proposition that came up," she wrote on August 27.

> At the dance at Hayden Friday night I met Ferry Carpenter, a young ranchman who lives ten miles out from there, and he told me of a school out there. At first, I said "Nothing doing" as I already had several such suggestions. But he began telling me about his model school with a cottage built for the two teachers, domestic science equipment, piano, electric lights, moving pictures, and so on, and I said I'd like to see the establishment, anyway. He urged that I have Floyd bring me out to his house Sunday, and he would show me the rest. We were all ready to rest from many festivities when Sunday came and I wasn't especially interested anyway. But they all began to tell me how wonderful this place was, and how many lovely winter sports there were, and how the dances out at this school were famous for miles around and attended by Hayden people, and what an enterprising community was out there, with many wealthy ranchers, and so on. This place is

> as much a community center, as a school. Mr. Carpenter still seemed anxious to have me come; so I caught a ride to Hayden Monday morning, saw him at his law office, was taken out to his ranch, ten miles, by another man, where I had dinner with his sister and a Chicago teacher who is also there for the summer. Then we all went over to the school. I found it fully up to specifications, and they offered me the job right off the bat. We stopped to see a woman on the board, and she said to tell Mr. Carpenter to go ahead and do what he saw fit. He isn't on the board, but it is his district and he used to be on, and the entire board told him to go ahead and get them a teacher since he was there in town. The first teachers they had in this new building were two girls from Smith, and it is the standard they are trying to keep up, it seems.[334]

Eunice Pleasant was thirty-one, unmarried and self-supporting. She had grown up in Lyndon, Kansas, a town of 808 residents, located 31 miles straight south of Topeka. She had four older brothers and two younger brothers. Her father was a small-town attorney. Her mother died when she was twenty-five. In the six years before she came to Elkhead, Eunice had been teaching school, going to college, and taking care of her father and two younger brothers. Her college education had come in fits and starts; she would attend for a semester and leave to teach in a small, rural school to raise money for her next semester. She eventually graduated Phi Beta Kappa from Kansas University in 1915, majoring in English. She got her first-class teaching certificate in 1918 and a high paying and prestigious job in Tulsa, Oklahoma. She was looking forward to living near her brother, Carl, and his wife, her former roommate and close friend, Gertrude.

Pleasant pondered her decision to cancel her contract in Tulsa to teach in Elkhead in many letters to her sister-in-law. Finally she sent a telegram to Superintendent Oberholzer in Tulsa: "Wish release from contract to take homestead here. Health has improved so much here that feel I ought not return." She did not say that she had accepted another teaching position. She told her sister-in-law that what she had telegrammed was "as near the truth as anything I could wire them."[335] The school board offered her $125 per month, the teacherage rent free, and all of her "light and fuel." Over the coming months, Pleasant continued to circle back to her decision to teach in Elkhead and she always found again the joys of independence, her own home, and recognized how much better she felt riding a horse and spending time outside under the clear skies.

Pleasant was also intrigued by a school that was a community center. She was aware that her qualifications as a teacher were more than sufficient for the job, but she was surprised by her central role in the community and the expectation that she would lead the community center. She described her interview with Paroda Fulton, the school board member, as one of the most unusual she had ever experienced.

> I have met all kinds of school boards, and been asked all kinds of questions, but this is the first time a school board member ever asked me whether I danced, with the idea that my being fond of dancing is in my favor. That, and whether I played the piano are the only qualifications, I believe, that the woman asked me about. There is a movable partition between the two rooms, which they roll up or back, and then they use the two rooms for dancing. How's that for an up-to-date country school?[336]

Pleasant began teaching in Elkhead in the first week of September, after Labor Day, but waited until the community made all the repairs she requested before she moved into the teacherage. For the first several weeks, Pleasant lived with her predecessor,

Art Horton with his fiddle. To his right, Elizabeth Stanwood and Ruth Carpenter Woodley. Horton and his brother, Reece, homesteaded between Elkhead Creek and Dry Fork on what was later was referred to as Horton Hill. Art Horton was prominent among many musicians in Elkhead who regularly played at dances.

the former high school teacher, Ruth Bodfish Fulton. The two became lasting friends, "the only good pal near," she wrote a few months later. Ruth was living with her new husband, Ed Fulton, on a mesa above Dry Fork. Pleasant learned to ride horseback and carefully chose and purchased her own horse which she named Partner. Of the horse she wrote, "it's as thrilling as having a new Steinway Baby Grand!"[337]

She explained her purpose in writing so many letters to her sister-in-law: "When I occasionally send you a long letter with account of things here, if you find it interesting, I wish you would save it, as I might use the bunch and write this up some day. First impressions are sometimes the most striking, and are hard to keep."[338] She held to that promise; she wrote over 31,000 words over the next eight months, detailing her experience living and teaching in Elkhead.

Enrollment at the Rock Schoolhouse was around thirty pupils when school began in September. Over the following months it grew to over forty. Iva Rench had twenty-five students in the primary grades, including seven in the first grade, presumably enrolled in school for the first time. Eunice Pleasant had somewhere between fifteen and twenty students in grades seven through twelve. The ages of the children did not necessarily correlate with their grade level. Rench taught a group that ranged in age from four to fifteen and Pleasant taught secondary students who ranged in age from eleven to twenty-one.

The Freeman family, who like the Fergusons, Morsbachs and Hayeses, came to Elkhead from Medicine Lodge, Kansas, had four children between the ages of four and ten. The Freeman boys were not enrolled in school for some time because Jimmie (age eight) and Paul (age seven) were both placed in first grade with their sister Elizabeth who was only four. Their oldest sister, Louise (age ten), had somehow kept up with her class and enrolled in fifth grade.

The Hayes family of Calf Creek listed five children on the school census but only three attended. Guy Hayes, back from WWI, was twenty or twenty-one and counted as a ninth grader but probably never attended school. His brother Ray, who was fifteen, was sent to the state mental institution in Pueblo in August 1919. The last grade listed for him was grade three in 1916 when he was twelve. Only a short note in the newspaper explained his removal from Routt County. In the article his name was confused with that of his older brother, Roy. "Roy Hayes of Elkhead was taken to Pueblo a few days ago as he has been mentally afflicted and it is hoped the change will help him."[339] He would become the youngest inmate at the insane asylum. Of his siblings, Ina (age sixteen) was a senior, Roy (age thirteen) was in seventh grade and Morgan, who had turned six over the summer, was in first grade.

The Jones family, who had moved to Elkhead from Michigan with eleven children in 1909, still had five children in school. Helen, a senior, was the oldest at twenty-one, followed by Florence (age seventeen) in ninth grade, Yoleta (age sixteen) also in ninth grade, Tommy (age fifteen) in fifth grade and Minnie (age nine) also in fifth grade.

Pleasant was fundamentally an English teacher. She was competent in other high school subjects, and willing to push her students to achieve in math and science, but her focus and her greatest ambitions for her students were to excel in expression—to be articulate—well-spoken and eloquent in written English.

Pleasant created a class for her high school students called "Oral English" in which students were asked to tell a story or make an argument out loud, in front of the whole class. She also started a Better Speakers Club to encourage the students to improve their public speaking.

All of the students in Elkhead had always received bountiful instruction in writing. The teachers insisted on good penmanship and, like other schools at that time, focused heavily on grammar.

The whole educational system was oriented to grammar and daily lessons in the subject were considered essential. Where Elkhead teachers diverged early on was in placing equal or more weight on expository and creative writing. Children typically created a play from a book they had read. They also wrote autobiographical essays and short stories. The best were performed or published for the community.

Beginning under Bodfish and flourishing under Pleasant, the students practiced a wide range of narrative writing about Elkhead itself. All the students contributed articles to the *Rimrock Echoes*, the handwritten community/school newspaper. For years, the students read the paper aloud every few weeks to whoever came to listen. Starting in 1917, the unsigned "Elkhead Items" published nearly every Friday in the Hayden newspaper were replaced with carefully polished and signed articles written by the students. Later in the year, the Regional Survey approach added further inspiration to the writing curriculum; students at all levels researched aspects of their home place and turned their work into essays.

Pleasant in particular was a careful critic and she did not consider a piece of writing finished until it had been edited and rewritten several times. Under her influence, the high school students worked on developing a clear, authoritative style. Pleasant had taken many courses in journalism and she favored essays that were full of information, mingled with a bit of wit. Leila Ferguson later commented that when she got to college her professors and fellow students assumed that she would be ill-prepared because she had come from such a small high school in a rural area. But the opposite was true. "When I went to college, I found I had college students coming to me for help with English."[340]

Through the fall, a friendship grew between Carpenter and Pleasant. Although he was immersed in several projects, Carpenter renewed his involvement in the Rock School. He organized a Boy Rangers group that practiced calisthenics and took camping and fishing trips together. He also taught a weekly civics class. When Pleasant rode to town for supplies she would stop by Carpenter's law office and when he came up to Elkhead he would drop by the teacherage. Carpenter gave Pleasant a pair of his old army trousers (known as puttees) for horseback riding and he brought her a barrel of homemade oatmeal cookies. He also made sure she had plenty of hay to feed her horse.

As was the custom, dances were frequent at the schoolhouse and the "come one, come all" invitation extended to Routt County, and sometimes beyond. Pleasant quickly adapted to local festivities: when she wasn't dancing, she was playing the piano. She preferred to accompany "community sings," as she called them, but when some percussion was needed for the dances, she willingly sat at the piano and pounded out the chords. She and Carpenter, who had met at a dance, were often dance partners. As she described in a letter:

> The dance out here was very different from the one in town, but lots of fun. The people out here do the old-fashioned square dances and quadrilles, and so on. They do the late dances, too, but sprinkle these others through the program. I had thought I couldn't do one at all; but when the first one was called, I happened to have it with Mr. Carpenter and he pushed and shoved me around through it, and it got along very well. After that I boldly sailed in. They are stacks of fun. I had never seen them except about once, I guess, in the days of my childhood, when I was taught that all dancing was one of the wiles of the devil. And the people out here do them nicely, too, and gracefully. Ever see a waltz quadrille?[341]

Carpenter and Pleasant were also serious readers. The two traded books and articles and talked regularly about how the Elkhead School and community could be improved. Both of them were reformers at heart, civic to their core, and they shared a love of conversation. One afternoon in early October, Pleasant stopped by Carpenter's office with her load of provisions after an efficient shopping trip through Hayden. She had left her horse in the town's livery barn and had a little time before she needed to ride back to Elkhead. Carpenter kept a fire going in his potbellied stove; his office was known for its coziness, with cowhides on the floor and wainscoting along the narrow walls.

Carpenter had just read an article in the *Christian Science Monitor* that he wanted to discuss with Pleasant. The article, titled "Regional Survey," described an educational vision developed by the Scottish sociologist Patrick Geddes.[342] Although best known for his work in urban planning, Geddes was a polymath and regularly crossed into other disciplines. He wanted school children to study their surroundings. His plan for British schools had children begin with an intensive study of topography or geographical features, and later move on to study botany and zoology. After these elements had been thoroughly researched, children studied humans from a local perspective. Geddes thought children could investigate the anthropology and sociology of their communities and form an understanding of, even discover on their own, the economy of their locale. Ultimately, the idea was that schools would become local depositories, like museums and libraries, for all the information the students had gathered and synthesized. The children would become experts in where they lived; the school would be the place to find facts and insights about the district that could be used as a base for improvement and reform.

The short and fairly abstract article in the *Monitor* inspired Pleasant. She and her fellow teacher, Iva Rench, were already inclined to study the region. They, like many Elkheaders, shared a vision of the school as the center of the community. Pleasant also felt that there were many interesting stories in Elkhead that were worthy of exploration: perhaps the students could prepare a history of the area, one that could become a book. Like Bodfish, she also understood that her students would do their best writing when they wrote about their own experience and what they knew.

The frequent mention of Mr. Carpenter in Pleasant's letters evidently caused Pleasant's sister-in-law to ask some pointed questions. Pleasant sent her this reply:

> No, Ferry Carpenter isn't married, which makes him all the more unique. He is responsible for this whole school and all its improvements, and still looks after things as you see, tho he is no longer on the school board here, but is on the board in town. His ranch is in this district and he has a law office in town. From inscriptions in his books, he was in Princeton about 907 and 909. From wind and weather, he looks older than Carl. He is very tall and lanky. All the men out here are thin. I haven't seen a fat man since I came. In his private library in his office he has all kinds of fine books (from which I helped myself to all the history reference books I wanted for school); and at that dance at which I met him in Hayden he appeared in a blue shirt with collar attached. Can you put the two together? I've never seen him with a white collar on—oftener with boots and spurs. But he and his office and his house are neat as a pin. And I never saw anyone so thoughtful or so generous. This whole community just idolizes him.
>
> I could make my headquarters in his office in Hayden for a day without anyone paying any attention; and have expected telegrams delivered to him; and so on and so on. He's all business—and kind friendliness—and immune to other sentiment. When he tells of some little incident, it's just a scream, it's so funny. He's just as good to everybody in Hayden and Elkhead as he has been to me.[343]

That fall, Carpenter and Pleasant found they had many common interests, but it was not until mid-winter 1919-1920, when the flu returned to Elkhead, that they became trusted colleagues and close friends.

The Spanish Flu, or "the Great Epidemic," first struck Elkhead in December 1918 when it took the life of George Hughes, Jr. His homesteading parents, George and Willmenia (Minnie) Hughes, were too sick to attend the funeral. After their son's death, the family sold their interest in the Bears Ears sawmill. George Hughes left Elkhead and went to work as a coal miner.[344] A week after Hughes died, a neighbor to the west, Mrs. Anton Balleck, also died; she left behind five young children. The local paper reported over fifty families sick with the flu in Mt. Harris. Men returning from war to the cramped quarters of the coal mines and company town hastened the spread of the disease. Hayden schools were closed from October 1918 until mid-January 1919 and all civic events were cancelled. Notices in the paper that winter reminded readers that there were no dances and that organizations had suspended all meetings and parties.

Flu viruses typically strike old people and young children the hardest, but this flu attacked those in the middle, young men and women between the ages of eighteen and forty. The Spanish Flu, as it was called, may have set off a "cytokine storm" in its victims—an over-reaction of the body's immune system—that caused the victim's lungs to fill with fluid. Death came very fast, sometimes within a few hours of being infected. This flu, which may have developed in China prior to WWI, took its name from the death-toll in Spain during the first wave of the disease. The war greatly aided the flu's spread; troops moved all over the world and young people carried the disease home when they left the front.

The first reported outbreak of the epidemic in the United States was in central Kansas in January 1918. In March, the flu struck Fort Riley and Camp Funston where Ferry Carpenter and others had gone to teach or be trained. A week later, it appeared in Queens, New York. The first wave, that winter and spring, was less deadly than the second, which began in August in Boston and other cities around the world. Eventually, one in five people in the United States came down with the flu; close to a third of the world's population was infected. In the United States, an estimated 500,000 to 675,000 people died. Globally, the numbers were similar or worse; an estimated 50 to 100 million people died, approximately three percent of the world's population—far more than perished in the war. The epidemic remains the most deadly of any in recorded history.[345]

Both Ferry Carpenter and Eunice Pleasant may have been exposed to the flu before it reached northwest Colorado. Pleasant was from Lyndon, Kansas, about ninety miles from Camp Funston. Carpenter was in Camp Funston in 1917 before he was transferred to Georgia and then to Arkansas. In October 1918 he was moved again to Brownsville, Texas, where he was in charge of training young college students for the war. A week after his first group of recruits arrived the unit was struck by the epidemic. Out of the 173 men in his charge, 122 became ill with the flu. Carpenter set up infirmaries and arranged for medical care. He battled the flu among his charges through the Armistice in November 1918. Only two men died under his care. In December the college students finally returned to their homes and colleges; they were never trained, much less deployed to war.[346]

Thus, in a curious coincidence, both Carpenter and Pleasant were near the epicenter of the flu as it emerged in Kansas in 1918. They did not know each other, nor were they likely aware they were located at the site of the flu's first appearance in the United States. They were probably exposed to the milder version of the flu, its first version, which gave them immunity to its later, more virulent forms. Neither of them got sick, even when they were both in nearly constant contact with sick people in subsequent years.

There was a lull in the flu's spread at the end of 1918. Schools in Hayden reopened; the parties and dances resumed. For most of

1919, there were no cases of the flu reported in Routt County. Then, just as Pleasant and Rench began the school year in September 1919, young people in Routt County began to fall ill with a flu that was deadlier than the earlier versions.

Frank Maynard fell sick but recovered in September 1919. A few months later, teacher Iva Rench was too ill to work. Ina Hayes and her fellow senior in high school, Leila Ferguson, were drafted as substitutes until a more permanent replacement could be found. Rench was bedridden for months.

All of the Fultons, including their year-old baby boy, were sick by January, as were the Freemans and the Jones families. In Hayden, the editor of the newspaper wrote on January 16, 1920, that "It would be fully as easy to give the names of those who have not been sick as to try to give the names of those who have been sick."[347] Carpenter drew on his experience in Brownsville and called in Dr. Lowell Little, a physician at Mt. Harris. Dr. Little arranged for a Red Cross nurse to come from Denver. Nurse Grace Dailey was headquartered at the teacherage, which was turned into a makeshift infirmary.

In mid-January, Jake and Ira Smith were working at the Pilot Knob sawmill and returned home in a hurry when they learned that Ira's wife and child were sick with the flu. Perhaps Jake was exposed to the virus at his brother's house: a few days later his entire family, Ed and Hannah Smith, and their four children came down with the flu as well.

The following week, Eunice Pleasant received news through the mutual telephone operator that her sister-in-law, Frances, was dying in Craig. The cause was a brain tumor but, given the timing and that others in her household were sick, it is likely that the flu contributed to her sudden decline. Pleasant rushed to Craig by wagon, horseback and automobile and arrived just before Frances died on Sunday. Pleasant's brother, Floyd, was soon enmeshed in a difficult family dispute. His wife's parents in Overton, Indiana, insisted in curt telegrams that the body of their daughter be returned home and that their three grandchildren be sent to them to be raised in Indiana. Floyd, with strong support from his sister, agreed to transport the body for burial but refused to give up his children. Pleasant and her brother, Floyd, decided that only the eldest son, Sid, would go on the train with his father for the funeral and burial. The baby, Floyd Junior, would stay with a family in Craig, and Rex, the middle child, who was ten years old and himself recovering from the flu, would go to Elkhead with Pleasant.

The Rock School had been closed for several days in January due to the flu but had reopened again just before Pleasant rushed to Craig. Pleasant worried that the students, particularly the seniors, would fall behind in their work. With Iva Rench still sick, the district decided it should not continue to use Leila and Ina as substitutes. The school board hired a temporary replacement from Craig, Mrs. Fairbrother, who took up lodgings in the teacherage, joining the Red Cross nurse who had been brought in from Denver while Pleasant was away.

On Wednesday, Pleasant, her brother, two nephews, and the casket traveled together on the early morning eastbound train from Craig. Pleasant and her nephew Rex got off in Hayden while her brother and nephew Sid continued on to Denver and then to Indiana. Ferry Carpenter, who knew Floyd well and had heard about Frances's death, came to Pleasant's aid. He borrowed a sled and team from Jack White and drove Eunice and Rex up to Elkhead that afternoon. Along the way they stopped at several homesteads to check on sick and grieving families. They learned that Elmer (Jake) Smith, age twenty-three, had died suddenly after he returned from the sawmill. He had gone out to do evening chores in the snow and when he came back into the house he acted as though he had pneumonia; he died that night. Jake was known for his ability to work with horses and for his inventive and mischievous sense of humor. Like nearly all the Smith children, he had sandy, red hair and blue eyes. No one could believe that a young man so healthy and strong could die so suddenly.[348]

Pleasant was very aware of her nephew Rex's state of mind and had promised him a horse to ride in Elkhead. On the long ride up from Hayden, she noticed that "he began to look awfully solemn" and worried that he would be lonely and distraught.[349] When Carpenter, Pleasant and Rex finally arrived at the teacherage late in the afternoon they were met by the Red Cross nurse, Grace Dailey, who according to Pleasant "rushed out from my house to meet us, threw up her hands and said to Ferry 'Never again!'" Pleasant made everyone lunch while Carpenter persuaded the nurse to take a horse and visit the ailing families they had seen along the way. Rex, she wrote, "looked out the west window toward the mountains and said, 'it looks awfully lonesome up here.'"[350]

Pleasant spent the next month taking care of Rex, teaching high school and running the infirmary in the teacherage. She also rode her horse all over the district attending to "flu-stricken" families. There was no medicine that would cure the flu, nor were there any sure remedies for the symptoms—high fevers and a rapid and severe lung congestion. People realized early on that good nursing could save lives, but even more essentially, people needed to rest and stop doing the ordinary labor that defined them as homesteaders. Feeding livestock, chopping wood and doing laundry by hand were arduous tasks, but in the middle of the winter they required more than ordinary strength. Jake Smith's death was among many warnings to Elkheaders that those with the flu needed to stay warm and in bed.

While school was closed for two weeks, Pleasant and other neighbors who were well went from homestead to homestead, tending to the sick and doing their chores. One morning Pleasant swept out Iva Rench's cabin and in the afternoon she did Fulton's washing. She bathed sick people and took food and "delicacies" to others. "Everything except caring for the sick," she said at the end of January, "has looked like a nonessential, to be omitted. If you could see the dreadful state of my clothes you would disown me. And school work is piled mountain high."[351]

By the time school began again in the second week of February, she was exhausted. "I've had the only blue days I've had on Elkhead these two weeks," she wrote, "but I know things will soon be all right again."[352] In the same paragraph, she apologized for feeling sorry for herself. Others were so much worse off. She told the story of Susie Jones Hood, wife of James Hood, who had just given birth to her second child in her parents' cabin near the school. "Monday, Mrs. Jones stopped at my room at school to show me that she had taken absorbent cotton and so on from the First Aid box at school, and told me that her daughter, Mrs. Hood, was going to have a baby, probably before the doctor could come out from town." After describing the humble cabin, she asked, "How would you like to be Mrs. Hood? And no one out here—of the natives, that is—seems to think the occurrence so very unusual. The only thing for which I was called upon, was safety pins, for the infant's clothes."[353]

Carpenter and Pleasant both marveled that they, among all their neighbors and friends, did not get sick in Kansas, Texas, or Colorado. Their work with the flu victims sealed the bond between them. During that long winter, the two became confidants. When Pleasant's home was full of sick students and the substitute teacher was driving her to distraction with her helplessness, she turned to Carpenter. The two found time alone on horseback to talk. She said she loved riding at any time, "but it is always more fun with someone, and Ferry Carpenter is a circus, all by himself." They would ride and talk for hours. "It surely is a grand relief to talk to someone to whom one can boil over a little after such a strenuous week," Pleasant wrote.[354]

After her sister-in-law Frances's death, Pleasant faced family pressure to quit her job teaching in Elkhead so that she could help her brother, Floyd, raise his family. It was the sort of thing that a good sister would do, especially given the pressures her brother was feeling from his wife's family in Indiana. Pleasant had evidently heard such questions before and she deftly said "no." "I wouldn't feel I could leave Elkhead this way in the middle of the year," she wrote. "It isn't like a city school where one is only a cog in the wheel. They simply wouldn't be able to find anyone to take my place up here."[355]

Ferry Carpenter and Eunice Pleasant on horseback in front of Carpenter's homestead, circa 1920.

In early February, another fear—darker and more personal than the flu—rippled through the Elkhead community. James Oldham had been sentenced to life at Canon City in 1916 for the death of Cliff Fulton. In September of 1919 he petitioned for a commutation of his sentence but was unsuccessful. A few months later, the warden at Canon City, faced with severe overcrowding, asked that forty-four prisoners be reviewed and possibly transferred to the state asylum in Pueblo. Oldham was among those investigated by the Lunacy Commission and in late February 1920, he was declared insane and eligible for the transfer

Many Elkheaders—the Fultons and Ferry Carpenter among them—immediately felt threatened. Oldham had expressed no remorse for his shooting spree. George Smith, the editor of the *Routt County Republican*, weighed in: escapes were common from the asylum, he said, and if Oldham returned to Routt County, lives would be in danger. The Fultons were particularly concerned. Even while he was in prison with little hope of release, Oldham had continued to petition courts in Colorado and Ohio for the money he claimed Charles Fulton owed him. He still imagined himself the injured party and contended that the Fultons unjustly claimed he was insane.

Ferry Carpenter was quick to respond to the Lunacy Commission. He wrote letters to the commission and to the Colorado governor on behalf of the Elkhead community, stating that Oldham was capable of escaping and would continue to kill if he was released. His interventions were successful. In early March, Governor Shoup sent a note to Carpenter assuring him that Oldham would not be moved from Canon City and added that the commission had found him to be a "dangerous character."[356]

Life finally got back to normal—Elkhead normal—in March. The flu had retreated. The Red Cross nurse went back to Denver. The new Hood baby, named Marjory, was doing well. There was a lot of snow on the ground and Elkheaders were running out of feed for their livestock. Attendance was high at school and the five seniors were back diligently leaning into their studies. Pleasant, who had tackled her mountain of schoolwork, now focused most of her attention on making sure that the seniors completed their final year of high school. She expected the students to pass all their examinations and to be ready for college. Graduation was on the horizon, an accomplishment not only for the five young promising students but for the entire community.

CHAPTER FIFTEEN

Graduation

(1920)

April 2, 1920

Mr. Carpenter gave his third lecture in Civics, "How a Bill Becomes a Law," on Friday afternoon to the High school room. The class acted as the House of Representatives and the Senate introducing, debating and voting on a bill.

Ina Hayes entertained the High school pupils with a big turkey dinner Sunday evening at her home.

The English class has just finished an analytic study of magazines including all types from the Atlantic to the Breeders' Gazette taking in consideration the make up, purpose and contents of each.

Elizabeth Freeman returned to school again after an absence of several months.

The English Literature class is now studying the Modern Drama and reading John Drinkwater's Abraham Lincoln.

Ferry Carpenter and Clarence Freeman have been the Elkhead mail carriers the past week.

A. Ferguson is spending a few weeks in Southern Colorado while on his way to Oregon.

The question of feed is becoming serious in this locality as the March storms have continued all week with several inches of snow daily.

Several of the young people here attended a dance at the Reed home in Long Gulch Friday evening and they report a very enjoyable time.

Mrs. U. F. Harrison has returned home after spending several weeks at Oak Creek with her daughter.

"East Elkhead," *Routt County Republican.*

Eunice Pleasant had a Kodak camera she treasured. One early spring day, after the flu had finally passed, she skied out from the teacherage on a path through a stand of oak brush, over the still-deep snow. Her close friend Sophia Neilson, now a teacher in Hayden, had given her the new pair of skis. Pleasant stopped on an open field, smooth and white with snow, the sagebrush and grass completely covered. She turned back to the north and took a photograph. The image centered on Bear's Ears, the two volcanic mounds that rise up several hundred feet from the surrounding ridge, nearly covered in snow, with sections of vertical rock and pine-covered slopes figuring as the only dark areas in the picture. To the left, the northwest, was the rugged outline of Aigner Mountain; to the right, the basalt dikes, a set of parallel stone walls that had been the source of rocks for the schoolhouse. Three single-room log cabins and a larger sawed log house with a high peaked roof stand out in the photo's foreground. In the background, further up the hill, away from the saddle where the school sits, and closer to the dike, is the teacherage, its prominent bay window looking west out of the upstairs attic bedroom. It is possible to see that the snow has melted off the schoolhouse roof, and around the base of the rock walls the ground looks tramped down and muddy. Just in front of the schoolhouse, what would have been about fifty feet downhill, is an open shed, where Pleasant sheltered her horse and stored her hay.

The whole scene is both wild and homey. With the big open sky and no trees taller than the oak brush, the view is unbroken and immense. The natural world is dominant. At the same time, there is ample evidence of people and their hard work: their school, their teacherage, their little houses and their shed for domestic animals.

When she took the photograph, in late March 1920, during so much hardship, but nearing a moment of crowning achievement, Pleasant had decided to stay in Elkhead. "I am about of the notion that this part of the country is the place for me to take permanent root," she wrote in one of her last letters from the teacherage. "I feel I can turn myself loose out here, and be myself, and not someone else's notion of what I ought to be, and I like it."[357]

Rock Schoolhouse and teacherage from the east. In the distance are Elkhead and Calf Creeks. March 1920.

A census taker, James Funk, traveled on horseback around Elkhead that spring. He enumerated 50 homes and took down the names and occupations of 190 residents in the 1920 census. It was a fairly accurate count, though for some reason, the census included neither Pleasant nor Carpenter. Although some families had moved out—the Galloways, Graves, Murphys, Robinsons and Rileys—others were moving in. Very few were able to start a new homestead, but it was common for newcomers to buy patented land if they could not take over a claim by buying a relinquishment. Two new families, the Ingles and the McBrides, had moved into Elkhead the previous winter.

The Rock School had been anchored on the hillside in the center of the community for nearly five years. In that time, various buildings and enterprises had sprung up around the school. No one seemed to mind that people were building private homes on the school grounds. With a forty-acre yard there was little need to squabble; the general feeling was that families should be encouraged to nestle around the schoolhouse in the winter, almost like boarders, if it helped keep their children in school. The Jones family moved into the Huguenin cabin near the schoolhouse, the one the early teachers had called a hog pen because at that time it was just log walls without a roof or floor. They operated a small grocery store and maintained the post office from the front room while they cooked and slept in the back room. After they recovered from the flu, the nine members of the Freeman family also moved into a vacant cabin near the school so that the children could finish the term. Iva Rench had built a one-room log cabin about a quarter mile north of the school on land she and her brother owned. Together, the five log houses and the stone teacherage formed a village cluster around the Rock School.

When Louis Charos did not return to Elkhead immediately after the war, Pleasant considered buying a pre-emption claim on his deserted homestead. She abandoned that idea when news filtered into the community that Charos was in Denver with a Russian wife and intended to return. She was then tempted by 160 acres that were "all proved up." This was most likely George and Mary Murphy's homestead on lower Dry Fork. The Murphys had been early supporters of a community center: the first votes were taken to form a school district at their home. When they departed in the summer of 1919 the community gave them a big party at the schoolhouse. The 160 acres was for sale for $2,000. Pleasant thought her mortgage would be too high; she deferred to Carpenter, who said he might buy it for pasture.

Carpenter rode his horse the five or so miles from his homestead cabin nearly every Thursday to teach the civics class and convene his group of Boy Scouts and Boy Pioneers. Pleasant was a stickler for standards but she delighted in Carpenter's teaching. "If I could get as much out of these youngsters as he can, I'd be proud of myself," she wrote. "But he is so fine with them, it isn't any wonder they adore him. And his civics class is a wonder. You would think he had had years of training in conducting classes, in addition to excellent aptitude for it."[358]

Pleasant and Carpenter fell into a habit of having lunch together in the teacherage on the days when Carpenter came up to teach. In the afternoon after the lesson, Pleasant would play the piano and Carpenter would lead the children in singing. His favorites were marching songs he had learned in the Army, like "Hurray, Hurrah, Father is going to be hung. Hurray, Hurrah, the dirty son of a gun. He used to treat me awful mean when I was very young. And now they will hang him, poor father." He also loved the Elkhead school song, sung to the tune of "Tipperary."

After school was dismissed, Carpenter led his troop in exercises outside on the new sidewalk. Then, in late afternoon, Pleasant often accompanied Carpenter on his ride back to his homestead or to Hayden. Carpenter encouraged her to pursue her career in education. He thought she might become an expert on incorporating motion pictures into the curriculum. The matched set of reformers were constantly exploring new ideas for the school and community.

Life in the school was rich and complex in the winter and spring months leading up to graduation. Geddes' idea of a rural school as a research station, and the traditions of interweaving the needs and interests of the community with the work of the students to study and record their home place, passed from teachers like Mary McDowell and Ruth Bodfish and onto Rench and Pleasant. By the spring of 1920 the school was experiencing a blossoming of extraordinary achievement by the Elkhead students.

Iva Rench, who shared a mutual respect with Pleasant, continued to turn the primary school students' attention to studying their homes and community. Instead of a focus on writing, she emphasized expression through drama, handicrafts and art. The primary classroom was bedecked with examples of the students' work. Described as "of great interest to all the visitors" and a "wonderful display," the walls were covered with "woven rugs, baskets, clay modeling, base relief maps of the school yard, the school district and the county, calendars and many paintings and works of art and designs."[359]

Studying and knowing who they were and where they were was part of the process by which students built a community, by which they became Elkheaders. It was also a means to tell outsiders, especially others in Routt County, how they were different and special. No longer were residents just individuals, with their personal names—they came to carry their community name. The school was the core of this process; students described the place, collected and published its stories, and preserved its history. They were like bees venturing out and returning to the hive, full of information and sentiment. Inside the hive, they turned their knowledge and experiences into essays and stories, plays and newspaper articles. They created honey in the form of pride and loyalty, which in turn nourished everyone and strengthened the sense of community.

The adults were working hard and generally alone on their homesteads. They didn't spend their days sitting at a desk in a furnace-heated room, chatting with their neighbors and writing about their lives and their place. Nor were parents in frequent contact with outsiders who noticed different things—like the view—and who asked different questions. Children, with the relative luxury of time and resources, with opportunity to reflect, and under the guidance of their devoted teachers, were in an

Eunice Pleasant at the Rock Schoolhouse door, 1919-1920.

environment where creativity thrived. Students were learning but they were also building, making, generating: contributing to the well-being of the whole.

Deep snow prevented Pleasant from taking the teachers' examination in Steamboat in December, so Carpenter arranged for her to take the test a few months later, in Craig. The road was passable in early March. Pleasant rode her horse the fifteen miles to Hayden. There, she found that the trains to Craig were not running. She encountered another teacher who had a horse, and together they rode seventeen miles to Craig through a heavy snowstorm. Pleasant described the two-day Colorado exams as the "old fogy kind of years ago in Kansas" and was confident that she had done well.[360] She spent a night with her brother and his children in Craig and then rode alone all the way back to the schoolhouse. When she got home, her face was burned and swollen. She wrote to her sister-in-law, "You've never saw such a wind-burned specimen as I am."[361]

Pleasant spent a following Sunday at home alone. Ezra and Ione Smith, her student boarders, skied down to Dry Fork to spend the weekend with their parents; Fairbrother and her young daughter had returned to Craig, leaving Pleasant the place to herself. She loved her cook stove and had no problems getting a good fire going, but she often struggled with the heater stove and depended on Ezra to keep it hot. With the boy gone, she fussed with the stove and tried to keep warm in her downstairs bedroom. She wanted to ride horseback to Hayden for supplies but the roads were so bad she decided against it. "The snow is now softening up, and the horses go through and fall down, so that the rider has to jump off, to help his horse out."[362]

She had a dinner invitation with the Hayes family on Calf Creek. She had planned to ride the nearly three miles to their house, a much shorter ride than to town, but her student Ina Hayes appeared on skis at the teacherage in the late afternoon and told her that the snow had drifted in the hard wind the night before and that a horse would not be able to get through. Pleasant considered skiing back with Ina but decided against it. "I feel somewhat like a piker not to ski back with her," she wrote. When the girl had left, Pleasant "went to the door to call to her that I was going, after all; but a blast of cold wind that I met changed my mind."[363] She settled down to study European history and to write her friend and sister-in-law a long letter. She reviewed the emerging crisis in the community with the heavy snows and the scarcity of food or feed for livestock. In closing her letter, she turned her attention back to Elkhead's first graduating class, the achievement that helped to balance out the growing sense of despair. "Now that the exams are off my hands," she wrote, "it is time to think about Commencement, for I really have a graduating class here, who deserve as nice a commencement as we can give them; and besides we have to uphold the reputation of the school."[364]

Ina Hayes on skis with one pole, 1920.

Pleasant began making plans that evening, but she knew that for an event to be successful it would need to be a community effort. First, she would check every detail with the seniors. Meeting in the optimistic warmth of the schoolhouse, the high school students decided to assemble a yearbook (which Pleasant referred to as an annual), put on a play, have a banquet for the graduates and their parents, invite a commencement speaker from outside the community, and wind it all up with a dance. Each class would perform exercises and the graduation itself would be a formal affair with a procession, speeches, diplomas and music. The students sent letters inviting a professor from Colorado University to give the commencement address and the Craig Orchestra to provide the music. Pleasant telegraphed an order to Denver for the script of a play, printed invitations, programs, and place cards for the banquet.

Train service between Denver and Hayden on the Moffat Line was erratic in March and came to a standstill in April. The Moffat railroad had been built on a pyramid of investors led by David Moffat. The business was coming apart again and the company was in receivership by March 1920. In addition to crippling financial troubles, the local paper reported that the train was "'tied up' by slides, snow drifts and other minor causes."[365] In mid-March there was a blockade of snow that stopped trains from going through Hot Sulphur Springs, a town on the west slope of the Rockies. There were more problems at Corona Pass, where the train crossed the Continental Divide and at various times slid off the rails; rescue trains were engulfed in avalanches of snow, forcing passengers to walk down the tracks to safety.

Without train service, no one in northwest Colorado could get mail. Two tons of undelivered mail piled up in a transit station. Some people resorted to taking the Denver and Rio Grande Railway to the station in Wolcott, in central Colorado, and walking the fourteen miles to State Bridge, where they could—at times—catch a train shuttling between stations on the west slope. Coal could not be shipped by rail and the mines decreased production and laid-off workers. Stores in Hayden, Mt. Harris and Craig were out of food.

It was not long before the animals began to suffer. Though there was still hay available for sale for a short time, at fifty dollars a ton, no one could afford it.[366] After the trains stopped running, there was no hay at all. Richard Ferguson remembered taking an axe to aspen trees to peel off the bark and feed it to cows and horses in a desperate effort to keep the animals from starving. His parents "had built up a small herd of highly productive Jersey cows and were doing well selling cream."[367] In the summer of 1919 they were milking over twenty cows and had several young shorthorn cattle and a few horses. "The winter had been very mild, but in March [1920] a tremendous blizzard came that lasted through April. We, the same as everyone else in the area, ran out of hay to feed the cattle."[368] Pleasant noted that she no longer had milk, cream or butter because the Armstrong milk cows had no feed and had presumably died. No one could get hay or grain for livestock. With the snow covering the ground, the animals could not even paw their way to something to eat. Many, including Pleasant, were miserable; they helplessly witnessed farm animals starving to death. "We may live in the city," she wrote, "and see a stray item in the paper that scarcely takes our eye, that stock is suffering, but you can have no idea what it is like until you live in the midst of it, and see what it means to people to see all their wealth disappear, and that in the pitiful way of seeing their livestock die of starvation."[369]

The sense of isolation was intense. Many people had arrived by train. They assumed that the train would always be available to take them to safety, or at least to bring in food for themselves and their domestic animals.

The snow continued to fall. At one point, the Oak Creek paper reported ten to twelve feet on the ground. The Hayden paper said that two new inches were falling every day. Pleasant wrote in late March that the telephone was still out, "and it leaves us rather cut off from the world."[370]

The crisis hit the families of Elkhead from many different directions. In late March, Leila Ferguson's father, Alex Ferguson, left home unexpectedly and did not come back. "The first thing we knew he went to Oregon," Leila Ferguson said.[371] He had traveled alone to Hayden, where he saw a doctor who advised him to go to a lower altitude. Then he went to Oak Creek and later to Montrose in southern Colorado where he found work. A few weeks later he had a massive stroke, but somehow continued his journey by train to Umatilla, Oregon. "His health failed completely," his daughter said.[372] The pressure was just too great. His prospects for paying even the interest on the debt were nearly nil given the heavy snow and the delayed spring. His livestock on which he depended for cash were dying. He could probably sense that even in the best of winters and the best of springs, he would not be able to make a living or pay off his debt because prices for agricultural products were falling steadily.[373]

The Fergusons had bought additional land and had at least twenty Jersey milk cows and several beef cattle. "There was mother left with the ranch and a bunch of dairy cattle," Leila said. "That was the spring of 1920, when people lost their cattle so. It snowed and snowed and snowed."[374] Her brother described the "tremendous blizzard" that came in March and "lasted through April." "We, the same as everyone else in the area, ran out of hay to feed the cattle. When grass did come, we only had four of the Jersey cows and a few yearlings left."[375]

Rench and Pleasant attempted to share what food they had with their students. Like the teachers before them, they were particularly concerned with the Jones family. "One after another they have all been sick, even to the tough little Tommy, undersized and fifteen," Pleasant wrote. "We have decided that they are a family of the 'underfed' children that you read about in sociology. All of the shelves of their grocery store are entirely empty, and we know for certain that they have had no groceries brought out from town since Christmas."[376] Rench invited children to her cabin for dinners and Pleasant rode horseback to take food and supplies to other students. She was particularly worried by one of her seniors, Helen Jones. "I have felt very sorry for Helen, who has taken care of all the rest, and now succumbed herself to ill-nourishment."[377] She invited Helen to spend the weekend at the teacherage with the purpose of giving her some "wholesome food." She also tried to give rest and comfort to Ina Hayes, who she felt was suffering under an emotional strain after the loss of her father and the mental illness of her brother. "I felt terribly sorry for her," she wrote. "Her father is dead, and they have a hard time to get along. Two brothers are feeble-minded and Ina fears it for all of them."[378] Pleasant described a night in the teacherage when Ina "shook, almost with nervous convulsions, all night long." She wrote that she "tried every method I could devise, psychological and otherwise, to put her to sleep, all in vain."[379]

Ione and Ezra Smith continued to live in the teacherage during the week while school was in session. Lewis Harrison, the other senior boy, broke his wrist and that spring he, too, moved into the teacherage to convalesce while still being able to attend school.

By mid-April, no one had enough to eat. Pleasant at one point reported that she hadn't had fresh meat in months, was out of milk, eggs, butter, fruit, potatoes and bacon. She had no ingredients for salad. She was also out of what she referred to as "substitutes," namely canned salmon and dried meat. Still she insisted she was much better off than her neighbors. She had "begged" a sack of flour from Mr. Freeman. Carpenter brought her a pound of butter in each pocket when he came up to teach his class at the end of April. No wonder she referred often to the luncheon for the graduates as a banquet and admitted it was her "pet plan at present."[380]

As graduation neared, Pleasant fretted. She had ordered supplies for the school and for the grand celebration the community envisioned, but the chances of receiving anything got smaller and smaller. "I heard today," Pleasant wrote near the end of April, "that there are two tons of mail over there for Routt County, waiting to be brought in. I have telegraphed for all sorts of materials that I have ordered for Commencement to be sent by first class mail, and even then, I do not get them."[381] Putting on a play was part of most school celebrations in Elkhead but without a script, practice could not begin. Nevertheless, the students and teachers continued to plan and prepare. Ione Smith and Yoleta Jones, younger sisters of two graduating seniors, hand lettered the invitations and programs; others prepared table decorations and planned the luncheon for the graduates and their families. Pleasant said, "I am going right ahead making plans galore for Commencement, but once in a while I get discouraged, and wonder whether there will be any good weather this side of July Fourth."[382] The students joined together and wrote their own play, dubbed a burlesque, which they titled: "A Day at Elk Head."

Pleasant was moved by a lengthy debate among the students about where to hold the senior banquet. The consensus that emerged was that if the midday dinner was to be by invitation it could not be held in the schoolhouse. Pleasant explained the sentiment of her students: "The class said that people would be offended if we had it at school, because the crowd comes early, and would be there before the dinner hour, and nothing has ever been given up here that excluded part of the community."[383] The public building must remain completely public and open to all. "Then I thought of the plan of giving it here in the teacherage," Pleasant wrote, and her high school students accepted her proposal.[384]

For forty-four days there was no train from Denver. The crisis became known as the Snow Blockade. In May, hundreds of workers and volunteers finally dug through the snow on Corona Pass. Miners from Mt. Harris, workers from the State Highway Commission, and hundreds of ordinary people shoveled through the packed snow to free the marooned rail cars and opened the line. On May 6, the first train made it over the divide from Denver, bringing passengers, mail and supplies. But it would be weeks, if not months, before life was back to normal.

The printed invitations on heavy cream paper came in the mail from Denver the week of May 7. They were delivered by hand and mailed in a hurry, but to be on the safe side the students included an invitation in the Hayden paper: "It is the earnest wish of the graduating class that everyone who has ever come to Elkhead return again and anyone who has never been here to make this an occasion for a visit."[385]

May 22 finally arrived. The weather was fine, but the mud was still too deep for motor vehicles. The Craig Orchestra could not come, a huge disappointment for Pleasant, who had put the orchestra on the agenda for both the class exercises in the afternoon and the graduation exercises in the evening. The mud did not deter the community: nearly every homesteader, rancher, cowpuncher, drifter, man, woman and child attended. They forded the surging creeks; they struggled on foot and on horseback through the clay. But they came.

At four in the afternoon "Class Day Exercises" began. Two local musicians, Joseph Cuber and Sam Reid, stepped in for the missing orchestra and opened with a selection of tunes.

Ina Hayes was the first speaker. She told the history of the class; she recalled her eighth-grade graduation exercises at the Rock School in 1915, the first ceremony in the new building. She and seven others took part in that graduation; four of them were now graduating from high school. She noted how "interwoven" her class was with the history of the school: "it is almost impossible to speak of the one without telling of the other," she said. The school had been built so that they "could continue their studies here at home." She described the long, bitterly cold winter of 1916-1917 when "in the mornings there were always at least a dozen small boys holding a crying concert around the furnace." She remembered how the students and teachers relished the winter sports—skiing and coasting over the snow. "We studied hard and played harder," she said of that year. Hayes recalled the two years with Bodfish, Neilson and Rench, when domestic science and manual training were added to the curriculum, though the emphasis was on the war. "Under the leadership of the teachers," she said, "school and community united in doing Red Cross work." Hayes said nothing of the double winter of 1919–1920, nor of the influenza pandemic, but she did not ignore the character traits that emerged from hardship.[386]

> It wasn't the easiest thing in the world to buck trail for two or three miles when the trail is drifted and your horse lunges and plunges; nor yet to ski, when the snow is loose and sticky. But, if as we are told, it is these things that develop grit, stick-to-it-ive-ness, and independence—well, the children who have gone to school on Elk Head, ought surely to have a superfluous amount of these qualities.[387]

She went on to describe the character of her community:

> And these hardships, shared by all the children of the community, have drawn the people of the community—the parents of the children, closer together; have made them better friends, and more loyal neighbors. And, if we had learned nothing else during our four years of high school here, I should count it worthwhile if we had absorbed even a little of the spirit—of that spirit of hospitality, loyalty, and friendship and true neighborliness, which characterizes Elk Head.[388]

The class song was next, a homemade ditty, with a rousing chorus of "Elk Head, our mountain school/Where pluck and loyalty are always the rule."

Leila Ferguson told the class prophecy and Ezra Smith delivered the class will. Leila predicted that Ezra would have "cattle sleek that roam the hills and bring him in carloads of bills." Ina would be a writer "famed is she, for stories of this wild country." Helen would be a cowgirl riding the range, and Lewis "a cook of great renown."

Ezra Smith read the "just disposal of all our scholastic effects" which gave "all future visitors of the school, the view from the west windows" and "the refrigerator, in which they have spent four cold and frosty winters" to Miss Rench's room. Each graduate gave their least favorite subject or textbook to a younger student and they appointed Pleasant executor "and direct that she shall serve without bond or security whatsoever."

The music provided an intermission followed by the burlesque "A Day at Elk Head." The students had ordered a script for a play in February but because the trains were blocked, nothing arrived until May 18, four days before graduation. Instead, the students had written their own play. No one kept the script, but portions of the story are threaded through the yearbook. One scene, titled *Routt County Hardship,* was recorded as follows:

> Miss P (in physiology class): If we had some fresh meat, we could perform this experiment. Can any of you bring meat to school?
>
> A boy (promptly and willingly): I can.
>
> Miss P (smiling and having in mind, delicious mutton or beef): Just ask your mother for a small piece. Beef is too costly to waste.
>
> The boy: It ain't beef—it's porcupine.

By this time, the attention of the whole room was attracted and Miss P, partially recovered from the shock, asks whether anyone can bring some fresh meat. Blank silence meets her request until a senior speaks up:

> "I can bring some porcupine, too!"[389]

Ezra Smith and Lewis Harrison graduation photo 1920.

Ina Hayes

Leila Ferguson

Helen Jones

The graduating girls, Helen Jones, Leila Ferguson and Ina Hayes, had ordered dresses for graduation in February. Two months of backed up mail came through on May 12th and "noon hour extended until 2:30 to open and read letters and packages" the students wrote.[390] But no dresses. The girls decided to make their own dresses, "very simply." In the photos that Pleasant took of the graduating class, the three young women are wearing white shirt waist dresses with big pockets. Ezra Smith and Lewis Harrison borrowed or bought suit jackets, which they wore over their best Sunday shirts.

Food was certainly on everyone's mind. Preparing the banquet for the seniors, their parents, the school board and invited guests was a preoccupation through the cold and snowy spring. Pleasant moved all her furniture and belongings in the teacherage upstairs and managed to fit tables and chairs to seat forty people in the downstairs rooms. The underclassmen worked as waiters. The guests were the graduates and their parents, past and present teachers, including Rosamond Underwood Perry and Ruth Bodfish Fulton, and former members of the school board, Paroda Fulton, Ed Smith and Ferry Carpenter. Special guests were the commencement speaker, J.F. Reynolds, an English professor from the University of Colorado in Boulder, and Emma Peck, Routt County Superintendent of Schools.

Everyone found a seat at a table adorned with arrangements of mountain wildflowers, name placards and the hand-lettered programs written by the younger students. These included the menu: Baked Ham, Creamed Potatoes, Scalloped Corn, Parker House Rolls, and Tomato Sponge Salad followed by Fruit Pudding, Cake and Coffee. Pleasant was the toastmistress and, as the meal was winding down, she opened the program for a series of short, prepared speeches:

Blazing the Trail by Mrs. Perry
Bronco Busting by Ina Hayes
The Open Range by Mr. Smith
The Round-up by Lewis Harrison
The Chuckwagon by Mrs. Fulton
Grass Grown Trails by Mrs. Peck
Locoed by Mr. Carpenter
Crossing the Divide by Professor Reynolds[391]

A short hour later, the dinner party concluded and all the guests walked back to the schoolhouse for the graduation exercises.

Fortunately, the programs had arrived in time. The newspaper in Steamboat, *The Pilot,* printed them using their hand press: a thick grey paper printed with ornate lettering and art deco designs in indigo blue ink. The front page featured an interesting design—two laurel branches formed a "V" around a scroll, a bottle of ink and a large feather. The Elkhead school was not only keeping up with the procession, they may have been outdoing it. The two local musicians stood in for the musical numbers and played what was expected to be "Poet and Peasant" overture by Von Suppe, but may have been a much more familiar tune. Reverend R.H. Warren then gave the invocation, followed by more music and the graduation address by J. F. Reynolds. Delcina Neilson's sister, Sophie Neilson, who taught school in Hayden, sang a solo, "Spring Song" by Rubinstein. Pleasant was always awed and moved by Sophia's "beautiful, rich contralto voice with a big range."[392]

Carpenter called out the names of the graduates: Leila Ferguson, Lewis Harrison, Ina Hayes, Helen Jones and Ezra Smith. They walked in front of the cheering crowd and received their diplomas. The Reverend gave the benediction, there was another musical interlude, and the ceremony ended.

No one expected to leave, even after the five or so hours of graduation celebrations. A few homesteaders got out their instruments—a fiddle, banjo and guitar—and Helen's mother, Minnie Mae Jones, no doubt played chords on the school piano. When Pleasant wrote of the dances that year she said, "Families come *en masse*, carrying bedding which they spread down behind the piano, or in some corner, and there, the babies are 'bedded down' for the night. There is always a midnight lunch of sandwiches, cake, and coffee." Everyone dances until "the cold, grey dawn."[393]

The high school graduation dance was no exception. Whoever wrote the report for the newspaper called it a "regular, old time Elkhead community dance [which] lasted till morning with supper served at midnight."[394] Quadrilles, squares, waltzes, polkas and something Pleasant called a 'waltz quadrille' kept people on their feet through the night.

For a few hours it was possible to forget, or at least set aside, the sickness and death caused by the flu, the father who had left his family and homestead, the snow, mud, suffering livestock, threatened foreclosures and hungry children. The schoolhouse was full of music, food and merriment. The five graduates had big plans. The Delco lights were on inside, illuminating the dancers as they spun around the floor. Outside, the summer constellations were just coming into view, the Milky Way, Venus, the Big Dipper, all bright and visible against the huge arc of night sky. Four years, four nine-month terms, six excellent teachers, five brand new high school graduates; the Elkhead community had proven they could run a school—and they could certainly celebrate with food and dance.

CHAPTER SIXTEEN

Leave Taking

(1920–)

October 8, 1920

Ezra Smith and Lewis Harrison left for Ft. Collins Saturday to attend the State Agricultural College this year.

Ruth Harrison has gone to Oak Creek to visit her brother Ed. She expects to remain until Christmas.

Ina Hayes writes that she likes it fine at Lawrence, Kansas where she is attending the University of Kansas.

Mrs. Anna White the high school teacher at the Elkhead school left for Ft. Morgan Saturday morning taking her granddaughter, Virginia with her. She found the altitude too high here.

Helen Jones who is training to be a nurse at St. Luke's Hospital in Denver writes to her friends that she finds the work hard but very interesting.

April 27, 1921

Ezra Smith and Lewis Harrison got home from Fort Collins after several days of hard traveling on the Moffat road. They said they did not walk or they would have arrived sooner. College life has fattened them up. Don't believe they rode skis much last winter.

December 21, 1921

The Hayden Republican says that the Elkhead school pays their teachers the highest of any country school. Well, they are worth it.

The boys at Elkhead are catching the coyotes and getting cash for the pelts, which is something the rancher cannot get for his wheat, butter or eggs.

Charlie Fulton upset with a two-ton load while coming down to Elkhead with coal. No damage was done.

December 27, 1922

Mrs. Harrison moved to Oak Creek last Friday where they will live. U.F. Harrison having gone there some time ago. This community thus loses one of its best public spirited and enterprising citizens. Our best wishes go with them.

"East Elkhead," *Routt County Republican.*

The summer that followed the terrible winter of 1920 was ordinary, though crops were better than normal because of heavy snowfall. Creeks and reservoirs were full of water for irrigation. The grass and other vegetation were late to emerge, but plentiful. In some places, there was too much water, a highly unusual problem. The finely crafted twenty-five-foot dam that Lewis Harrison's father, U.F. Harrison, built on Calf Creek gave way in early summer and sent a wall of water into Elkhead Creek at the Adair Ranch. No one was hurt, but apparently John Adair was caught in the flood while crossing a bridge with six horses. He and the horses swam to shore. Harrison simply decided to rebuild his dam with a bigger spillway.

The graduates had grand plans. Ina Hayes was on her way to the University of Kansas, Eunice Pleasant's alma mater. Lewis Harrison and Ezra Smith were both going to Colorado Agricultural

College in Fort Collins. Helen Jones was leaving in early summer to begin a nursing course in Denver. No one doubted that Leila Ferguson would go to college—she was such a capable student—but after graduation her plans were still uncertain. She aspired to go but her responsibilities to her family came first.

Rosamond Underwood, now Rosamond Perry, had come to Elkhead for the graduation. Her mother, Mrs. George (Grace) Underwood, joined with Ferry Carpenter's mother, Belle Reed Carpenter, to set up a scholarship fund for Elkhead graduates. All five would have their tuition and fees paid.

Leila Ferguson's situation was complicated and troublesome. Her father, Alex, was in Oregon. Her mother, Jesse, proving her grit, refused to leave the homestead. Jesse had two sons in Elkhead: Richard, who was thirteen, and James Hood, her son from an earlier marriage, who was married to Susie Jones. The Fergusons had lost nearly all their livestock and were destitute. Richard explained that he and his mother and sister were living on porcupine meat and dandelions. Dandelions referred to any edible greens found in swales and along creek banks.

Whatever it took, Jesse Ferguson did not want to lose the land they had so recently won. It had only been a year since they had proven up and gotten the deed to their 160 acres. She was also one of the most fiercely loyal Elkheaders. She had fought hard for the school bond issue that paid for the Rock Schoolhouse; she had worked to get a post office and a voting precinct. The post office was especially important to her: she kept most of the letters she received that were addressed to Elkhead or Elk Head, Colorado, as if to prove that it was a real place on the map.

Richard also wanted to keep the homestead in Elkhead. It was his dream as a young man to live there permanently. He wanted to rebuild the herd and try again. Nobody wanted to sell out, and the family recoiled from the idea of selling to Isadore Bolten, their neighbor to the west. Bolten was always on the lookout for property, and the family considered him a threat, ready to take advantage of a neighbor in distress.[395]

Yet, 1920 was not a promising year for Bolten, either. Bolten's venture in Nampa, Idaho, so widely touted in the papers in 1919, failed miserably. He later told Carpenter's sister, Ruth, that when he left Idaho in late 1920, he was completely broke and in debt. He made his way back to Routt County, where he still owned his homestead and the Oldham ranch. In the spring of 1921, Bolten got a job working in a store in Hayden and somehow managed to buy 3,600 sheep.[396] Bolten herded the sheep alone in the Red Desert in Wyoming the following fall and winter. He said he lived on rice and mutton and went without a bath or a haircut for six months. "I commenced to get along; I made up my mind that nothing would stop me."[397] As he had done before in his life, Bolten managed to rebuild his fortune and reappear with money to invest. Bolten wanted to buy places like the Fergusons' because it was perfect sheep pasture, on a south-facing slope. He was looking to expand his sheep ranch.

Sheep were fast replacing cattle in Elkhead, though the community was sharply divided on whether this was a right and good thing. Some ranchers and homesteaders, like Bill Kleckner, Fred Schaefermeyer, Reece Horton and U.F. Harrison, had kept small bands of sheep on their land over the previous decade.[398] But most people held an intense bias against sheep for a long list of reasons: they smelled bad, their meat did not taste good, they were dimwitted and would allow themselves to be buried in the snow. Cattle would at least turn their backs to a storm and brave it out. Sheep ate the grass and shrubs down to a nub; their sharp hooves chewed up the ground, damaged the roots of native grasses, and left behind pulverized dust, covered with their little round droppings. Worst of all, they walked right through fences that were good enough for horses and cattle. Three strands of barbed wire held up by cedar or oak brush posts would not even give pause to ewes and lambs. Ewes could get down on their knees and crawl under an ordinary fence and lambs hopped or wriggled through. And once on the other side, they were nearly impossible to catch or push back out. They didn't herd like cattle: they ran fast through the sagebrush and could change direction in a blink.

No matter how people personally thought about sheep, these domestic animals had much better economic prospects in the 1920s than cattle or grain crops. The price of lamb and mutton was steadier than the price of veal or beef. Moreover, sheep ranchers had another commodity besides meat—they could sell wool, a precious material, when every soldier wore wool socks and often had wool pants and a wool jacket.[399]

Bolten was the first in Elkhead to see the future in sheep and he had no compunctions about taking care of the animals himself. He began styling himself as a big sheepman as early as 1917, and by the 1920s he was buying and selling thousands of sheep every year. Except for his misadventure in Idaho, he was consistently making a profit and could attract capital both from the bank and private investors. Ferry Carpenter later described Bolten spending hours in his law office reading law books and quizzing Carpenter about the law—particularly contract and business law. "He was one of the best students I ever had," Carpenter said.[400] Knowledge of the law informed Bolten's decisions to form and dissolve partnerships, invest and speculate in livestock and land.

Few things made Jesse Ferguson angrier than the thought of selling out to Bolten. Leila and Richard shared her sentiment, as did many in the Elkhead community. They said Bolten was only out for himself. Bolten, at the same time, described himself as a businessman and entrepreneur; he was determined to prove that a Russian who had come to Colorado with nothing could become wealthy and influential. Elkheaders had watched as Bolten quickly bought Oldham's ranch after the shooting, and some criticized Bolten for having no feelings for the Fulton family. People muttered that any generous act by Bolten, any donation to a good cause, had to be recorded in the newspaper; even scholarships had to be paid back with interest.[401] Bolten was single; he was not supporting a wife and children. His thrift and business sense were renowned. But as his neighbors in Elkhead began to fail, what was felt as his ruthlessness also became legendary—and feared.

The Fergusons were in debt, with few livestock and no savings in 1920. Instead of going to college, as she was expected to do and as she so fervently wished, Leila worked through the summer cooking for hay crews and tending other people's children. In October, she got on the train and went to find her father in Oregon. When she got back to Routt County a few months later, she decided to support her mother and brother by teaching in one-room schools where her high school diploma was more than sufficient qualification.

Although Leila postponed college to support her family, two years later the Fergusons lost their homestead. Leila understood the Agricultural Depression better than most Elkheaders. She later described her family's situation the early 1920s:

> Mother and Dick, he was just a boy, thirteen, they had milk cows and they went ahead and milked the cows. I started in teaching. I sent home money to buy food and help take care of things. They managed to build up the herd until it was in pretty good shape. Then the bank took it. It was about two years, I guess. We managed to feed them through a couple of winters and the bank took it. Just came and took it. So my mother was heartbroken to lose all her stock. They foreclosed the mortgage on the ranch.
>
> It was happening to everybody, the whole country, because it was just the way they did it; it sounds heartless but that is the way it was done. No one had a chance to recuperate because cattle hadn't risen since WWI. I can remember so well their talking about the high prices for cattle during WWI: "Oh

> cattle can't possible go down, they can't possibly go down." They can go down just like they did then.[402]

Even while many families were in a state of crisis, ordinary life continued, and most, if not all, looked forward to what they hoped would be a brighter future. Looking back, the decline of the Elkhead community appears swift and irreversible. Precipitous. But in the moment people felt they just needed a bit of luck or to work harder. No one predicted failure.

Ferry Carpenter and Eunice Pleasant married in September 1920. They honeymooned at the homestead cabin and rented a house in Hayden for the winter where Ferry could have easy access to his law office and Eunice could set up house and continue her community work. Eunice was certain that she did not want to spend another winter in Elkhead, and she did not want to give birth in a log cabin far from a doctor or hospital. She was ready to stop teaching full time and live in town. Ferry Carpenter continued his various enterprises in Elkhead—he was still Jack White's partner with a herd of Hereford cattle and he was in the dairy business with a stone barn and Ayrshire dairy cattle on Dry Fork. He was no longer on the Elkhead district school board, but he visited frequently and continued to help recruit teachers for the Rock Schoolhouse. He also continued to attend the dances in Elkhead and often brought a sleigh of partiers up from Hayden to dance all night at the Rock Schoolhouse.

Iva Rench was rehired to teach the lower grades again in the fall of 1920. Mrs. Anna White took over for Eunice Pleasant teaching the high school. Mrs. White, as she was known, was a widow, and she brought along her granddaughter to live with her in the teacherage. She didn't last long. In October, she returned to Denver—she said the altitude was too high in Elkhead. Her abrupt departure interrupted the term. Fortunately, Hazel Watkins, a teacher from Texas, was willing to take her place and competently led the high school through another year.

The following year, Carpenter stepped in again and recruited George Norvell, a Rhodes Scholar and well-liked educator who had been superintendent of schools in neighboring Moffat County. Norvell served as the principal and the high school teacher for the next two years and, under his leadership, a large group of boys who had resisted schooling finally graduated from the eighth grade. According to Richard Ferguson, it was Norvell who persuaded him to attend to his studies and stay in school.

In 1923, Rudolph, Jesse and Oliver Morsbach, Ecil and Elsie Scott, Florence Fredrickson, and Minnie Jones graduated from the primary grades. Ione Smith, who had lived with Eunice Pleasant in the teacherage, was the sole high school graduate. It made her the sixth—and the last—high school graduate from the Elkhead district.[403] Ferry Carpenter rode up to the school to give the commencement address. The paper noted that his talk was inspiring and that he had fallen from a horse, badly injuring his arm.

Carpenter was on the Hayden school board and adamant about the advantages of a union high school. He did not advocate consolidating districts at that time, but he felt that a proper high school education included a range of courses and extracurricular activities that could only be taught by several teachers and justified by a larger group of students. He wanted the high school in Hayden to be the hub for advanced education in the western part of Routt County and he tried to talk the various little districts into sending their students to town. He was only partly successful at first. After Ione Smith graduated in 1923, the Elkhead district gave up the idea of having a full four-year high school. As families began moving out and enrollment declined, the Elkhead district began paying tuition for students to attend high school in town. Students lived in Hayden because there were no school buses and the distance was too great to go back and forth every day.

This shift was not without pain. Families did not like to be split up. There was a significant extra cost in supporting a young person living in town, either as a boarder with another family, or in temporary housing with a parent. When Richard Ferguson's mother faced the choice, she opted to send her son to live with an uncle in Illinois to finish high school. He went for one year and returned. "My Dad had told me when he first became sick to take care of my Mother, so I tried to do so," he explained.[404] He went to high school in Hayden for a few terms, but never graduated. Florence Fredrickson, another graduate of the eighth grade, boarded in Hayden and rode horseback the ten miles home and back every weekend.[405]

Elkhead's primary problem was a lack of money. Homesteaders who were accustomed to earning some cash from the sale of livestock and grain in the fall were suddenly unable to sell any product for a profit. In November 1921, a student reporter for the "Elkhead News" column wrote in the *Steamboat Pilot*, "It seems as if Uncle Sam would find some way for the farmers to get a little cash for their wheat and cattle so they could buy some of the government securities he is so keen to sell."[406] Prices for nearly all agricultural products were less than half, and sometimes less than a third, of what they had been during the war. As the Agricultural Depression deepened into the Great Depression, consumers had less money to spend on food and were more likely to buy lean, cheap meats.

Elkheaders struggled and did what they had always done in difficult times—the men went to work in the mines, at the sawmill or as ranch hands in the Yampa Valley. The women took on jobs as cooks, housekeepers or child minders and tried to find buyers for eggs, butter and cream. Some took in laundry. Some, like Leila Ferguson, used their education to teach.

Children pitched in. If they were old enough, they went to work in the mines. When Ezra Smith came home from his first year of college, he immediately went to work at Mt. Harris as a miner. Other children earned money by killing coyotes and skinning them for their pelts. Wolves had been exterminated from the area by around 1916, and by the early 1920s, coyotes had taken their place as chief predators. The local livestock association placed a bounty on coyotes, making for a profitable source of income for a few. The paper reported: "The boys at Elkhead are catching the coyotes and getting cash for the pelts which is something the rancher cannot get for his wheat, butter or eggs."[407] A year later "Elkhead News" followed up: "The boys are making good pocket money trapping, running the trap lines as they go to and from school. The Jim Barnes boys have ten coyotes and Walter Davis four already. Catch them boys, St. Louis wants them."[408]

Another group of homesteaders decided to try growing lettuce. It seemed like a far-fetched idea even at the time and there were plenty of snickers about "those afflicted with lettuce" and "lettuce heads" but for several years homesteaders around California Park, like Ed Knowles, John Jykadorke, Jim Barnes and Lerch Covert, tried to raise and sell the vegetable.

Ed Smith and his sons continued to run a sawmill on Pilot Knob. Every winter, they packed a trail to haul lumber to the rail depot in Hayden.

Henry Morsbach, the loyal and determined mail-carrier, earned extra money by building complex wooden silos—tall structures made with short lengths of wood that were assembled like a sixteen-sided log cabin. In 1923, he built one for Carpenter's dairy and several around Elkhead and in the valley. The silos were intended for silage—a mixture of hay and chopped sunflower plants. Morsbach also operated a small shingle mill, hauling timber down from the forest and slicing it into shingles that his neighbors used for their roofs and gables.

None of these efforts provided a stable income and all were eventually abandoned.

Coal remained a prospect and lure to investors. Its price had soared during the war, and, unlike lettuce, was not perishable. After Clarence Horton returned from the military, he and his cousin Otto reopened and expanded a punch mine on the eastern side of the district, along a flank of Pilot Knob. The mine was called the Cottonwood Mine, named for a small intermittent creek nearby. Otto soon returned to farming with his uncle Reece, while Clarence persisted. The Hortons' neighbor on Dry Fork, Charles Fulton, contracted to haul coal from the mine to the railroad depot in town. He could carry a few tons at a time with his team of horses. At one point, in a flurry of optimism, the paper reported that the mine had a fourteen-foot seam of coal and was planning to lay tracks. But that never happened.

Speculation on coal reserves in California Park and around Pilot Knob continued; every few years there would be a notice that vast reserves had been discovered and were about to be mined. Small mines opened and closed but no one ever opened a large mine in the area. The amount of coal in relation to how far it needed to travel to a market eventually discouraged even the most avid investor.

Isadore Bolten did not sell his holdings in Elkhead, but he moved to Rawlings, Wyoming, and began acquiring land in the Red Desert, south of Rawlings, where he could winter his increasingly large herd of sheep. In 1926, at the age of 41, he married Ethel Fuiks, a librarian he met at the Rawlins library. He used his Elkhead lands for summer grazing and took tens of thousands of sheep into the public lands in California Park to nibble down the lush vegetation in the national forest. Slowly, and piece by piece, he bought up land in Elkhead. Over the next several decades, he bought the Morsbach, Hayes and Murphy places on Calf Creek. He bought the homestead of Jesse Ferguson's son, James Hood, when Hood was not able to pay his mortgage.[409] He bought out Herbert and Minnie Mae Jones. And he eventually acquired Clarence, Otto and Reece Horton's lands above Dry Fork. He acquired some of the land by challenging the homesteading process—a few residents had never had their land surveyed and had improved land without legally claiming it. Others had never paid the fee to receive a patent on their homestead and were left with nothing but a paper claim, easily challenged at the courthouse.

As Bolten amassed more and more land in Elkhead, he became impatient with his neighbors and more inclined to see them as adversaries. In the summer of 1927, he accused Izaiah Scott, a homesteader on upper Calf Creek, of stealing sheep. Scott was arrested and charged with larceny for fifty sheep found in his pasture. The *Steamboat Pilot* noted that Bolten was "running large bands of sheep in that vicinity," implying that it was little surprise that sheep might get through a fence and into a neighbor's pasture. A jury trial a few months later found Scott not guilty.[410]

In 1933, Bolten bought the Adair Ranch, a huge holding with over 1,200 acres of grazing land and hundreds of acres of irrigated hay meadows. By his own account, Bolten became a millionaire. He eventually owned over 80,000 acres in Colorado and Wyoming. Bolten had an aversion to paying taxes and regularly contested the county appraisals. He also routinely tore down any structures he found on the land after his purchase. All of the homestead cabins, barns and outbuildings he bought in Elkhead were either sold and moved or hauled away for firewood. The sole exception was the cabin he built when he first came to Elkhead. He leased it, along with his 160-acre homestead near the schoolhouse, to struggling homesteaders.

In 1925, Carpenter was asked to take on the management of the Dawson Ranch, on the Yampa River, about four miles east of Hayden. This was the same ranch where he had worked in his youth and on his summer vacations from college. John B. (J.B.) Dawson had sold the ranch to the Colorado Anthracite Coal Company in 1915 and the coal company had been leasing it on very difficult terms to a local rancher. Carpenter brought his herd of cattle down from Elkhead and put them on the irrigated hay meadows of the Dawson Ranch. He bought out his partner Jack White and the LX Bar became his cattle business. Eunice gave birth to their first child at home, in Hayden, in 1922. Their second child, Rosamond, was born at the newly completed Solandt Memorial Hospital in 1923. The family moved onto the former Dawson Ranch as tenants in 1927 and Ferry and Eunice spent the rest of their lives (with a few year-long forays in Denver and Washington, D.C.) at that ranch in the Yampa Valley. They kept the homestead in Elkhead but occupied it only in the summer months.[411]

Ezra Smith and Lewis Harrison did spectacularly well at college. They came home after the first year "fattened up" and ready to apply what they had learned to the challenges of agriculture in Elkhead.[412]

Helen Jones earned her degree and became a nurse at St. Luke's Hospital in Denver. Leila Ferguson taught in small, one-room schools for years, got married and finally, when she was in her fifties, earned her college degree. Ina Hayes initially thrived in Kansas at the university. She kept in touch with her teacher, Eunice Pleasant, and the paper proudly recorded her successes, but in her spring semester she fell ill, probably with scarlet fever, and was hospitalized for months. She returned to Routt County and married a young man in Craig. After sizing up the economy in Routt County, they left Colorado for good and moved to San Diego, California.

Throughout the 1920s, families leaked out of Elkhead and sold their homesteads. James Clarence and Ethel Freeman, whose seven children had almost all fallen sick with the flu and recovered, worked for Ferry Carpenter on the dairy for a while. Freeman then took a job in the coal mine at Mt. Harris, working in his former trade as a plumber. His wife and children stayed in Elkhead until nearly the whole family got diphtheria. Their youngest child, Earl, died of the disease and the family left Elkhead to live in Mt. Harris in June 1921.

Young men like Frank Harrison, Guy and Percy Hayes, Galen Kleckner and Paul Jones came home after the war with a little money and a strong desire to have a ranch in Elkhead. None of them succeeded. They found that their parents needed their cash earnings and that there was no path to accumulate the capital needed to buy their own land. They tried. Frank Harrison made an offer on some unclaimed state land in Elkhead, but Bolten outbid him. Guy Hayes came home for a time to help his mother and look for a place of his own, but he was limited by insufficient funds and his health was not good. He eventually moved to Chicago and never returned to Colorado. Perry Barnes, a young man from Missouri who homesteaded around 1910, enlisted just months before the war ended. On his way home in early 1919, he married Adelaide Riley, the widow of Joshua Riley, and they returned together to Routt County.[413] Perry worked as a ranch hand and partnered with Isadore Bolten briefly in the sheep business, but they were unable to "get a hold." The family returned to New Jersey to live near Adelaide's parents, and according to the 1930 census, Perry got a job working for Atlantic City Electric.

Clarence and Otto Horton returned to Elkhead after the war and were able to survive economically, at least for a few years. Both married local women and worked and farmed in Elkhead. Clarence married Vada Smith and they lived on Dry Fork while Clarence worked in the coal mine on Cottonwood Creek. Otto Horton married Myrtle Castor and worked for his uncle and aunt, Reece and Orpha Horton, on their land on Dry Fork. In the late 1920s, like most of their neighbors, the Hortons moved into Hayden and took various jobs on ranches in the valley.

Mary and U.F. Harrison, who had hosted the first Rock Schoolhouse teachers on their small ranch on Calf Creek, moved to Oak Creek in southern Routt County in the winter of 1922.

Mary McDowell, one of the first teachers in the early one-room schoolhouses in Elkhead, married in 1924, sold her homestead, and settled in Oak Creek.

The Hallers bought the Fredrickson homestead in 1925 and then sold all their property above Elkhead Creek to Irl and Lola Rhodes in 1934. The Fredricksons stayed in the area for several more years and then left to live with their daughter in Fort Collins, Colorado.

The Morsbachs, Henry and Ethyl and their boys, Rudolph, Jesse, Oliver and Frank, were joined by a sister, Ethyl Olive, born in 1922. Despite the family's well-known industriousness, they could not make a living in Elkhead; they left for eastern Oklahoma in 1925.[414]

Charles and Julia Smith Pizor sold both their homesteads in 1926 to pay off a debt. "We had bought a few cattle and had to buy some feed for them every year," Julia Smith Pizor explained, "so we ended up selling both homesteads and coming out $200 in debt. We didn't think it honest to take bankruptcy, so we finally managed to pay off the $200 and 'felt free again.'" The couple moved with their two children to Hayden where "times were *very* hard." Pizor worked in the coal mines, as a plumber's helper in Hayden, and later as an electrician.[415]

Earl and Vella Rice and their daughter, Okla, left Elkhead in the early 1930s and moved south of Hayden.

Jesse Ferguson, never to be a broken woman, homesteaded again after she lost her Elkhead land. She somehow disassembled and hauled up to her new land an unused one-room schoolhouse she purchased from the district. She proved up on her new homestead in 1931 and stayed in Elkhead until she sold her land to one of the Fultons in 1943. Only at age seventy-two did she leave Elkhead.

The Fultons' story is equal in tragedy and determination, the familiar mix of relentless hard work, crushing circumstances, and renewal and optimism.

Like most of their neighbors, Charles and Paroda Fulton borrowed money to expand their ranch during the war. Both were industrious. Paroda was raising five boys—John, Ben, Bill, Cliff and Charles—and remained an active member of the school board. Charles Fulton was constantly at work trying to bring water to their fields and raising horses. Even so, after ranching on upper Dry Fork for twenty-two years, the Fultons lost the ranch in 1925.

They moved into Hayden, where Paroda found work as a cook in the grade school. Although she was an accomplished teacher and had taught in many rural schools in Snake River, the Williams Forks and Hayden, her teaching certificate had expired; the family was desperate for a steady income.

The following summer, the bank that had foreclosed on their Elkhead ranch leased it back to them. Charles Fulton and his sons moved into their former bunkhouse and worked the land. Fulton cashed in a $1,000 insurance policy and bought a saddle horse and a few cows back from the bank. He also filed another homestead claim on Bull Gulch to the north of their former ranch. "I heard Dad say if we could have come up with $5,000 we could have gotten the ranch back," Ben Fulton recalled. "We couldn't get it. I got disheartened. Couldn't make anything. That was my attitude. I got so sick of working on a ranch and ending up with nothing."[416]

Bolten contested Fulton's filing and the government eventually withdrew the acreage, making it ineligible for homesteading.

The Fulton family struggled in Hayden and kept trying to find a way to regain their land. "We weren't destitute," Ben said. "I never missed a meal, but we never had money."[417] In 1924, the Fultons' middle son, Bill, died at age eleven of rheumatic fever. The losses were piling up but "Dad said the best cure for our grief was to get to work, which we did."[418] The Fultons were finally able to buy some Elkhead land from Iva and her brother, Emil Rench, in the 1930s. They also bought the Rileys' homestead from his widow, Adelaide, and eventually bought Jesse Ferguson's second homestead in Little Arkansas. The Fultons used this acreage as summer pasture. They built a barn on Bull Gulch in the late 1930s, but the family stayed in Hayden, eventually acquiring acreage along the Yampa River, just north of Hayden.

Charles Fulton's brother Ed, who had moved to Elkhead permanently after their brother Cliff was murdered, lived for a time on Cliff's homestead on upper Dry Fork and then homesteaded. He claimed a mesa above Dry Fork, in the far southern corner of the district. He married Ruth Bodfish and devoted himself to raising wheat on a gentle slope above the creek. Bolten also contested his claim, and that of his deceased brother, but Ed and Ruth Fulton were able to keep their place and did not sell out and move to Hayden until the Great Depression.[419]

Animosity toward Isadore Bolten swelled in Elkhead through the 1930s and persisted until he died in 1951. Ben Fulton recalled that one chilly spring night at their ranch along upper Dry Fork, his father, Charles, heard a strange noise coming from the creek. He went over to investigate and pulled a drowning Bolten out of the freezing water. "It could be dangerous," Ben Fulton said, and added that his father "always said he should have left him."[420]

The 1920 census enumerated 53 households and 190 people, but the 1930 census found only 19 households and 45 people. The exodus was fast and never reversed. In the 1930s, a few more families tried to survive in Elkhead. Walter and Anna Dickerson and their two children held on, and the Coverts and the Castors scrambled together a living for a few years. Ed and Hannah Smith lived on Dry Fork well into their seventies and their neighbors, the Lighthizers, also held onto their land. Fewer and fewer people living in Elkhead had children. Those who did often spent the winter in Hayden. The Elkhead district closed what it then called "the branch schools," the one-room seasonal schools in the more remote corners of the district, in 1923.

Allie Kleckner, who had grown up on the Bears Ears ranch with her brother, Galen, returned to teach in the 1932-1933 school year. She found the conditions of her fifteen students dire: "No food, no overshoes, no nothing . . . Sometimes we were pretty much on starvation rations."[421]

In 1938 the school district abandoned the Rock Schoolhouse and made many unsuccessful attempts to sell the building, the rock or the flooring. The district continued to receive property tax revenue and there were still a few young children needing schooling. In the mid 1940s Bolten donated an acre of land across from the entrance to the Elkhead Ranch. The district built a small one-room cinderblock schoolhouse equipped with a small kitchen and a wood floor suitable for dancing. That school was only open for a few years before the Hayden district absorbed the Elkhead district in the 1950s. Before the district consolidation was finalized, the Elkhead district deeded the acre and the school building to the Elkhead community as a social and educational center.

In the 1930s and 40s the last stragglers gradually left, until the only families living year round in Elkhead were the Carns (who had bought the Ed Fulton place), the Rhodes (on the Fredrickson homestead) and ranch hands on the Adair Ranch, which Bolten had renamed Sheep Haven.

There were several aspects of life that were unique to that time, or which don't seem within the range of possibility anymore. One was the idea of free land: the whole concept turned on the assumption that it was right and correct to remove Native American people from the land they inhabited, and the idea that "citizens"—wherever they were from originally, or whatever their circumstances—could claim that land as theirs.

A second concept that was considered ordinary at the time but now seems incredible (and unlikely to be replicated) was that residents of a place could establish their own political entity and unit of governance. They could raise and spend public money as they saw fit. If they wanted to build a rock schoolhouse of classical proportions, hire the finest teachers, and orient the curriculum to the study of their place and people, the law allowed them—no one, no governmental entity, stood in their way. While people can form nonprofits in the current system, and they can ask for donations and grants to do the charitable or educational work of their group, those structures are very different from local government. Local government gave a vote and a voice to every adult who lived within the precinct or district, rich or poor, landed or tenant.

In the late 1920s and 30s, loss and failure were scattered like the logs and stones of collapsed homesteads. Ben Fulton's sentiment was not uncommon: "My ambition when I was a little kid was to be a cowpuncher. After starving out, I decided to do something else. There was nothing attractive about ranching. I wanted to go out and work."[422] Ben Fulton took his fine education and became an engineer, far from Routt County. His youngest brother, Charles, better known as Chuck, stayed. He bought and leased more land in Elkhead and kept the family ranch near Hayden.

Given that so many people left—or more accurately, lost their home ground—some might call the whole span of time, the aspirations and idealism, a massive failure. Yet, most Elkheaders were able to leave with some capital, at least a bit more than they arrived with and they left with an enduring experience of a functioning community. Homesteading usurped Ute land from communal use and ownership, moving it into the public domain and then into private hands. The Ute were forcefully removed; the mostly white settlers arrived with very little and left with very little. The Ute were confined to a reservation hundreds of miles away in Utah. The homesteaders, though they failed at ranching, usually left with a few hundred or thousand dollars which enabled them to buy a house in Hayden, or another small piece of land.

John Jykadorke, the bachelor homesteader in California Park, sold his land to Bolten in 1936 for $800 and moved his log cabin to Hayden. Fannie Hayes took the money she received from Bolten and bought a small house in San Diego to be near her daughter, Ina. Jesse Ferguson received $2,500 for her homestead and moved to Yampa to be near her daughter, Leila.

Very few Elkhead children inherited land from their parents. None except for Chuck Fulton were able to expand or even maintain their parents' homestead or ranch. Yet, that generation of Elkheaders, the children of homesteaders, had an opportunity for schooling that most of their parents never had. In a sense, they became educated out of subsistence homesteading, farming or ranching. A few, like Richard Ferguson and Frank Harrison, would have stayed to live in Elkhead if they could, but many more deliberately sought opportunities outside of the community.

Elkheaders like the Carpenters and Fultons, Julia Smith Pizor, Allie Kleckner Lasnick, Vada Smith Horton and Marie Huguenin Holderness infused Hayden with Elkhead spirit. Those who came to Hayden brought their optimism, social capital and high ideals. They were key people in developing the fundamental social institutions in Hayden. The friendships and trust built between people like Eunice Pleasant, Ruth Bodfish and Paroda Fulton in Elkhead was crucial when it came to building the new union high school, the Solandt Memorial Hospital and the first Hayden Public Library.

They, and virtually everyone who experienced living in Elkhead, proudly remembered their stamina, their hard work, their ability to survive in an isolated place with long, snowy winters—what Ina Hayes called "grit" in her graduation speech. They also remembered working together, sharing what they had, and helping others in need, despite having arrived from different places and walks of life. They knew "real neighborliness," Julia Smith Pizor explained. Throughout their lives, long after they left Elkhead, they expressed their appreciation for a good school that is also a gathering place. As Eunice Pleasant wrote in her first letter about the Rock School, reversing the emphasis, "this place is as much a community center, as a school."

Even if they failed financially, abandoned homesteading, and left the beautiful Bears Ears country, Elkheaders did not lose the knowledge of what can happen when people create and unify with a common vision. Wherever they went, to Hayden or much farther away, the sense of being part of a community and knowing what a community working together is capable of, remained at their core.

Epilogue

I am on Bear's Ears, the north ear, after a long walk and a scramble up loose rock held at the angle of repose. The wind is strong. The sun is strong. There is no trail; sometimes I grab hold with my hands because the climb is so steep. The view from the top is astoundingly immense and complex; for me, it is a place of wondrous beauty. In the boundless sky overhead, wispy and fleecy puffs of clouds swirl south and gather at the horizon; raptors swoop and play in the updrafts. I find the line where the sky meets the land and follow it the full 360 degrees. I face south. The sun has come up on my left and is going down on my right, clockwise. I sit down and wait. Close by are rocks covered with lichen. Between the rocks are tiny tufts of grass, wooly yellow daisy, pussytoes and juniper shrubs, all dwarfed by the wind and pressed down in the winter by the snow.

From Bear's Ears it is clear to me that my love for the earth, and the place—Elkhead, below me, to the south—is accompanied and sustained by an intense curiosity about people. What creates community? What breaks community? I think we all carry a longing for community, a nostalgia for another way of life where we were less defined as individuals alone in the world with our singular ambitions. We have a soft spot in our hearts—some might say a lingering sentiment—for another way of life, where we belonged to a community; where we felt in unison with others; where our singular *I* melted into *our* collective accomplishments and tragedies. That sentiment is linked to place: a sense of belonging and being in harmony with our land and its people. We want to be part of a people. Our ancestors were all members of a group, a tribe, and not so long ago, we all lived off the land, with the land, belonging to the land. Somewhere inside each of us is that memory of our past connection, but for most of us, through centuries of being "cultured" and becoming consumers, of being trained away from the collective and the shared, we have moved into defining ourselves as private people, solitary, self-defining, self-improving, self-actualizing, and in many cases self-centered. My land, my house, my spirituality, my ambition, my future.

Every time I read of the Ute asking to return to the Bear River Valley or the Bears Ears country, I could feel that tug back to this place. And to that way of life. Everyone I interviewed who had lived in Elkhead remembered what it was like to live in a tight community. They so dearly wanted to return to the harmony they had known among themselves and with the land they inhabited. But that singular connection to their group and a place was no longer possible. For the Ute in the 1800s, it was knowing that others had moved in, strangers in dresses and coats and ties, living in log and frame houses, speaking new languages, with odd beliefs and customs. Their land had been divided: private ownership and personal gain appeared to be the only way forward. There was no room in the mostly white culture for collective ownership and mutual gain. Competition, brother against brother, sister against sister, neighbor against neighbor, settlement against settlement; for the most part these new people thought that competition was essential. They all wanted to be land owners, if not successful capitalists, and "get ahead." But ahead of whom?

Historically, the Ute, who knew community and held a deep connection to their land, were nearly beaten—by the military, by the reservation system, by boarding schools that sought to educate children by removing them from their homes and communities, and by the many diseases non-natives brought from the Old World. The stories present-day Ute tell about themselves emphasize resilience and resistance. They do not want ot be known as subjugated, conquered, or dominated. They are warriors who carry on their heritage and customs with honor and pride.

My grandmother Eunice is no longer a mysterious person to me. I now read her letters as kin, as a granddaughter, knowing the people she speaks of and the allusions she makes to the work she is doing. I feel she left messages for me along the way, including in an article she wrote about the abandonment of the Elkhead School. In the 1930s, she had a regular column in the local paper called "On Thinking it Over" in which she told stories of ranch life, mused on the prospects for world peace, and addressed issues of common concern in the county. In October 1938, a news item about boarding up the doors and windows of the Rock School prompted her to write a column that began: "Thus passes the Elkhead School, one of the earliest consolidated schools in the state, and, though set in an isolated district in the high mountains, one of the most modern in equipment, in standards of school work, and in social service to its community. As such, its history merits some attention."[423]

The Rock Schoolhouse stands today where it has for over a century, high up near the dike, the roof just barely visible from Bears Ears. It is a private summer residence, not a public school. A sense of absence blankets the whole Elkhead district. The sagebrush and bluestem have returned to the fields and pastures, roads have grown over, bridges have washed away, ditches have filled with dirt. This land is now most profitably used for hunting, an irony that the Ute might appreciate: their ancestors knew this was not a place to be in the winter, it was a place to hunt deer, elk and antelope, a place to gather the abundant sarvis and chokecherries in the summer and early fall. There is more than one paradox to ponder: a place of failure and loss, and yet, victory and unique accomplishment; a flicker in time, and a place of some permanent vital truths; a long-gone community, and yet, a beacon, an example, a place with a memory, for the truths of community.

Acknowledgments

People who had faith in me, never doubted and were patient. Over the years these people would write me encouraging notes with new snippets of information and insight—or pass along a photograph that had recently surfaced. Deep thanks to Venita Taveapout, Betsy Chapoose, Floyd O'Neil, Julia Pizor, Leila Ferguson Ault, Flo Hein, Allie Kleckner Lasnick, Chuck Fulton, the Dwight and Barbara Green family, Marie Huguenin Holderness, and Robert "Bobbie" Robinson. Thanks, too, to all the former Elkheaders who agreed to be interviewed and so generously shared their stories. I am also indebted to their children, nieces, nephews and grandchildren who told stories, unearthed photographs and documents from their family's time in Elkhead: the extended Ferguson family, the Robinsons, the Rice/Barbiero descendants, the Morsbach family, especially Nancy Woolery, and the Frank and Fannie Hayes family—especially Jo Buchanan, Ina Hayes' daughter, who trekked up Calf Creek and shared so many insights about her grandparents and great uncles. The Fredrickson family, especially Essam Welch. And all the Fultons, most prominently Rebecca and Vance, who were alongside me, sharing their keen interest and love for the place. Thank you to Laurel Watson of the Hayden Heritage Museum, who was always willing to dig for details and retained her curiosity and anticipation over many years.

My grandparents, Ros and Ferry Carpenter, emanated kindness and exuberance even when they were a little mystified by my fascination with Elkhead. When I walk through the ranch house today where they lived for so many years, I can hear their voices and feel their love in every room, every closet and drawer. They have a huge presence in this book and in my heart. My Uncle Ed (Edward F. Carpenter) wrote his own book, *The First Grazier*, and we enjoyed several lively arguments. He had an amazing memory for names and dates. I'll never forget his thrill when he read through my collection of news items from the *Routt County Republican*. Uncle Bill (Willis V. Carpenter), who also has an amazing memory and is a consummate storyteller, helped me at many points along the way. We share a deep love of his mother, my grandmother, Eunice Pleasant, and I will always treasure our conversations and evolving understanding and appreciation of her.

Further back, and in somewhat broader circle, I am more of a complete person, and therefore a better writer, for the teaching and care of several people: Sheafe Satterthwaite, who trained my eye to better read a landscape and who holds a powerful reverence for good questions; and David Park, a physicist who primarily studied time, who was my best writing teacher. He had no patience for foggy thinking or writing. He helped me join what was in my head with what came through my fingers and onto the page. Robert (Bob) Gaudino, human being extraordinare, could make you laugh while basically removing your skin and heaving you overboard into icy waters. How did he make his students feel so safe and loved and yet shift and deepen our thinking so profoundly? His attention was powerfully nutritious. I feel his spirit and kindness daily. And I remember his words: "confusion is necessary for learning."

My heartfelt gratitude for their teaching and as exemplars of scholarship: Patricia Albjerg Graham, Patty Limerick and Alan Brinkley. Bernadette Frances (Bern) Giannini read my dissertation so many years ago, sitting in her cabin in Hayden. She turned to me and said, This is good. She lives within me as an honorary aunt, critic, and "get off your duff" force of nature.

There were many more hearts and hands along the way, from scholars to skeptics, friends who read transcripts and helped me make sense of a mass of material that threatened to choke me at times. I hope you know who you are. Thank you.

And friends. Who could live without friends? Not me. I think it was from my realization of how crucial, how much of a life force, my friends are that I developed my reverence for community. I thrive inside a community of friends. They and the "we" we form hold me up, circulate my blood, bring air into my lungs, put spring in my step. I have no idea how to properly acknowledge you and your contributions to my work. A list will have to do: Barbara Wilson, Mary Palmer, Kit Miller, Don Rosiello, Bill May, Ned Sullivan, David Chapin Weeks, Ellen Toll, Deb Marshall, Bob Anderson, David Blanchett, Penny Howe, Guy Baird and Joel Baird—you inspired me, shared your courage with me, gave me fuel, made me laugh, made me work harder. More recent friends and colleagues have listened, shared insights about Elkhead, and in some cases gone through the manuscript with a fine-toothed comb. You have given me invaluable help: Allen Cooper, Lisa Ubelake, Elizabeth Szatkowski, Charlene Elliott, Abigail Maldonado Elliott, Jenny Blair, Toni Rockwell, Sarah Swearer, Jonathan Tamez and Keith Walters, Jennifer O'Donnell, Kaye Edwards, Sandy Fails, Negin Nabavi, Joan Piaseki, Penny Thron-Weber, Ben Colkitt, Helen Thorpe, Dorothy Wickenden and Marj Perry. Thank you, beloved nieces—Cordelia, Emily and Frances and beloved nephews—Levin and Tilden.

Becky Fernald and Mary Palmer were with me at the beginning of this project. They took the leap with me and we spent a summer interviewing children of homesteaders, students of the Elkhead school, anyone who seemed to know anything about the community. In between times, and to keep ourselves in groceries, Becky taught swimming in Craig while Mary and I tutored children in reading. We stopped at the Hayden Merc on our way back from Craig and shared a pint of sherbet before we headed up the dirt road to the homestead in Elkhead. Mary suggested we write an epic poem and I hope this manuscript at least partially lives up to that vision.

My brothers, Reed and Hugh Zars, are so close to me I can barely distinguish their presence. How can I thank my brothers for their knuckle sandwiches, their teasing, their constancy, their rock-solid dependable love and respect? We grew up together; we are still growing up together. I can't imagine life without them.

To Bernadette, Vivian, Yoarlin (Yoli), and Carmen, three daughters and one granddaughter. I hope I send you at least some measure of the love I receive from you every day.

About the Author

Belle Zars is an independent researcher and historian. She grew up in and around Hayden, Colorado, the granddaughter of local homesteaders. As a Quaker she has long been fascinated with the experience and practice of belonging in community. She holds a doctorate from Harvard University where she wrote her dissertation on the Elkhead School and district consolidation.

Endnotes

1. Eunice Pleasant to Gertrude Pleasant, August 27, 1919.
2. The State of Colorado completed the sale of the land to the Elkhead School District 11 for $197.25 on February 20, 1930. There is no deed transferring the property to the Hayden District. Hayden District sold the schoolhouse and surrounding forty (39.45) acres to Ira Benedec, the highest bidder, for $1304.00 in June 1961. Benedec sold it to Charles Fulton, minus two acres, for $1750, in July 1961. Fulton kept thirty-three acres for pasture and sold the schoolhouse, teacherage, and seven acres around the buildings to Dwight and Barbara Green in October 1962. The Green's four daughters now own the property and use it as a private residence.
3. Ferry Carpenter soon after filed on an adjoining 160 acres opened under the Desert Claims Act. He added another 640 acres of grazing land and bought 640 acres, a "school section 36" directly north of his homestead. Farrington Carpenter, *Confessions of a Maverick*, (Denver, CO: Colorado State Historical Association, 1984), 45.
4. Wall text, "Written on the Land: Ute Voices, Ute History." Colorado History Museum, Denver, CO.
5. Ibid.
6. Ibid.
7. The Yampa plant's Latin name is *Perideridia americana*.
8. I am indebted to the assistance of Venita Taveapont, a member of the Ute Indian Tribe of the Uintah and Ouray Reservation, who was the Ute Language Coordinator at the Ute Indian Tribe, headquartered

at Fort Duschene, Utah. She was exceptionally generous in her response to my many questions. She intended to visit Elkhead and to go to California Park to gather Osha (a medicinal plant), but sadly she died before she was able to make the trip. My deepest appreciation for her wise counsel. I also wish to thank Floyd O'Neil, former history professor at the University of Utah, who advised me in many ways, and who sent me to Ms. Taveapont.

9. James A. Goss, "Traditional Cosmology, Ecology and Language of the Ute Indians" in William Worth, ed. *Ute Indian Arts and Culture* (Colorado Springs, CO: Colorado Springs Fine Arts Council, 2000), 27-52
10. William Worth, "Ute Civilization in Prehistory and the Spanish Colonial Period," in William Worth ed., *Ute Indian Arts and Culture* (Colorado Springs, CO: Colorado Springs Fine Arts Council, 2000), 53.
11. J. Alden Mason, "Myths of the Uintah Utes: 'Bears Ears Country,' story told by Andrew Frank" *The Journal of American Folklore* 23, no. 89 (1910):317.
12. Bears Ears, the twin peaks in NW Colorado should not be confused with Bears Ears in southeastern Utah. Venita Taveapont, member of the Ute Indian Tribe of the Uintah and Ouray Reservation, confirmed the importance of Bears Ears Peaks for the northern Colorado Ute and the distinction between the buttes in Utah and the peaks in Colorado. Utah's Bears Ears, now a part of Bears Ears National Monument, are generally described as a pair of buttes. Five area tribes have ancestral ties to the region: the Ute Mountain Ute Tribe, the Ute Indian Tribe (which includes descendants of the Yamparika), and Southern Ute Indian Tribe, the Navajo Nation, the Hopi and the Pueblo of Zuni. The Elkhead Mountains were first described in detail by a government expedition under the direction of Clarence King, but carried out by Arnold Hague and Samuel Emmons between 1867 and 1873. Emmons describes the Elkhead Mountains as " a singularly picturesque and beautiful group of high volcanic peaks . . . Their steep, rugged slopes are covered for the most part to their very summits with a dense growth of pine forests, while the valleys which are enclosed between them present a pleasing variety of open glades and groves of quaking-asp and

pine." S.F. Emmons, "Elkhead Mountains," Section 7, *Descriptive Geology,* Arnold Hague and Samuel Emmons, (U.S. Government Printing Office, 1877), 167-180.

13. J. Alden Mason, "Myths: 'Origin of the Bear Dance,' story told by Snake John," 363. Wickiup is the term used in this story to describe shelters. "Ute stick home" or nuu ivi kahn is the term preferred by present day Ute. According to wall text, " Some Ute groups started using tipis instead of stick houses after the introduction of the horse. The horses could carry the long poles and covers to the next camp." From Wall Text in "Written on the Land: Ute Voices, Ute History," Colorado History Museum, Denver, CO.
14. Wall Text, Ute Indian Museum History Colorado, Montrose, Colorado and Wall Text, "Written on the Land: Ute Voices, Ute History." History Colorado Museum, Denver, CO. Further wall text states: "The Cumumba, Pahvant, Parianuche, San Pitch, Sheberetch, Tabeguache, Tumpanawach, Uinta-ats, and Yamparika bands became the Ute Indian Tribe of the Uintah and Ouray Reservation. The Weenuche band (later called the Weeminuche) became the Ute Mountain Ute Tribe. The Capote and Mouache bands became the Southern Ute Indian Tribe. The names of the bands have many different spellings."
15. Goss, *Ute Indian Arts,* 35.
16. Floyd A. O'Neil. "The Utes, Paiutes and Goshutes. Peoples of Utah," in *The Peoples of Utah* ed. Helen Z. Papanikolas. Salt Lake City: 1976, 27-59.
17. Ibid.
18. J. Alden Mason, "Myths: 'Indians of Long Ago,' story told by John Duncan," 362-363.
19. John Star testimony in *Minutes of Councils held by James McLaughlin, U.S. Indian Inspector, with the Uintah and White River Ute at Uintah Agency, Utah, From May 18 to May 23,1903,* 63.
20. Silvestre Vélez de Escalante, *The Dominguez-Escalante Journal: Their Expedition through Colorado, Utah, Arizona, New Mexico in 1776.* Ed. Ted J. Warner. Translated by Fray Angelico Chavez. (Salt Lake City: University of Utah 1995), 44.

21. Wall text, Ute Indian Museum History Colorado, Montrose, CO.
22. P.J. DeSmet, S.J. *Letters and Sketches, with a Narrative of a Year's Residence among the Indian Tribes of the Rocky Mountains.* (Philadelphia:1843), 168.
23. John C. Fremont, *Report of the Exploring Expedition to the Rocky Mountains in the Year 1842.* (Washington DC: Blair and Rives Printers, 1845), 280.
24. Ibid, 276.
25. Ibid, 280. In Fremont's account of camping on the Yampa River he confused the Little Snake with the Elkhead River. This may be the first written mention of Elkhead.
26. John Wesley Powell, *Explorations of the Colorado River of the West and Its Tributaries; Explored in 1869, 1870, and 1871.* Under the Direction of the Secretary of the Smithsonian Institution. (Washington, DC: U. S. Government Printing Office 1875), 321.
27. Treaty with the Utah, 1849. Signed Dec. 30, 1849. 9 Stats.,984. Ratified, Sept. 9, 1850. Proclaimed, Sept. 9, 1850. Published in *Indian Affairs: Laws and Treaties. Vol.II, Treaties.* Compiled and edited by Charles J. Kappler. (Washington: Government Printing Office, 1904), 585-586. Referred to as the 1849 Treaty at Abiquiu because the signing took place at Abiquiu, New Mexico.
28. Ibid.
29. Ibid.
30. Treaty with the Utah—Tabeguache Band, 1863. Signed October 7, 1863. 13 Stat., 673. Ratified, March 25, 1864. Proclaimed, Dec. 14, 1864. Published in *Indian Affairs: Laws and Treaties. Vol.II,* 856-859. Compiled and edited by Charles J. Kappler. (Washington D.C.: Government Printing Office, 1904). Referred to as the Treaty at Conejos because the signing took place at Conejos, Colorado.
31. Treaty with the Uintah and Yampa or Grand River Bands of the Utah Indians. Signed August 29, 1866. Unratified. Published in *Indian Affairs: Laws and Treaties. Vol.V,* 705-706. Compiled and edited by Charles J. Kappler. (Washington D.C.: Government Printing Office, 1941). Referred to as the Hot Sulphur Springs or Kit Carson Treaty.

32. Ibid.
33. Ibid.
34. Undated statement discussing affairs of Ute and their treaty, subscribed by Gov. Hunt, Kit Carson, and others. National Archives (Enclosure of report of Mar. 13, 1868, ID, LR). In 4. Comr. of Indian Affairs to Sec. of Interior, Mar. 13, 1868, reporting on treaty; Oct. 31, 1868, as amended.
35. Ibid.
36. Ibid.
37. Ibid.
38. Ibid.
39. Ibid.
40. Ibid.
41. Treaty with the Eastern Shoshoni, 1863. Signed July 2, 1863. 18Stats.,685. Ratified March 7, 1864. Proclaimed, June 7, 1869. Published in *Indian Affairs: Laws and Treaties. Vol.II,* 849-850. Compiled and edited by Charles J. Kappler. (Washington, D.C.: Government Printing Office, 1904).
42. *Annual Report of the Commissioner of Indian Affairs to the Secretary of the Interior for the Year 1881.* Washington D.C.: Government Printing Office, 1881, xxxiv.
43. *Annual Report of the Department of Interior for the Fiscal Year ended June 30, 1902. Indian Affairs, Part 1, Report of the Commissioner and Appendixes,* (Washington D.C.: Government Printing Office, 1903). 352. Indian Agent H.P. Myton writes: "There are two schools on this reservation, viz, the Uinta and the Ouray. [The Yamparika Ute were removed to the Uintah reservation in 1881]. These Indians are very much opposed to the schools, and it is very difficult to get them to send their children to school; in fact, there are a large number of them that can only be put in school by force. I have coaxed and threatened ever since I have been here. I have discharged Indian employees, for refusing, and have withheld all favors from Indians who refused to place their children in school. But I am convinced that nothing but force will reach a number of them.

"I don't think reservation schools do as much good as the non-reservation schools do. It is very difficult to keep them from talking their own language. And during vacation they go back to their camps, and when they come back to school in the Fall they seem to have forgotten much that they learned the year before."

The agent's account is reiterated by the acting Superintendent of Schools, James W. Reynolds on page 353: "The attitude of the older Indians toward the school is one of animosity. Everything that can possibly be charged to the detriment of the school is brought up, and every effort is made to keep children out of school. The medicine man is one of the greatest enemies of the school and should be suppressed."

44. Meeker's threat referred to a real initiative by Colorado legislators in Congress to have the state's entire Ute population removed to Indian Territory in Kansas. See: Russel D. Santala, "The Ute Campaign of 1879: A Study in the Use of the Military Instrument." Masters Thesis, (U.S. Army Command and General Staff College, Fort Leavenworth, KS, 1993.) 76.
45. *White River Ute Commission Investigation*, Ex. Doc. 83, House of Representatives, 46th Congress, 2nd session, Submitted May 14, 1880. 7-8. Generally referred to as the "Los Piños Commission" because the hearings were held at Los Piños, Colorado over several days in the winter of 1879 and the spring of 1880 following Meeker's death.
46. Ibid. General John Pope was a Civil War Union Army general who was in charge of the Army's Missouri division.
47. The BIA combined the Ouray and Uintah reservations in 1886. Today the name of the reservation is the Uintah and Ouray Reservation. The proper name of the tribe is the Ute Indian Tribe of the Uintah and Ouray Reservation. There are two other federally recognized Ute tribes that are part of the Ute Nation: the Ute Mountain Ute who are primarily descendants of the Weeminuche Band who were forced onto to the Ute Mountain Ute Reservation in 1897; and the Southern Ute Indian Tribe who are primarily descendants of the Caputa (Capote) and Mouache Bands who were forced onto the

Southern Ute Indian Reservation in 1895. The acreage of all three reservations has been greatly diminished over time. By 1933, 91% of the Uintah Ouray Reservation was taken in an allotment process called severalty.

48. Sondra Jones, "'Redeeming' the Indian: The Enslavement of Indian Children in New Mexico and Utah," *Utah Historical Quarterly* 67, no.3 (1999):232.
49. *White River Ute Commission Investigation*, 7–8.
50. "Testimony of Captain Jack, of the White River Utes, December 3 & 4, 1879." Appendix P. *White River Ute Commission Investigation*, 66.
51. "Testimony of Douglas, chief of the White River Utes, November 13, 1879." Appendix P. *White River Ute Commission Investigation*, 3.
52. "Testimony of Captain Jack, of the White River Utes, December 3 & 4, 1879." 67.
53. Ibid, 67-68.
54. Dan Davidson, director of the Northwest Colorado Museum in Craig, Colorado provided invaluable assistance in figuring out who H.E. Peck and family were and where they lived.
55. "Testimony of Captain Jack, of the White River Utes, December 3 & 4, 1879." 68.
56. Ibid.
57. Ibid.
58. Ibid, 69.
59. Ibid.
60. Ibid, 65.
61. Ibid, 69-70.
62. Ibid, 70-71.
63. Ibid, 71.
64. Ibid.
65. Ibid, 72.
66. Ibid.
67. According to Beth Simmons, *Colorow: A Colorado Photographic Chronicle* Morrison, CO: Friends of Dinosaur Ridge, 2015d, Colorow

was born a Comanche around 1913. He was captured as a child by the Mouache Ute. He married three Yamparika sisters, Recha, Siah and Poopa and had thirteen children. He died in 1888, nine years after the Battle of Milk Creek

68. "Testimony of Captain Jack, of the White River Utes, December 3 & 4, 1879." 72-73.
69. In "Testimony of Sow-er-ick of the White River Utes, November 14, 1879." 12.
70. *White River Ute Commission Investigation,* 70.
71. "Testimony of Colorado, chief of the White River Utes, December 1, 1879" Appendix O. *White River Ute Commission Investigation,* 64.
72. Ibid.
73. Indian Citizenship Act (Snyder Act) of 1924. (43 Stat.253). 68th Congress. Enacted June 2, 1924. There were various attempts to give U.S. citizenship to Native Americans prior to 1924, and estimates vary as to how many Native Americans were paying taxes and considered citizens before 1924. There were also widespread efforts to undo or subvert laws bestowing citizenship on Native Americans. Citizenship did not ensure the right to vote. The right to vote depended on state laws; for example, New Mexico and Arizona denied Native Americans the vote until laws were passed in 1957 and in 1965 when Native Americans were included in the Voting Rights Act. Colorado denied Ute people living on reservations in Colorado the right to vote for five years after the passage of the 1965 Voting Rights Act. "Tribal members living on reservations in Colorado could not vote until 1970." *What Does Equal Suffrage Mean?* Dawn Di Prince. Colorado History document published online August 16, 2020.
74. Willis Carpenter to author, June 27, 2013. Colorado became a Territory in 1861.
75. David McMillan and David Chavis, "Sense of Community: A Definition and Theory" *Journal of Community Psychology,* Vol. 14. January 1986.
76. David D. Hall, "Peace, Love, Puritanism" *New York Times.* Nov. 23, 2010. Hall published a book on the same topic, *A Reforming People*

and the Transformation of Public Life in New England, (Chapel Hill: UNC Press, 2011).

77. *Statement of Pit-she-shook, Concerning the Certain Indians in Colorado, in October 1897.* Prepared by Special Agent E. B. Reynolds. Submitted December 16, 1897, 1.
78. *Annual Reports of the Department of Interior: Indian Affairs, For the Fiscal Year Ended June 30, 1898.* (Washington D.C.: Government Printing Office,) 8, 72.
79. Ibid, 73.
80. *Statement of Nannatchaav, Concerning the Certain Indians in Colorado, in October 1897.* Prepared by Special Agent E. B. Reynolds. Submitted December 16, 1897, 1.
81. *Statement of Pit-she-shook*, 1897, 1.
82. William H. Beck, Capt. U.S. Army Acting U.S. Agent to Commissioner of Indian Affairs, July 26, 1897.
83. Ibid.
84. *Statement of Un-gut-she-one-Starr, Concerning the Certain Indians in Colorado, in October 1897.* Prepared by Special Agent E. B. Reynolds. Submitted December 16, 1897, 2.
85. *Statement of Sir-e-outs, Concerning the Certain Indians in Colorado, in October 1897,* Prepared by Special Agent E. B. Reynolds. Submitted December 16, 1897, 1.
86. *Annual Reports of the Department of the Interior: Indian Affairs 1898*, 71.
87. *Statement of Nannatchaav, 1897*, 2.
88. *Statement of Un-gut-she-one-Starr, 1897*, 4.
89. Ibid.
90. "Utes Killed in Colorado; They Fired on Game Warden Wilcox and His Party and A Fight Followed. The Whites Also Suffered Gen. Otis Says Troops Will Be Sent Out If Necessary—The Indians Crossed the Line from Utah," *New York Times*, October 27, 1897, 1.
91. "Pale Faces at Fault," *Salt Lake Tribune*. November 30, 1897.
92. "Settlers are Warned," *Deseret News*, October 28, 1897.

93. Agent E.B. Reynolds to Commissioner of Indian Affairs, T.J. Morgan, December 16, 1897.

94. *Annual Report of the Commissioner of Indian Affairs to the Secretary of the Interior for the Year, 1898.* (Washington D.C.: Government Printing Office), p. 73.

95. *Report of the Commissioner of Indian Affairs, Office of Indian Affairs Sept. 30, 1907.* (Washington D.C.: Government Printing Office), 130.

96. "Disgruntled Utes. No Use for the Soldiers. Provisions are Already Running Short and Wild Game Scarce, But They Continue on Northward." *Vernal Express*, June 9, 1906.

97. "Crossing the Range. Utes Gather their Stock and Bid Farewell to the Uintah Reservation," *Vernal Express*, May 26, 1906. The article ends with the sentence: "They give as a reason for going that they do not want to live on their allotments among the white people, but want to be by themselves."

98. Photo identifications from Clifford Duncan, "The Northern Utes of Utah," *A History of Utah's American Indians* (2000), 206.

99. Agent H.P. Myton to Commissioner of Indian Affairs, February 19, 1899 cited in Floyd A. O'Neil and Kathryn L. MacKay, "A History of the Uintah-Ouray Ute Lands," *American West Center Occasional Papers*, no date. 26. See also Floyd O'Neil, "An Anguished Odyssey: The Flight of the Utes 1906-1908," *Utah Historical Quarterly*, Fall 1968, vol. 36, no.4, 315-327.

100. The name Sow-er-ick may be a written variation of Sowawick. Sowawick was a prominent Ute who led a group from the Uintah Reservation back to Colorado in 1899.

101. *Annual Reports of the Department of Interior. 1906. Indian Affairs: Report of the Commissioner and Appendixes.* (Washington, D.C.: Government Printing Office, 1906), 78.

102. Ibid.

103. Acting Commissioner Larabee to The Secretary of the Interior conveying the report made by Lieut. Co. Frank West, June 9, 1905.

104. *Annual Reports of the Department of Interior. 1907. Indian Affairs: Report of the Commissioner and Appendixes.* (Washington, D.C.: Government Printing Office, 1906), 130.

105. *Annual Reports, Indian Affairs, 1906*, 79.

106. Ibid, 368.

107. "Department of the Missouri Report," *War Department Annual Report, Vol.3, 1907.* (Washington, D.C.: Government Printing Office, 1907), 123-126.

108. Ibid.

109. Ibid.

110. Captain Carter P. Johnson quoted in "Department of the Missouri Report," *War Department Annual Report Vol. 3, 1907,* 124.

111. Ibid, 125.

112. Photo identifications from Clifford Duncan, "The Northern Utes of Utah," *A History of Utah's American Indians* (2000), 207.

113. *Annual Reports, Indian Affairs, 1906*, 79.

114. *Report of the Commissioner of Indian Affairs to the Secretary of the Interior 1907,* (Washington, D.C.: Government Printing Office, 1907), 158.

115. "Myton Trespass Fines collected," Archives Branch, Denver Federal Records Center, RG 75, Records of the BIA, Uintah and Ouray Agency, Misc. Letters Received. FRC 37120.

116. Agent H.P. Myton to Commissioner of Indian Affairs, July 11, 1902. Archives Branch, Denver Federal Records Center, RG 75, Records of the BIA, Uintah and Ouray Agency, Misc. Letters Received. Letter ID 35563.

117. "Minutes of Councils Held by James McLaughlin, U.S. Indian Inspector with the Uintah and White River Ute Indians at Uintah Agency, Utah From May 18 to May 23, 1903," (Washington, D.C.: Department of Interior, Indian Office, 1903), 13.

118. Ibid, 19.

119. Ibid, 20.

120. Ibid, 15.

121. Ibid, 19.

122. Ibid, 39-40.
123. Ibid, 58.
124. Ibid, 59.
125. Ibid, 63.
126. Ibid, 17.
127. Ibid, 62-63.
128. Ibid, 33.
129. Ibid, 20.
130. Ibid, 63.
131. Ibid, 48.
132. Ibid, 63.
133. Ibid, 89.
134. Ibid, 39.
135. James McLaughlin to Secretary of Interior, May 30, 1903, 5.
136. Ibid.
137. "The Ute Campaign," *War Department, U.S.A. Annual Reports, 1907,* vol. 3, 71.
138. *Annual Reports, Indian Affairs, 1907,* 130.
139. "Utes Must Work, Says Roosevelt," *New York Times,* November 3, 1907.
140. "Bureau Clashes Over Ute Indians," *New York Times,* November 2, 1907.
141. James McLaughlin, U.S. Indian Inspector to Captain C.G. Hall, Acting Indian Agent, Uintah Agency, White Rocks, Utah, August 1, 1907.
142. "Bureau Clashes Over Ute Indians," *New York Times,* November 2, 1907.
143. *Report of the Commissioner of Indian Affairs to the Secretary of the Interior 1908,* (Washington, D.C.: Government Printing Office, 1908), 120.
144. Quaker mountain was named for its abundant aspen trees whose leaves, locals noted, "quaked" or trembled in the slightest wind.
145. John Wesley Powell, *Report on the Lands of the Arid Region of the United States, with a More Detailed Account of the Lands of Utah. With Maps.* (Washington, D.C.: Government Printing Office, 1879), 2.
146. Ibid.
147. Ibid.

148. Ibid, 23.

149. Great Plains Drought Area Committee, *Report of the Great Plains Drought Area Committee August 1936,* Morris Cook, et.al. (Washington, D.C.: Government Printing Office, 1936).

150. George Vaile, testimony in James W. Oldham, Plaintiff in Error V. The People of the State of Colorado, Defendant in Error, Colorado State Supreme Court filed January 22, 1915. 61 Colo. 413 (1916) No. 8557. 262:904.

151. Ibid, 263:905-906.

152. Ibid. Rose's last name remains unknown.

153. "J.H. Ratliff Experiences 1905 -1914 U.S. Forest Service." *History of Routt National Forest, 1905-1972,* 104. Bound typescript at Bud Warner Library, Steamboat Springs, CO. "The big cattle outfits were the Sevens, owned by Mr. Jeffy Pierce and Mr. Joseph Reefe; the Two Bars, owned by Ora Haley; the Circle Bar, owned by the Carey Family; the Ayers outfit chiefly financed by the American Livestock Company; the OVO, a local organization formed by the settlers on the Little Snake River which flows along the Colorado Wyoming border, all organizations of men or individuals who imported yearlings steers from South Texas, New Mexico, Arizona and sometimes form Nevada, Oregon and Idaho. These outfits controlled 75% (a conservative estimate) of the livestock occupying the public range on the west slopes of the Continental Divide. For years these men or cattle companies had used public grazing lands unhindered and without control except that forced upon them by necessity, such as storms, cattle thieves or the encroaching or invasion by nomadic roaming bands of sheep owned by equally large corporations and individuals in Wyoming."

154. *History of the Routt National Forest 1905-1972,* 18.

155. "J.H. Ratliff Experiences," *History of Routt National Forest,* 118. Ratliff added on the same page: "To understand the difficulties of managing this range, it must be remembered the boundaries of the Forest Reserve were loosely drawn."

156. "Old History of the Routt National Forest as told by Ray Peck," *History of Routt National Forest,* 163.
157. Ratliff, *History of Routt National Forest,* 119.
158. The most interesting lawsuit was one brought against Ratliff for fraud. Elkhead homesteader, U.F. Harrison apparently sold a stallion to Ratliff but kept a chattel mortgage of $600 on the stallion. When Ratliff decided to take the job with the forest service, he sold the stallion to a neighbor, Matt Gates, with Harrison's permission. A year later, Harrison demanded his horse back from Ratliff and eventually took it back from Gates. Harrison then had Ratliff arrested and charged with "selling mortgaged goods without the consent of the mortgagee" and "using false pretenses to obtain something of value." Ratliff, *History of Routt National Forest,* 115. The U.S. Forest Service got involved, all the way up to the first Chief of USFS, Gifford Pinchot, because Harrison had recently purchased a large cattle ranch, Ora Haley's Two Bar, and the assumption was that he was trying to discredit Ratliff on behalf of the large cattle outfits. John Rolphe Burroughs, *Where the Old West Stayed Young,* New York: 1962, 287.
159. The fence was along the western boundary, close to Elkhead. Ratliff describes the fence in his memoir essay. "From Four-mile Creek north to Baker's Peak," *History of Routt National Forest,"* 163.
160. George and Willmenia (Minnie) Hughes, homesteaders in Elkhead also owned this sawmill, or perhaps a different one, on Bears Ears which the local newspaper reported they sold in 1918.
161. Farrington R. Carpenter, testimony in James W. Oldham, Plaintiff in Error V. The People of the State of Colorado, Defendant in Error, Colorado State Supreme Court filed January 22, 1915. 61 Colo. 413 (1916) No. 8557. 200:624.
162. Ibid, 201.
163. Ibid, 206.
164. Farrington Carpenter to Mother and Family, August 8, 1909.
165. Farrington Carpenter, Interviewed by Bill May. Transcription of tape recording. Routt County, August 19, 1979. See also Farrington

Carpenter to Edward and Belle Carpenter, undated but presumed to be 1909.

166. Farrington Carpenter to Edward and Belle Carpenter, circa 1909.
167. Farrington Carpenter to James W. Oldham, no date. Included as Exhibit K in James W. Oldham, Plaintiff in Error V. The People of the State of Colorado, Defendant in Error, Colorado State Supreme Court filed January 22, 1915. 61 Colo. 413 (1916) No. 8557. 158.
168. James W. Oldham to Farrington R. Carpenter, 1910. Included as Exhibit L in James W. Oldham, Plaintiff in Error V. The People of the State of Colorado, Defendant in Error, Colorado State Supreme Court filed January 22, 1915. 61 Colo. 413 (1916) No. 8557. 200:624. 208.
169. Ibid.
170. Ibid.
171. Arie Keitel, testimony in James W. Oldham, Plaintiff in Error V. The People of the State of Colorado, Defendant in Error, Colorado State Supreme Court filed January 22, 1915. 61 Colo. 413 (1916) No. 8557. 247:859.
172. "Mustang Stallions," *Routt County Republican*, July 20, 1906. Included as Exhibit J, James W. Oldham, Plaintiff in Error V. The People of the State of Colorado, Defendant in Error, Colorado State Supreme Court filed January 22, 1915. 61 Colo. 413 (1916) No. 8557. 192.
173. "Third and Last Warning," *Routt County Republican*, April 5, 1907. Included as Exhibit J in James W. Oldham, Plaintiff in Error V. The People of the State of Colorado, Defendant in Error, Colorado State Supreme Court filed January 22, 1915. 61 Colo. 413 (1916) No. 8557. 192.
174. Edgar Knowles, testimony in James W. Oldham, Plaintiff in Error V. The People of the State of Colorado, Defendant in Error, Colorado State Supreme Court filed January 22, 1915. 61 Colo. 413 (1916) No. 8557. 132:422-423.
175. Elkhead East, *Routt County Republican*, May 29, 1908.
176. Surveying land and designating it "open" for homesteading began after the Homesteading law was enacted in 1862. The peak of homesteading applications didn't occur in the U.S. until around 1920. Elkhead was relatively late in becoming available for homesteaders

but shares a similar timeline with the U.S. in that 1920 was when homesteading applications and patents crested in Elkhead.

177. Carpenter, Farrington, *Confessions of a Maverick,* Denver, CO: Colorado State Historical Association, 1984, 75.
178. Farrington R. Carpenter, "Stockman of the Year Award" (Speech, Colorado State University, 1967).
179. "Railroad Came to Steamboat 100 Years Ago," *Steamboat Pilot,* January 16, 2009.
180. "Rush of Homesteaders Begins," *Routt County Republican,* April 30, 1909. States that $50,000 was spent advertising the rail line and that the Moffat Road company sent out 10,000 letters in response to enquiries.
181. Minnie Jones Camelletti. Interviewed by author, Becky Fernald and Mary Palmer. Hayden, CO., July 5, 1973.
182. Ibid.
183. Elkhead was one of the many areas in Colorado that was over hunted to the point that by 1919 there was concern that many wild mammals would become extinct. According to the *History of Routt National Forest,* 58: "In 1919 the supervisor recommended that the deer season be closed indefinitely. The elk season had been closed for some years but poaching was reported. In 1921 there were reported 400 elk, 155 mountain sheep, 200 deer, 2450 beaver and 240 bear on the Routt forest. Not a very impressive showing. Only 5 elk, 10 deer, 100 beaver and 10 bear were reported on the Bears Ears District, the nationally famous hunting ground of the 1890s." The Bears Ears District, closest to Elkhead, was a subsection of the Routt National Forest.
184. "Homesteads are Being Entered," *Steamboat Pilot,* June 9, 1909.
185. Farrington Carpenter. Interviewed by author. Routt County, CO., August 8 and 12, 1973.
186. Isadore Bolten. Interviewed by Ruth Carpenter Woodley. Rawlings, WY, 1926.
187. Ibid.
188. Farrington R. Carpenter. Interviewed by Herbert White. Tape Recording, Routt County, July 11, 1970. Western History Division,

Denver Public Library, Denver, CO. The entire interview is about Bolten. This is from a long section on Bolten's name and Jewish identity.

189. Ibid.
190. Gambel oak, *Quercus gambelii,* is sometimes referred to as scrub oak or white oak. It spouts from acorns but mainly spreads from root spouts, called lignotubers. Because all the trees in a grove are interconnected through their common root system, it is very hardy. From the point of view of a homesteader trying to clear land, oak brush can be very difficult to remove.
191. John Fulton, "The Reclamation Man," unpublished essay, 1958.
192. Ibid.
193. Elkhead East, *Routt County Republican,* August 14, 1910 states Herbie died of "cholera Infantum."
194. "America's Most Unusual Storyteller." *The Saturday Evening Post,* April 12, 1952, 76.
195. Elkhead East, *Routt County Republican,* August 19, 1910.
196. The new Elkhead district carved out of two earlier formed districts, contained 220 square miles or 140,800 acres. Most of the land was held either by the federal or the state government: 120 square miles (76,800 acres) was part of what became the Routt National Forest and 1440 were public lands later held by the Bureau of Land Management; 5.25 square miles (3360 acres) were owned by State of Colorado. Public lands claimed by homesteaders through the homesteading laws or by pre-emption amounted to 92.5 square miles (59,200 acres). Mineral holdings are separate from surface holdings. The district was able to tax valuable private mineral holdings under privately held land.
197. Edward F. Carpenter, *America's First Grazier,* (Wellington, CO: Vestige Press, 2004), 45, and Farrington R. Carpenter, *Confessions of a Maverick,* Colorado State Historical Association, 50.
198. Rosamond Underwood to George Underwood, July 30, 1916.
199. Julia Smith Pizor. Interviewed by author, Becky Fernald and Mary Palmer. Tape recording. Hayden, CO., June 26, 1973.
200. Ibid.
201. Elkhead East, *Routt County Republican,* July 1, 1910.

202. Some Notes on the Life of Emma Hull Peck and Her Work in Routt Co. *Steamboat Pilot*, April 13, 1934 and April 27, 1934.
203. Women gained the right to vote in Colorado by referendum in 1893. In 1876, in the original Colorado Constitution, women gained suffrage in school elections. Article VII Suffrage and Elections, Section 1, part 2: "That no person shall be denied the right to vote at any school district election, nor to hold any school district office, on account of sex."
204. Elkhead East, *Routt County Republican*, August 5, 1910.
205. *Routt County Republican*, March 10, 1911.
206. The spelling of Jykadorke name is based on how it appears in the 1910 census. People in Hayden pronounce it Jack-a-dow-ski. In census records and newspapers his name is spelled variously: Jykadorske, Jakodovske, Jodske, Jackodovske, Jadorkey, Jykadorke.
207. Elkhead East, *Routt County Republican*, September 9, 1910.
208. It was not until 1916 that the government automatically reserved all minerals under any homestead claim. Colorado surface owners were, and still are today, subservient to the rights of the mineral owner. If the mineral owner wants to mine, the surface owner cannot deny entry or use of the surface.
209. "County School Notes," *Routt County Republican*, March 17, 1911. Part of a longer article reviewing the status of schools in the county and various other petitions.
210. Elkhead East, *Routt County Republican*, April 21, 1911.
211. Leila Ferguson Ault. Interviewed by author, Mary Palmer and Becky Fernald. Tape recording. Yampa, CO., July 7, 1973.
212. Ibid.
213. Ibid.
214. "East Elkhead," *Routt County Republican*, December 15, 1911.
215. Questions for the County Examination of Teachers for First, Second and Third Grade Certificates, August 18 and 19, 1910. Prepared by Katherine M. Cooks, Superintendent of Public Instruction, Denver, Colo. Archives, Colorado State Normal School, Greeley, Colorado. Currently held at University of Northern Colorado, Greeley.

216. The school on the Adair Ranch was usually called the Red Top School because its red roof.

217. Leila Ferguson Ault. Interview by author, Mary Palmer and Becky Fernald. Tape recording. Yampa, CO., July 16, 1973.

218. Ibid.

219. Steve's full name was James Steven Cook. He was born around 1862 in Illinois and was married twice before he married Gratis. Her maiden name is unknown to the author. She was 13 years younger than Steve Cook. The census in 1910 listed her, and her parents, as being from Tennessee.

220. Leila Ferguson Ault, interview July 16, 1973.

221. Ibid.

222. Ibid.

223. *Steamboat Pilot,* June 28, 1911.

224. Leila Ferguson Ault, interview July 16, 1973

225. *Routt County Republican,* April 12, 1912.

226. "C.D. Hayes Killed By Lightning" *Routt County Republican,* May 10, 1912. For more information on the Clayborn and Margrett (Maggie) Gallager Hayes family, see Edna J. Hayes, "Hayes, William Clayborn," in *History of Hayden and West Routt County, 1876-1989,* Dallas, TX: Curtis Media Corporation 197.

227. *Routt County Republican,* July 1, 1909.

228. Edith W. Smith, "Smith, A.M. Family," in *History of Hayden and West Routt County 1876-1989,* Dallas, TX: Curtis Media Corporation, 286-287.

229. Opal Bisel to Chuck Fulton, April 28, 1994. Hayden Heritage Museum archives.

230. Ibid.

231. *Routt County Republican,* August 16,1912. Census records do not appear to confirm the J.C. Freeman family in Medicine Bow. The Routt County Republican mentions J.C. Freeman, James Freeman and Clarence Freeman. These may refer to the same person or they may refer to J.C. and Ethel Freeman's son whom they named James

C. According to the 1920 Census, James C. and Ethel were living Dry Fork March 8, 1920. Children listed are Louise, age 11, James C. 9, Carl P. 8, Elizabeth L. 6, Louis R. 3½, Lester L. 3½, and Earl 1½. The story of the Freeman's claim on Wolf Mountain is drawn from James G. Hood and Evangeline Ames Hood, "The Country that Boomed and Faded 1913-1933," unpublished manuscript. "Clarence and Ethel Freeman had a homestead on Wolf Mountain. They lived there with their children, Jim, Louise, Paul, the twins, and Betty. One of the Freeman's neighbors was Tom Prevo and wife."

232. *Routt County Republican*, Sept 27, 1912.
233. Ibid
234. Leila Ferguson Ault, interview July 16, 1973.
235. Dr. John V. Solandt, testimony in James W. Oldham, Plaintiff in Error V. The People of the State of Colorado, Defendant in Error, Colorado State Supreme Court filed January 22, 1915. 61 Colo. 413 (1916) No. 8557. 149:477 thru 153:488.
236. George W. Smith, testimony in James W. Oldham, Plaintiff in Error V. The People of the State of Colorado, Defendant in Error, Colorado State Supreme Court filed January 22, 1915. 61 Colo. 413 (1916) No. 8557. 186:587.
237. "James W. Oldham Will Leave Upon Payment of $1000 Cash," *Routt County Sentinel*, August 8, 1913.
238. Judge Chas. A Morning, testimony in James W. Oldham, Plaintiff in Error V. The People of the State of Colorado, Defendant in Error, Colorado State Supreme Court filed January 22, 1915. 61 Colo. 413 (1916) No. 8557. 113:369. Morning testified, "I never saw James Oldham jubilant over anything, he was always a very sad man."
239. Present at the school board meeting: Romaine and Angelina Haller, Arthur Fredrickson, George Murphy, Jim Barnes, Alex Ferguson, Sam Lighthizer, Frank Corbin, Ferry Carpenter, James Oldham, Isadore Bolten, Charles and Cliff Fulton, Ed Smith, William and Ida Kleckner.
240. Mary McDowell Glanville. Interview by author. August 1, 1973.
241. Sam Lighthizer, testimony in James W. Oldham, Plaintiff in Error V. The People of the State of Colorado, Defendant in Error, Colorado

State Supreme Court filed January 22, 1915. 61 Colo. 413 (1916) No. 8557. 34:132.

242. William Kleckner, testimony in James W. Oldham, Plaintiff in Error V. The People of the State of Colorado, Defendant in Error, Colorado State Supreme Court filed January 22, 1915. 61 Colo. 413 (1916) No. 8557. 21:98.
243. Charles Fulton, testimony in James W. Oldham, Plaintiff in Error V. The People of the State of Colorado, Defendant in Error, Colorado State Supreme Court filed January 22, 1915. 61 Colo. 413 (1916) No. 8557. 82:281.
244. Frank Corbin, testimony James W. Oldham, Plaintiff in Error V. The People of the State of Colorado, Defendant in Error, Colorado State Supreme Court filed January 22, 1915. 61 Colo. 413 (1916) No. 8557. 69:240.
245. Dr. R.J. Enochs testimony, *Coroner's Inquest upon the body of Clifton Fulton deceased.* May 5, 1914. 1.
246. "Eph Donnelson is Murdered Shot to Death by Simp Tipton a Neighboring Ranchman," *Steamboat Pilot,* July 29, 1908.
247. "Clifford Fulton," *Routt County Republican,* May 15, 1914. The funeral was on Wednesday following Fulton's death on Monday.
248. Frank Corbin, testimony James W. Oldham, Plaintiff in Error V. The People of the State of Colorado, Defendant in Error, Colorado State Supreme Court filed January 22, 1915. 61 Colo. 413 (1916) No. 8557. 69:240.
249. Mary Officer Brunner. Interview by author, Mary Palmer and Becky Fernald. July 18, 1973.
250. Ibid.
251. Ibid. Although I had an extensive interview with Mary McDowell, she never mentioned Cliff Fulton or the murder. Mary Officer was paid $50 per month; Mary McDowell $75 per month. Both taught six-month terms in 1914.
252. Julia Smith and Myrtle Barnes attended high school in Hayden because there was not a high school in Elkhead yet.
253. "Award of Premiums," *Routt County Republican* October 5, 1917 and October 4, 1918.

254. The Graves were not in Elkhead for very long and exactly where they lived is still in question. The newspaper said that Iva Rench bought "the Graves ranch" in 1917, but there is no record of their owning land or a house.
255. See later footnote on mineral ownership and assessor's records. It was sometimes difficult to collect taxes from the mineral owners. "Sam Perry objects to an assessment of $33,000 on his $500,000 property. There are a lot of Sam Perry's in the country and we can't see why they should not dig up just as well as we little fellows." *Routt County Republican,* September 2, 1910.
256. "Routt County Coal," *Routt County Republican,* January 2, 1914.
257. "$4,000,000 For Hayden," *Routt County Republican,* June 3, 1910 and "Hayden—Caspar," *Routt County Republican,* June 13, 1913, announces plans for a railroad between Hayden and shipping points in Wyoming that would pass through California Park on the eastern side of Elkhead. "Anthracite Coal Hayden's Future as a Coal Center Now Assured. Hayden to Become Greatest Shipping Point in West," *Routt County Republican,* August 28, 1908, contains more promotional material for David Moffat and coal interests in general.
258. "Model Rural School: Community Celebrates Opening of New Educational Building," *Steamboat Pilot,* November 10, 1915. Valuation according to the county assessor. Valuation was up from $175.000 in 1911. Eunice Pleasant Carpenter in "The Passing of the Elkhead School," *Steamboat Pilot,* October 19,1938 says the 1916 valuation was $609,316 when the district voted in a 4 mil tax.
259. "School Meetings" *Routt County Republican,* May 7, 1915.
260. Leila Ferguson Ault, interview, July 16, 1973.
261. Farrington R. Carpenter. Interview by author, Mary Palmer and Becky Fernald. Tape recording. Routt County, CO., August 8, 1973.
262. Leila Ferguson Ault interview, July 16, 1973.
263. Farrington R. Carpenter interview August 8, 1973.
264. Leila Ferguson Ault interview, July 16,1973.

265. Ben Bisel later married Anna Maynard whose family had homesteaded earlier in Elkhead. Opal Bisel Rowe. Interview by author. Tape Recording. Routt County, CO., Summer 1976.

266. "Model Rural School" *Steamboat Pilot,* November 10, 1915.

267. Leila Ferguson Ault interview, July 16, 1973.

268. Gladys Mitchell Shuttlesworth, "Tribute to an Institution." Typescript circa 1955.

269. Story of serving wine from Galen Kleckner. Interviewed by author, Mary Palmer and Becky Fernald. Tape Recording. Hayden, CO., July 9, 1973.

270. *Routt County Republican,* May 5, 1916. "A petition was circulated asking the county commissioners to establish District 11 into a voting precinct with the new school house for a polling place; upon discussion it was ascertained that of about 70 legal voters in the district, only about 10 to 15 were able to get to Hayden to vote and that had to travel and average distance of 15 miles to get there."

271. Farrington R. Carpenter to Rosamond Underwood and Dorothy Woodruff, July 14, 1916.

272. Farrington R. Carpenter, "Treasurer's Report, June 30, 1916" Elkhead District 11 Schoolboard minutes. Final report published in *Routt County Republican,* August 25, 1916.

273. R.N. "Bobby" Robinson. Interview with author, Mary Palmer and Becky Fernald. Tape Recording. Hayden, CO., August 7, 1973. Robinson said Maynard died a very painful death due to locked bowels after his parents refused to allow Dr. Solandt to perform surgery.

274. Farrington R. Carpenter to Rosamond Underwood and Dorothy Woodruff, July 18, 1916.

275. Charlotte Perry (Smith 1911) met Portia Mansfield Swett (Smith 1910) at Smith College and in 1915 they started a dance school which later became the Perry-Mansfield Dance Camp. Portia is mentioned as Portia Sweet or Swett in Rosamond Underwood's letters.

276. Marj Harrison Marr was listed as Margaret in the 1900 census when she was 10. She married Evan Marr in March 1916. Only Ruth and Frank attended her wedding. She would have been 15 or 16.

Virginia Marr was born in 1918 and Elizabeth Marr was born in 1920 according to Edward F. Carpenter, "Marr, Evan G," *History of Hayden and West Routt County, 1876–1989,* 236.

277. Frank Harrison. Interviewed by author, Mary Palmer and Becky Fernald. Tape Recording. Hayden, CO., July 18, 1973.
278. "Model Rural School," *Steamboat Pilot,* November 10, 1915. "The graduation exercises of the two schools were held Friday night in the new building the following class being given diplomas: Lela [Leila] Ferguson, Frank Barnes, Ina Hayes, Eleanor Haller, Galen Kleckner, Florence Jones, Helen Jones and Ezra Smith." Also, Rosamond Underwood to Grace Underwood, August 6, 1916 wrote, "I have six girls, five of them in 9th grade." She also says she has Lewis age 12 in 8th grade and Ezra age 11 in 6th grade.
279. Robert N. Robinson. Interview, August 7, 1973.
280. Ibid.
281. Ibid.
282. Leila Ferguson Ault. Interview. July 16, 1973.
283. Gladys Mitchell Shuttlesworth, "Tribute to an Institution," circa 1955, unpublished manuscript, 4.
284. Dorothy Woodruff to Papa, September 30, 1916.
285. Liberty Hyde Bailey, *The Country Life Movement in the United States,* (New York: McMillan Co. 1915). In 1908 Bailey was appointed by President Theodore Roosevelt to chair a Commission on Country Life. The commission's report was published in 1909.
286. "Dr. Solandt Killed in Automobile Accident: Crushed Beneath Car on Trull Road," *Routt County Republican.* September 29, 1916. Jane Sprague was the widowed mother of Si Michaels and Gertrude (Gertie) Sprague who married Thomas McManus at the Rock School house.
287. Dorothy Woodruff to Mother, no date but assumed to be soon after October 31, 1916, and was likely included in a bundle of letters begun on October 26, 1916.
288. *Routt County Republican,* August 20, 1916.

289. "too dictatorial," Dorothy Woodruff to Milly September 6, 1916. "Typical old maid," Ben Fulton. Interviewed by author, Mary Palmer and Becky Fernald. Hayden, CO., August 16, 1973.

290. Rosamond Underwood to Papa, August 27, 1916.

291. Dorothy Woodruff to Anna, August 27, 1916.

292. Marie Huguenin Holderness. Interviewed by author, Mary Palmer and Becky Fernald. Routt County, CO., July 14, 1973 and August 27, 1973.

293. Ibid.

294. Rosamond Underwood to Papa, September 8-11, 1916.

295. Rosamond Underwood to Mother, October 22, 1916.

296. Dorothy Woodruff to Anna, October 1916.

297. Land transfer Frank Oldham to Isadore Bolten, March 13, 1915. Routt County Assessor, *Grantor and Grantee Index Books by Range, Township and Section,* Routt County Courthouse, Steamboat Springs, CO. Bolten deeded the land to his father, Alia Boloten, on May 17, 1915. Alia Boloten deeded it back to Isadore Bolten in 1924.

298. Charles Fulton. Interviewed by author, Mary Palmer and Becky Fernald. Hayden, CO., July 27, 1973 and Ben Fulton interview, August 16, 1973. See also John Fulton Christmas Letter 1958.

299. Dorothy Woodruff to Herm, December 12, 1916.

300. *Routt County Republican,* July 20, 1917.

301. *"An Act to authorize the President to increase temporarily the military establishment of the United States,"* Public Law 65-12. *Statutes at Large* 40 (1917): 76 Chapter 15, 76-83.

302. "June 5 Designated as Day of Service Registration," *Steamboat Pilot,* May 23, 1917.

303. *Routt County Sentinel,* July 13, 1917. The full list for Elkhead was: Everett W. Adair, Frank C. Corbin, Farrington R. Carpenter, Earl C. Callen, Ernest B. Sargent, Earl M. Rice, Thomas E. Mathis, Paul J. Jones, Ed. C. Hughes, James C. Hood, Louis Charos, Clarence E. Horton, Otto C. Horton, and Frederick H. Eshom.

304. *Routt County Republican,* December 17, 1917.

305. Israel Boloten (later Isadore Bolten) was born on March 28, 1885. He died on February 16, 1951.
306. *Routt County Republican,* November 23, 1917.
307. *Routt County Republican,* March 29, 1918.
308. *Routt County Republican,* October 10, 1919.
309. *Routt County Sentinel,* December 12, 1919.
310. Richard Ferguson. Interviewed by author, Mary Palmer and Becky Fernald, Lakewood, CO., July 31, 1973. He mentions prices as starting at $90 and going down to $60 in one year (assumed to be 1920) and down to $30 in 1921. See also Charles I. Bray, "Financing Western Cattlemen," *Colorado Agricultural College Bulletin 338.* Fort Collins, CO.: December 1928, 24.
311. Routt County Assessors tax records, 1915. Colorado Anthracite: $159. Routt Co. Anthracite $13. U.S. Marble and Iron $52.80. Sam Perry's holding is listed as Colorado Anthracite.
312. Helen Fulton White to author, December 14, 1984.
313. Marie Huguenin Holderness interviews, July 14 and August 27, 1973.
314. Ibid.
315. *Routt County Republican,* "Elkhead War Work" December 16, 1918.
316. Ruth (Bodfish) Fulton, *Day Book/Diary 1918-1922.* January 29 and 30, 1918. Typescript prepared by Mary Wright, 2020. Janie's full name was Jane Gertrude Robinson.
317. Marie Huguenin Holderness interviews, 1973.
318. Ruth (Bodfish) Fulton, *Day Book/Diary 1918-1922.* February 4 and 6, 1918. Typescript prepared by Mary Wright, 2020.
319. Ibid.
320. Jo Buchanan to author, August 2012. Guy Hayes was not able to leave Chicago due to his poor health.
321. *Routt County Republican,* February 8, 1918.
322. Galen Kleckner interview, July 9, 1973.
323. Allie Kleckner Lasnick. Interviewed by author. Hayden, CO.: August 25, 1973.

324. "Routt County Man Murders His War Bride in Denver," *Steamboat Pilot,* October 19, 1921.
325. *Routt County Republican,* November 7, 1919. Sophia is reported as waiting in San Francisco and the Red Cross helping her get to Denver. Later articles say she was left in Russia.
326. "Three-year-old Boy Again is Safe in His Mother's Arms," *The Saturday Blade,* Chicago, May 22, 1920, 1.
327. "Routt County Man Murders," *Steamboat Pilot,* October 19, 1921.
328. John O'Brien, "Boy Left Orphan by Murder of Mother Loses Playmates." *Denver Post,* May 19, 1923.
329. Louis Charos died in April 1976 at the age of 81 in Mosca, Colorado.
330. In 1930s Routt County courthouse records show that Charos proved up on his homestead and received his patent. A few months later the land was transferred to Isadore Bolten.
331. Ruth Bodfish Fulton, *Day Book/Diary 1918-1922.* Entry January 29, 1918.
332. Rosamond Underwood to Mother, August 6, 1916.
333. Helen's sister, Bessie, was married to Ira Smith and her sister, Susan, was married to James Hood. Her sister, Susan, had a baby that winter, Marjory.
334. Eunice Pleasant to Gertrude Pleasant, August 27, 1919.
335. Ibid.
336. Eunice Pleasant to Gertrude Pleasant, October 26, 1919.
337. Eunice Pleasant to Gertrude Pleasant, October 10, 1919.
338. Eunice Pleasant to Gertrude Pleasant, August 27, 1919.
339. *Routt County Republican,* August 15, 1919.
340. Leila Ferguson interview, July 16, 1973.
341. Eunice Pleasant to Gertrude Pleasant, October 26, 1919.
342. "Regional Survey in British Schools," *Christian Science Monitor,* November 7, 1919.
343. Eunice Pleasant to Gertrude Pleasant, October 10, 1919.
344. *Routt County Republican,* December 13, 1918.

345. Centers for Disease Control and Prevention, National Center for Immunization and Respiratory Diseases (NCIRD)

346. Edward F. Carpenter, *America's First Grazier,* (Wellington, CO: Vestige Press 2004), 58-59.

347. "Much Sickness," *Routt County Republican,* January 16, 1920.

348. "Influenza Wave Past Its Crest: Epidemic of Dread Disease Abates, Few New Cases Developing—13 Die This Week," *Routt County Sentinel,* January 30, 1920. See also Ione Smith Ratcliff. Interviewed by author, Mary Palmer and Becky Fernald. Craig, CO., June 29, 1973.

349. Eunice Pleasant to Gertrude Pleasant, January 23, 1920.

350. Ibid.

351. Eunice Pleasant to Gertrude Pleasant, January 29, 1920.

352. Eunice Pleasant to Gertrude Pleasant, February 13, 1920.

353. Ibid. The baby's name was Marjory Hood. Her older sister, Lois, is listed in the 1920 census taken in March 1920 as one year and ten months old. Susie Jones Hood and James Hood later had two more daughters, Mary and Julia. The family left Elkhead in 1920 after mortgaging their homestead. They moved to California and later to Illinois where they saved up money to pay the mortgage. When they returned to Elkhead in 1932, however, they found their homestead loan had been foreclosed. As Julia Hood Milner later told me, "It was hard to make a living on that ground." Julia Hood Milner. Interviewed by author, Steamboat Springs, CO., July 1, 2018.

354. Eunice Pleasant to Gertrude Pleasant, February 13, 1920.

355. Eunice Pleasant to Gertrude Pleasant, January 29, 1920.

356. "Among Our Neighbors," *Routt County Sentinel,* March 5, 1920.

357. Eunice Pleasant to Gertrude Pleasant, March 28, 1920.

358. Eunice Pleasant to Gertrude Pleasant, April 23, 1920.

359. "Elkhead Commencement," *Routt County Republican,* May 28, 1920.

360. Eunice Pleasant to Gertrude Pleasant, March 22, 1920.

361. Ibid.

362. Eunice Pleasant to Gertrude Pleasant, March 28, 1920

363. Ibid.
364. Eunice Pleasant to Gertrude Pleasant, March 22,1920.
365. *Routt County Republican,* March 19, 1920.
366. *Routt County Republican,* January 23, 1929.
367. Richard Ferguson, interview. July 31, 1973.
368. Ibid.
369. Eunice Pleasant to Gertrude Pleasant, April 23, 1920.
370. Eunice Pleasant to Gertrude Pleasant, March 28, 1920.
371. Leila Ferguson Ault, interview, July 16, 1973.
372. Ibid.
373. Leila Ferguson Ault, interview, July 16, 1973. Richard Ferguson, interview, July 31, 1973. Julia Hood Milner, interview, July 1, 2018. Julia Hood Milner told me that she thought Alex Ferguson ended up at the Insane Asylum in Pueblo, CO. The asylum was renamed the Colorado State Hospital in 1917 and indeed Alex Ferguson apparently spent the last four years of his life there. According to an obituary in the Steamboat Pilot, November 17, 1926, Ferguson (misspelled as Furguson) was diagnosed with Chronic Nephritis—a then incurable injury to the kidney that can be inherited or can be caused by an earlier illness like scarlet fever. Ferguson died at the State Hospital on November 12, 1926 of a massive stroke.
374. Leila Ferguson Ault, interview, July 16, 1973.
375. Richard Ferguson, interview, July 31, 1973.
376. Eunice Pleasant to Gertrude Pleasant, March 28, 1920.
377. Ibid.
378. Eunice Pleasant to Gertrude Pleasant, November 15, 1919.
379. Ibid.
380. Elkhead School, *Manahna* (Elkhead, CO: 1920) Manahna means "years" in Mandan, the language spoken by the Mandan American Indian tribe. The Mandans originally lived in North and South Dakota.
381. Eunice Pleasant to Gertrude Pleasant, April 23, 1920.
382. Ibid.

383. Eunice Pleasant to Gertrude Pleasant, April 23, 1920.
384. Ibid.
385. *Routt County Republican,* May 21, 1920.
386. *Manahna,* 10–13.
387. Ibid.
388. Ibid.
389. *Manahna,* 14
390. *Manahna,* 31.
391. "Elkhead Commencement," *Routt County Republican,* May 28, 1920.
392. Eunice Pleasant to Gertrude Pleasant, December 31, 1919.
393. Eunice Pleasant to Gertrude Pleasant, November 15, 1919.
394. "Elkhead Commencement," *Routt County Republican,* May 28, 1920.
395. Galan Kleckner, Leila Ferguson, Richard Ferguson interviews.
396. Isadore Bolten interviewed by Ruth Carpenter Woodley. Rawlings, WY, 1926.
397. Ibid.
398. First mention of sheep in Elkhead was in the Hayden paper in 1910 when Kitchens and Kleckner are said to own sheep. Later, Harrison sheep are noted as being on Galloway place over winter 1916.
399. "Fresh Meat Prices Decline Steadily Throughout 1921," *Weather, Crops and Markets,* Vol. 1, 1922. (Washington D.C.: United States Department of Agriculture, 1922–1924, 21. "An outstanding feature of the year's trade with respect to prices was the uneven distribution of declines among the various classes of fresh meat. For example, at the four markets under review pork loins led the downward movement with a loss of approximately $10.50 per 100 lbs. for the year, while good mutton showed a net decrease of only $1. Good beef, veal, and choice lamb showed declines of approximately $3.80, $4.73 and $1.75 respectively."
400. Farrington Carpenter interviewed by Herbert White, Routt County, CO., July 11, 1970. Western History Collection, Denver Public Library.
401. Galen Kleckner interview, July 9, 1973.
402. Leila Ferguson Ault interview, July 16, 1973.

403. Ione Smith Ratcliff returned to Elkhead to teach in the lower Elkhead School in 1952. She was one of the last teachers to teach in the Elkhead District 11.

404. Richard Ferguson interview, July 31, 1973.

405. Essam Welch. Interviewed by author. Hayden, CO., August 2018. Welch is Florence Fredrickson's grandson.

406. *Steamboat Pilot,* November 9, 1921.

407. *Routt County Republican,* December 21, 1921.

408. *Routt County Republican,* December 6, 1922.

409. Julia Hood Milner. Interviewed by author. Steamboat Springs, CO., July 1, 2018.

410. *Steamboat Pilot,* July 13, 1927 and November 18, 1927. Izaiah Scott was from Flat Creek, Missouri where he was a tenant farmer. He came to Routt County in 1912 with his wife, Eva, and five children: Ecil, Elzie, Gilbert, Homer and Alma. Together they homesteaded on upper Calf Creek, near the Morsbach, Jones, Hayes and Hood families.

After the resolution of the court case, the Scott sold out in 1928 to Homer and Mary Murphy (no relation to early homeseteaders, George and Mary Murphy) who were soon joined in the Calf Creek-Aigner mountain area by George and Bertha Murphy, Rose Murphy Parks, Mary Murphy's father, Franklin Comstock, and their friend, Jim Campbell. Homer, George and Rose grew up in a large farming family in Hillsboro, Ohio. In 1931 George and Bertha Murphy's son, Cecil married Gladys Rhodes. Cecil taught in the one-room school on the McKinlay ranch from 1931-1935 and he and his new wife lived in Elkhead until 1935. After the Cecil Murphys left Elkhead, Cecil's sister, Rose taught at the Adair School. Descendants of the Homer Murphy family still own land in Elkhead. Jean Coverston Marshall (Wixon) also taught in Elkhead in the 1920s and 1930s.

411. It was not until the 1940s that the Carpenters got a mortgage and purchased the Dawson Ranch. The ranch had been in bankruptcy for a long time. Carpenter said that it was his brother-in-law, Hugh B. Pleasant, who suggested that he and Eunice buy the ranch. Carpenter thought it was not possible but apparently the coal company was ready to get rid of the ranch they found a financial

liability. Carpenter kept his homestead in Elkhead and used it along with other lands for summer grazing.

412. *Routt County Republican,* March 23, 1921. Actual quote says new methods of farming.
413. "Local News," *Routt County Republican,* January 24, 1919. "Jo Covert said he saw Perry Barnes who is now married to Mrs. Riley."
414. Nancy Woolery, "The Morsbach Family in Elkhead and Beyond," unpublished manuscript. Henry and Ethyl Morsbach family reconvened in the early 1940s in Wichita, Kansas where the Morsbach brothers, Rudolph, Jesse and Oliver had jobs in the aircraft plants. The youngest son, Frank Morsbach, who was born in Elkhead in July 1918, suffered from various disabilities and died at age 30.
415. Julia Smith Pizor to author December 10, 1974.
416. Ben Fulton. Interviewed by author, Mary Palmer and Becky Fernald, Hayden, CO., August 16, 1973.
417. Ibid.
418. John Fulton, Christmas Letter 1958.
419. Ed and Ruth Bodfish Fulton sold their land to Jim and Elin Rhodes Carns after WW2. Members of the Carns family still live on the homestead and still farm on the shelf where the Fultons lived.
420. Ben Fulton. Interview. August 16, 1973.
421. Allie Kleckner Lasnick. Interview. August 25, 1925.
422. Ben Fulton. Interview. 1973.
423. Eunice Carpenter, "The Passing of the Elkhead School," On Thinking it Over, *Steamboat* Pilot, October 19, 1938. The reference to the Rock Schoolhouse as a "consolidated" school refers to the practice of closing small, remote school buildings in order to consolidate resources and teachers for a larger school with higher enrollment. The district itself, in this case Elkhead, initiated this type of consolidation. Later, larger, wealthier districts, encouraged and funded by state government, forced small districts to disband and "consolidate".

Bibliography

Testimony, interviews, letters, diaries, unpublished reminiscences, newspaper articles, schoolboard minutes, criminal trial testimony—first-hand accounts—form the basis of this history of Bears Ears country/Elkhead. Testimony given by members of the Ute tribe can be found in various commission reports. These are all available online through the University of Wisconsin's digital library. Interviews with members of the Ute tribe are part of the Doris Duke Oral History Project at the University of Utah. Interviews of Elkheaders are in the possession of the Hayden Heritage Center, Hayden, Colorado. Dorothy Woodruff Hillman's letters are now in the Sophia Smith Collection at Smith College. Rosamond Underwood Perry Carpenter's letters are held by the Perry and Cosel families. Eunice Pleasant's letters are held by the Carpenter family. Photographs of Ute people are used by permission noted in the captions. Photographs of Elkhead people are all held at the Hayden Heritage Center. The diary kept by Ruth Bodfish Fulton, reminiscences by John Fulton and a letter from Mary McDowell to Paroda Bailey Fulton are held by the Fulton and Wattles families. Gladys Mitchell Shuttlesworth, Lewis Harrison and James Hood's unpublished manuscripts are available at the Hayden Heritage Center as is the *Mananha,* the Elkhead School's 1920 yearbook. Land transactions for Routt County starting in the 1880s are documented in Land Books located in the Assessors office in the courthouse in Steamboat

Springs. Applications for homestead patents were published in the local paper. Back issues of the Routt County Republican and the Steamboat Pilot are available for reading at Colorado Historic Newspapers, an online repository. Back issues in physical form are also held in the Hayden Heritage Center in Hayden and the Tread of the Pioneers Museum in Steamboat Springs. The bound manuscript, Routt National Forest, is available for reading at the Steamboat Springs Public Library. The compilation of personal histories published in History of West Routt County is available at the Hayden Public Library and the Hayden Heritage Center. Schoolboard minutes from Elkhead District 11 are in the archives of the Hayden Heritage Center. Documents relating to the trial of James W. Oldham, including testimony and cross examination as well as exhibits, are held at the Colorado State Archives, Denver, Colorado. Census records, ship manifests, draft registration cards and similar records are available from many internet sites including MyHeritage and Ancestry.

Published books and a selection of articles referenced in the text are listed here.

"America's Most Unusual Storyteller." *Saturday Evening Post,* April 12, 1952.

An Act to authorize the President to increase temporarily the military establishment of the United States, Pub. L. No. 65–12, Chapter 15 Statutes at Large 40 76 (1917).

Bailey, Liberty Hyde. *The Country Life Movement in the United States.* New York: McMillan Co, 1915.

Beck, William H. Capt. U.S. Army. Letter to Commissioner of Indian Affairs. "William H. Beck, Capt. U.S. Army Acting U.S. Agent to Commissioner of Indian Affairs," July 26, 1897.

Bray, Charles I. "Financing Western Cattlemen." *Colorado Agricultural College Bulletin* 338 (December 1928).

"Bureau Clashes Over Ute Indians." *New York Times,* November 2, 1907.

Burroughs, John Rolfe. *Where the Old West Stayed Young.* New York: William Morrow and Co., 1962.

Carpenter, Edward F. *America's First Grazier.* Wellington, CO: Vestige Press, 2004.

Carpenter, Farrington R. *Confessions of a Maverick.* Denver: State Historic Society of Colorado, 2004.

Cook, Morris, et.al. "Report of the Great Plains Drought Area Committee." Washington, D.C.: G.P.O., August 1936.

Cuch, Forrest. *History Of Utah's American Indians.* Logan: Utah State University Press, 2003.

DeSmet, Pierre-Jean. *Letters and Sketches, with a Narrative of a Year's Residence among the Indian Tribes of the Rocky Mountains.* Philadelphia, 1843.

Duncan, Clifford. "The Northern Utes of Utah." In *History Of Utah's American Indians,* by Forrest Cuch. Logan: Utah State University Press, 2003.

Escalante, Silvestre Velez. *The Dominguez-Escalante Journal: Their Expedition through Colorado, Utah, Arizona, New Mexico in 1776.* Edited by Ted J. Warner. Translated by Fray Angelico Chavez. Salt Lake City, 1995.

Fremont, John C. "Report of the Exploring Expedition to the Rocky Mountains in the Year 1842." Washington, D.C.: Blair and Rives Printers, 1845.

Goss, James A. "Traditional Cosmology, Ecology and Language of the Ute Indians." In *Ute Indian Arts and Culture,* edited by William Wroth. Colorado Springs, CO: Colorado Springs Fine Arts Center, 2000.

Hague, Arnold, and Samuel Emmons. "Elkhead Mountains, Section 7." In *Descriptive Geology.* US Government Printing Office, 1877.

Hall, David. *A Reforming People and the Transformation of Public Life in New England.* Chapel Hill: UNC Press, 2011.

"History of Routt National Forest, 1905-1972." Bound Typescript. Bud Warner Memorial Library, Steamboat Springs, CO., 1973.

Holderness, Pat, ed. *History of Hayden and West Routt County 1876-1989.* Dallas, TX: Curtis Media Corporation, 1990.

Indian Citizenship Act (Snyder Act) of 1924, 43 Stat.253 § (1924).

Jones, Sondra. "'Redeeming' the Indian: The Enslavement of Indian Children in New Mexico and Utah" 67, no. 3 (1999).

Kappler, Charles J., ed. *Indian Affairs: Laws and Treaties. Vol.II, Treaties.* Washington, D.C.: GPO, 1904.

Leslie, Jan. *Routt County Rural Schools, 1883-1960: Windows to Yesterday.* Steamboat Springs, CO: Legacy Books and Resources, 1998.

Mason, J. Alden. "Myths of the Uintah Utes." *The Journal of American Folklore* 23, no. 89 (1910): 1–65.

McLaughlin, James. Letter to Secretary of Interior, May 30, 1903.

McMillan, David, and David Chavis. "Sense of Community: A Definition and Theory." *Journal of Community Psychology* 14 (January 1986).

O'Neil, Floyd A. "An Anguished Odyssey: The Flight of the Utes 1906-1908." *Utah Historical Quarterly* 36, no. 4 (Fall 1968): 315–27.

———. "The Utes, Paiutes and Goshutes." In *The Peoples of Utah,* edited by Helen Z. Papanikolas. Salt Lake City: Utah State Historical Society, 1976.

O'Neil, Floyd A., and Kathryn L. MacKay. "A History of the Uintah-Ouray Ute Lands, American West Center Occasional Papers." Salt Lake City, no date

Powell, John Wesley. *Explorations of the Colorado River of the West and Its Tributaries; Explored in 1869, 1870, and 1871. Under the Direction of the Secretary of the Smithsonian Institution.* Washington, D.C.: GPO, 1875.

———. *John Wesley Powell, Report on the Lands of the Arid Region of the United States, with a More Detailed Account of the Lands of Utah. With Maps.* Washington, D.C.: GPO, 1879.

Pritchett, Lulita Crawford. *The Cabin at Medicine Springs.* New and Revised edition. Steamboat Springs, CO: Tread of Pioneers Historical Commission, 1958.

Ratliff, J.H. "Experiences 1905 -1914 U.S. Forest Service." In *History of Routt National Forest, 1905-1972*. Steamboat Springs, CO: Bound Manuscript, 1973.

Santala, Russel D. "The Ute Campaign of 1879: A Study in the Use of the Military Instrument." Masters Thesis, U.S. Army Command and General Staff College, 1993.

Smith, Anne M. *Ethnography of the Northern Utes*. Papers in Antropology 17. Santa Fe, NM: Santa Fe Museum of New Mexico Press, 1974.

Smith, Anne M. *Ute Tales*. Vol. 29. University of Utah Publications in the American West, 1992.

Stories of Our Ancestors: A Collection of Northern-Ute Indian Tales. Uintah-Ouray Ute Tribe, 1975.

Taveapont, Venita. Interview by Nancy Green, no date. KUED University of Utah.

United States. "Acting Commissioner Larabee to The Secretary of the Interior Conveying the Report Made by Lieut. Co. Frank West," June 9, 1905.

United States. "Annual Report of the Commissioner of Indian Affairs to the Secretary of the Interior for the Year 1881." Washington, D.C.: G.P.O., 1881.

United States. "Annual Report of the Commissioner of Indian Affairs to the Secretary of the Interior for the Year, 1898." Washington, D.C.: G.P.O., 1898.

United States. "Annual Report of the Department of Interior for the Fiscal Year Ended June 30, 1902. Indian Affairs, Part 1, Report of the Commissioner and Appendixes." Washington, D.C.: G.P.O., 1903.

United States. "Annual Report of the Commissioner of Indian Affairs." Washington, D.C.: G.P.O., 1906.

United States. "Annual Report of the Commissioner of Indian Affairs to the Secretary of the Interior." Washington, D.C.: GPO, 1908.

United States. Minutes of Councils Held by James McLaughlin, U.S. Indian Inspector with the Uintah and White River Ute Indians at Uintah Agency, Utah From May 18 to May 23, 1903, § Department of Interior: Indian Office (1903).

United States. "The Ute Campaign," *War Department Annual Reports.*, Department of Missouri Report, 3 (1907).

United States. "White River Ute Commission Investigation." House of Representatives, 46th Congress, 2nd Session. Washington, D.C., May 14, 1880.

Wickenden, Dorothy. *Nothing Daunted: The Unexpected Education of Two Society Girls in the West*. New York, NY: Scribner, 2011.

Wroth, William. "Ute Civilization in Prehistory and the Spanish Colonial Period." In *Ute Indian Arts and Culture,* edited by William Wroth. Colorado Springs, CO: Colorado Springs Fine Arts Center, 2000.

Wall text, Ute Indian Museum, History Colorado. Montrose, CO.

"Written on the Land: Ute Voices, Ute History." Wall text, Colorado History Museum. Denver, CO.

Index

G

P

Q

R

S

T

www.ingramcontent.com/pod-product-compliance
Lightning Source LLC
Chambersburg PA
CBHW021959090426
42811CB00001B/90
9781735122502